C000056728

'Herein may be seen noble chyvalrye, curtoseye, humanitye, friendlynesse, hardynesse, love, frendship, cowardyse, murdre, hate, virtue, and synne. Doo after the good, and leve the evyl, and it shal brynge you to good fame and renommee.'

William Caxton's preface to Sir Thomas Malory's ' Morte d'Arthur.'

TO
MY FRIEND AND
RELATIVE, SIR HENRY NEWBOLT,
WHOSE EXCELLENT ROMANCE ENTITLED 'THE
NEW JUNE' FIRST GAVE ME THE IDEA
OF WRITING THIS BOOK, I DEDI-
CATE MY UNROMANCING
HISTORY

PREFACE

THE motto of the Knutsford branch of Hollands is ' Respice, Aspice, Prospice.' I have written this book primarily for the benefit of existing Hollands and those more numerous, I hope, as yet unborn, so that they may be the better able to practise the precept of ' Respice,' and may have some consecutive information as to the men and women who bore their name in times past. I do not agree with those people who, as a philosopher says, ' Nowadays attach much more importance to the pedigrees of domestic animals than to the pedigrees of men.' The book may also, I hope, be of interest to others who have a taste for history, public and private, or patriotic feeling for Lancashire.

Except now and then, as this does not pretend to be a didactic history, I do not worry the reader's eye by detailed footnote references to the authorities, but I append a list of the chief sources of information, and I ask readers to credit me with not having stated any fact without some authority. In the period between the thirteenth century and the sixteenth, one has to depend mainly upon the old chroniclers, English and French ; for these centuries are sadly deficient in that written correspondence from which one learns so much of the character of men and women in later times. These chroniclers mostly give the mere outward show of things, and hardly before de Commines does one obtain any attempt to analyse character. They are also sometimes obviously inaccurate as to facts, and it is never clear how far they are poetically composing the words which

vii

they put into the mouths of their characters, or how far
they are reporting on more or less trustworthy evidence.
When two chroniclers narrate the same event, they usually
give varying versions which are the despair of the modern
conscientious historian. He has to use his judgment and
make out the course of events which seems the most probable.
At the same time, I feel sure, from internal evidence, that
men like Froissart and de Wavrin did their best to ascertain
what did happen, and greatly are we indebted to them for
their trouble. As to facts of drier order, there is plenty
of record in legal and administrative documents. The
writer who deals with Lancashire, as is my fortune in respect
to part of the story, has the advantage that no county
provides such ample printed materials for local history.
The great patriotism and modern wealth of Lancashire
men has wrought this. In addition to Baines' older county
history, there is the copious series of the Chetham Society
publications, the distinct works of men like Booker and
Croston, and, above all, the 'Victorian County History of
Lancashire' published within the last few years. This
splendid monument of well-directed labour is, I should say,
the best designed and most complete of all county histories,
ancient and modern. It would have been impossible not
many years ago to write the present book without far more
time and original research than I could have afforded to give,
although this book has cost me quite enough, and possibly
too much, time and trouble, but books like the Victorian
County History and, on national affairs, like those of Sir
James Ramsay, Mr. Wylie, and others, men who have given
all the spare time of their lives to mediaeval history, make
things much easier now for the amateur historian.

I have derived special advantage from Mr. James
Croston's pedigree of the Hollands of Upholland in his
admirable 'History of the Ancient Hall of Samlesbury,'

published in 1871, and from the Upholland, Denton and Mobberley pedigrees in Mr. Wm. Fergusson Irvine's 'History of the Family of Holland of Mobberley and Knutsford,' which appeared in 1902. Mr. Irvine's book was partly based upon materials collected by the late Edgar Swinton Holland, who seems to have meditated writing a general history of the family.

I have entitled this book, 'The Lancashire Hollands.' Those of them who played a great part on the national stage for four generations, in the fourteenth and fifteenth centuries, lived mainly, it is true, in the South of England, but they were by origin pure bred Lancastrians, and other branches of the family lived in or near Lancashire till modern times, and some still live there. Therefore the Hollands, like many another vigorous clan, may salute the Red Rose County with 'Salve, magna Parens.'

I began to compose this book in hours of leisure before the great war broke out in August 1914, though I have finished it since. It would not have been easy to start upon a mere family history after the outbreak of volcanic events which make even great affairs in former history seem pale, and writing seem rather a shadowy occupation.

The best justification of histories of this kind is that given by the wise Gibbon in his Autobiography. He says :

'A lively desire of knowing and recording our ancestors so generally prevails that it must depend on the influence of some common principle in the minds of men. We seem to have lived in the persons of our forefathers ; it is the labour and reward of verity to extend the term of this ideal longevity. . . . The satirist may laugh, the philosopher may preach, but Reason herself will respect the prejudice and habits which have been consecrated by the experience of mankind.'

BERNARD HOLLAND.

HARBLEDOWN, NEAR CANTERBURY.

CONTENTS

xi

ILLUSTRATIONS

PEDIGREE TABLES

HOLLANDS OF UPHOLLAND IN LANCASHIRE

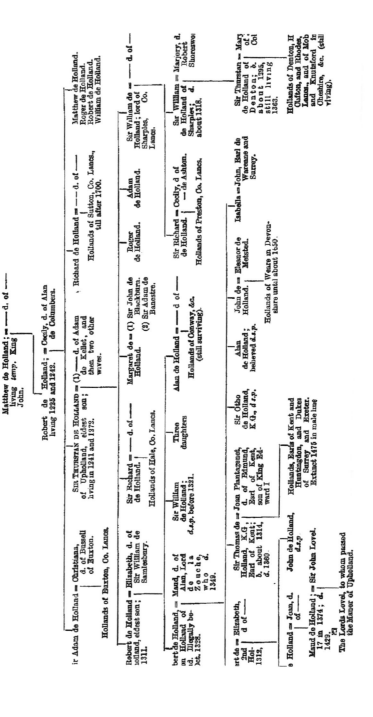

THE LANCASHIRE HOLLANDS

ERRATA.

Page 17, line 12. Warren should be Warenne.

Page 83. In quotation at head, Charles II should be Charles **I**

Page 160, line 21. 1306 should be 1406.

Page 160, line 22. 1307 should be 1407.

Page 304 In the Pedigree a generation has been omitted. Thomas Holland (line 6) was father of William Holland and Catherine (Atherton). William Holland was father of Humphrey Holland, who died, and was not born, in 1528.

Page 335. Frederick Holland, Capt. R.N., died in 1860, not 1857.

Edward IV, came to violent ends, as befitted an ambitious and fighting family in stormy English times, when politics was a game played with lives for stakes.

The village of Upholland is about four miles west of Wigan. The place is now blackened by coal-mining, but must once have been a pleasant enough region. Not far off there is another village called Down-holland, where also a Holland family lived, from, at least, the reign of Henry II to that of Henry VIII, but they seem to have been unconnected with the Hollands of Upholland, and with them this book is not concerned. There was also a Lincolnshire family

B

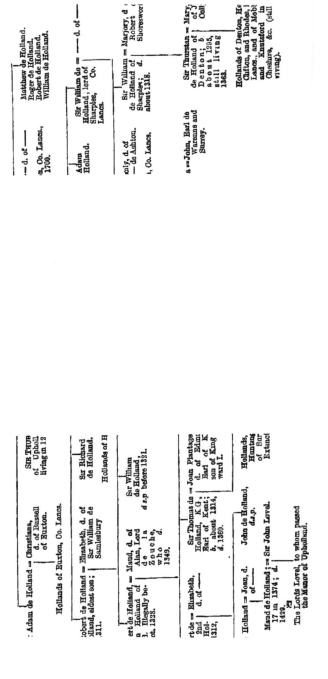

THE LANCASHIRE HOLLANDS

CHAPTER I

HOLLANDS OF UPHOLLAND

Memento dierum antiquorum ;
Cogita generationes singulas
CANTICLE OF MOSES

'THERE has existed no family in Lancashire,' wrote a distinguished antiquary of that county, Mr. Langton, ' whose
career has been so remarkable as that of the Hollands.
Playing an active part in the most picturesque and chivalrous
period of English history, they figured among the founders
of the Order of the Garter, allied themselves with the royal
family, and attained the highest rank in the peerage.'

The vicissitudes of their fortunes were great. If they
rose to the heights they also tasted of the depths. Most of
the chiefs of the race, from the time of Edward II to that of
Edward IV, came to violent ends, as befitted an ambitious
and fighting family in stormy English times, when politics
was a game played with lives for stakes.

The village of Upholland is about four miles west of
Wigan. The place is now blackened by coal-mining, but
must once have been a pleasant enough region. Not far
off there is another village called Down-holland, where also
a Holland family lived, from, at least, the reign of Henry II
to that of Henry VIII, but they seem to have been unconnected with the Hollands of Upholland, and with them this
book is not concerned. There was also a Lincolnshire family

of Hollands, but unrelated to those of Lancashire.[1] Down
to the fifteenth century the name was always spelt Holand
(or Holande), and its bearers were called John de Holand,
Thomas de Holand, &c., but in this book the later spelling
has, as a rule, been used throughout.

The manor of Upholland appears in Domesday Book as
'Hoiland,' and was in the possession of 'Steinulf' in the
days of Edward the Confessor. The Hollands appear in
the reign of John as donors to Cockersand Abbey, but their
name is first mentioned in connection with this manor in
a 'final concord' made at the Lancaster Assizes dated
November 5, 1202.[2] In this deed Uhctred de Chyrche
releases his right in fourteen oxgangs of land in Upholland
to Matthew de Holland. This would mean about 210
acres of arable land together with rights of meadowing and
pasturage, perhaps the manor as a whole, under this form.
Two later deeds show that between 1212 and 1224 Matthew
de Holland died and was succeeded by his son Robert.
Robert de Holland was still alive in 1241. In that year he
and his son Thurstan were in prison on the charge of having
set fire to a house belonging to the Rector of Wigan and
occupied by John Mansel. The Sheriff, however, was directed
to release them on bail. Thurstan did not appear on the
day appointed for trial, 'but Robert came and defended
his whole action and put himself for good or evil upon the
country, to wit, upon twelve knights above suspicion and

---

[1] The record of these Lincolnshire Hollands, who owned Estovening Manor in
the parish of Swineshead, begins with an Otho Holland before the Conquest, and
continued in that region down to the end of the sixteenth century. One of them,
Sir Thomas Holland, *temp.* Henry VI, 'spent his life in the Holy Land and came
home but every seventh year.' No wonder, for he was married to Elizabeth,
daughter of Sir Piers Tempest, whom men called ' the Devilish Dame.' One would
like to know more about this couple, who would have been a good subject for an
' Ingoldsby Legend.'

[2] In the Cockersand Chartulary, published by the Chetham Society, are
printed two deeds of grant of land in Upholland to the then new Abbey,
one by Matthew de Holland, the second by his son Robert.

four vills of the neighbourhood of Wigan.' A day was given him by the Justices at the next Assizes, and the Sheriff was directed in the meantime to ' let him have peace, and in no wise to trouble him or permit him to be troubled.' Thurstan appeared before the Justices on July 23, but no prosecutor attended the Court. The Justices asked Thurstan ' how he would acquit himself concerning the fire if any one would speak against him,' and he too claimed trial by jury, and was given a day at the Assizes. It does not appear what further happened in this case.

In 1242–3 Thurstan had probably succeeded to his father, for he represented the family in an inquiry then held to ascertain the knights' fees in that ' Hundred ' chargeable to the Gascon Scutage. Robert de Holland had other sons besides Thurstan : Adam, the ancestor of the Hollands of Euxton ; Richard, from whom came the Hollands of Sutton ; Matthew, Robert, Roger, and William. In 1268 Thurstan Holland, with his brothers Matthew, Richard, Robert and William, and Thurstan's own son Robert, were all summoned to answer a charge of trespass.

Thurstan de Holland first married the daughter of Adam de Kellet, through whom the Hollands acquired manors in north Lancashire, as Lonsdale, Furness, and Cartmel. By this wife he had five sons, Robert, William, Richard, Roger, Adam, and a daughter, Margaret. Thurstan next married Juliana, a daughter of John Gellibrand, and had four more sons, Thurstan, Adam, Elias, and Simon. He married thirdly a daughter of Henry de Hale, an illegitimate son of Richard de Meath, Lord of Hale. An old Norman-French petition from the ' loyal tenants of Hale ' states that as Henry de Hale lay dying ' came one Thurstan de Holland, who had married the daughter of the said Henry and as he lay at the point of death [*come il launguist a la mort*] his memory lost, the said Thurstan took the said

Henry's seal which he had round his neck, and made use of the seal to issue charters granting the said manor of Hale to himself, the said Thurstan, and Robert his son.' He had then put out some old tenants, and introduced new ones, which, perhaps, accounts for the allegation.

This accusation may not have been true, but evidently Thurstan de Holland was one of those vigorous and not too scrupulous men who, by local efforts and marriages, found families. Thurstan lived long. He is described as ' Sir Thurstan de Holland' in witnessing a charter to Stanlaw Abbey in 1272. He signed it with a cross, and his seal showed three bulls' heads.

Robert de Holland was the eldest son of Thurstan. William, another son of Thurstan, became Sir William de Holland, and he was ancestor of several Lancashire families, Hollands of Denton, Clifton, and their branches, a numerous posterity which, through descendants from the Clifton line, endures to the present day.

Sir Thurstan de Holland's eldest son Robert is on the main line of the present history. He married Elizabeth, the youngest of three daughters and co-heiress of William de Samlesbury. This Robert received knighthood about the year 1281. His eldest son was also named Robert, and he had another son, William, and three daughters who married into Lancastrian families, Joan, Margery, and Ameria. William died before 1321, without issue. Joan married first Sir Edward Talbot of Bashall, and next Sir Hugh de Dutton, and lastly Sir John de Redcliffe. Margery married John la Warre, from whom descended the baronial families of West and de la Warre. Ameria married Adam, son of Sir John Ireland, knight, from whom also came a numerous posterity.

Sir Robert de Holland, son of Robert and grandson of Thurstan, was a great man in his day, and first brought this energetic family of Upholland into the domain of national history. Beginning as a well-to-do Lancashire Squire, he owed his advance to his position in the household of that feudal lord of vast domains, Thomas, Earl of Lancaster, grandson of King Henry III through that King's second son Edmund, and nephew of Edward I. Robert de Holland took part in the Scottish wars at the end of the reign of Edward I and the beginning of that of Edward II. In the first year of the latter reign he received from the Crown seven manors in Derbyshire. By this time he had become a leading ' Member of Society.' In 1307 he rode at a tournament, held outside London, in the fields of Stepney, where he bore for arms ' azure, semé of fleurs de lys, a lion rampant guardant, argent,' and in the same year he obtained further territorial grants from the Crown. This was the first year of Edward II's unhappy reign. In the same year Robert de Holland obtained leave to fortify (' kernellare ') his mansions of Holland in Lancashire and Bagsworth in Leicestershire, and was appointed Chief Justice of Chester, with the charge of the royal castles of Chester, Rhudlaw, and Flint. In 1308 he made a great marriage with Maud, then aged twenty-four, younger daughter and co-heiress of Alan, Lord de la Zouche of Ashby de la Zouche in the county of Leicester, who was great grandson of King Henry II by the fair and frail Rosamond de Clifford. Maud de la Zouche, on her father's death, five years later, brought him several more manors in Northamptonshire, Oxfordshire, and Hertfordshire. In the year of his marriage, Robert de Holland was summoned to appear at Newcastle-on-Tyne to repel the invading Scots, and two years later was appointed to superintend military levies in the counties of Lancaster, Leicester, Stafford, and Derby He was summoned to Parliament in 1814 and 1321 as ' Roberto de Holland, Baron Holland.'

It has already been said that Robert de Holland owed

his rise to Thomas, Earl of Lancaster, Leicester, and Derby, and cousin to the King. This great lord had given to his follower, who was his chief agent and adviser in Lancashire, a number of manors in Cheshire, Staffordshire, Yorkshire, and Buckinghamshire.

Robert de Holland, perhaps in order to give his wife a title to dower, obtained a re-grant of his inherited territorial manors of Upholland and Hale upon new and interesting conditions. Thomas, Earl of Lancaster, by charter, granted these two manors to him and to Maud his wife, to hold of the chief lord by the service of distributing each year for the said Earl's soul on St. Thomas the Martyr's Day and on Christmas Day to the poor folk on the manor of Upholland twenty heaped up measures of wheated flour, and ox, and swine, and calf's flesh to the value of £10, and of providing a repast of two courses for 240 poor persons in the Hall of Upholland on the same feast, to be served on dishes after the manner of gentlefolk, and a repast of one course the following day, a pair of shoes or 4d. being given to each of the poor persons on departing.

The gifts of land and mesne manors, both from the Crown and from his chief and patron, made Robert de Holland rich and powerful, and his marriage, besides bringing more manors, made him well connected; but his fortune fell, as it had risen, with that of the Earl of Lancaster.

Throughout English history, from the time, at any rate, of Henry III to that of George III, there has been a struggle, now and then volcanically breaking forth, between the King and his intimate advisers on the one side, and, on the other, the party of the territorial aristocracy who always tried to put the royal power in commission, and so rule themselves. The reign of Edward II, like those of Richard II and James II, was one of the explosive epochs in this struggle, and the Earl of Lancaster was at the head of the feudal party, in opposition to the Crown.

A KNIGHT OF THE HOUSE OF HOLLAND IN THE CENTRE. A KNIGHT OF THE
HOUSE OF LANCASTER ON THE RIGHT

This drawing is in the Harleian MSS (oll 2129 fol 218) It was copied in 1640 from painted glass
then in the window of Warrington Church Baines says ('Hist Lanc' vol iii. p 672 'The surcoat of the
first knight, representing a Banastre, was or that of the second sable, pummel of his sword or, and blade
argent. The arms on the pennon are those of Holland, and the third knight is probably Thomas Earl of
Lancaster'

Robert de Holland accompanied the Earl of Lancaster in the military operations which, in 1312, led to the overthrow of King Edward's favourite Piers Gaveston and his execution on Blacklow Hill near Warwick on July 1, 1312. But in 1315 broke out a rebellion against the Earl in his own county of Lancashire. This was led by Sir Adam de Banastre, chief of a numerous and powerful family, who had married Margaret Holland,[1] the aunt of Sir Robert, now Lord Holland. This rising against their patron the Earl of Lancaster brought the loyal Hollands into violent collision with the rebel Banastres, notwithstanding the marriage alliance. 'The Hollands,' say the authors of the 'Victorian History of Lancashire,' 'were a numerous clan in south-west Lancashire ; their importance greatly increased with the rise of their chief ; and probably they presumed upon it.' The Banastre faction had some success at first, and plundered the houses of the Hollands and their friends, but they were happily routed in a pitched fight, banners flying, near Preston, on November 4, 1315. Sir William de Holland, Sir Robert's brother, captured Sir Thomas de Banastre, at Charnock, and at once beheaded him on Leyland Moor. Sir Adam was also afterwards caught and beheaded at Martinmas.

After Gaveston's illegal execution, Sir Robert de Holland took the precaution to obtain a royal pardon for his share in that outrage. In 1321 (the year, by the way, that Dante died at Ravenna) he was ordered to abstain from attending the meeting of the so-called 'Good Peers' whom Lancaster had illegally convened to meet in November. That Earl, who was so popular that after his death his admirers tried to get him canonised as a saint, was engaged in his attempt to oust the reigning favourites, the

---

[1] Adam de Banastre was Margaret's second husband. The Harringtons of Hornby and Wolfage descended from Katharine, daughter of Margaret by Sir Adam de Banastre. She married Sir John Harrington.

Despensers, from the council of his cousin the King. In 1322 Robert, Lord Holland, was sent by him into Lancashire to raise a force there in aid of this enterprise, and, despite the King's prohibition expressly addressed to him, marched his levy to join the Earl. In the meantime, one of his younger brothers, Sir Richard de Holland, with another levy, tried to cross the Mersey at Runcorn into Cheshire to attack a royal force in that county, led by Sir Oliver de Ingham, but failed because all the boats had been withdrawn to the Cheshire side. This was in the middle of March 1322. The Earl of Lancaster, operating on the Trent, placed a body of foot soldiers at Burton, to keep the bridge, and to prevent the royal army, estimated at 30,000 men, from crossing the river. He was out-manœuvred by the King's army, which passed the Trent at Walton, lower down the river, and thereby turned the Earl's flank and compelled his retreat across the Dove. The retreat was accomplished in such haste that the Earl's army chest, containing 100,000 silver pieces, fell into the river, where it was discovered in the year 1831. The Earl retreated as far as Boroughbridge in Yorkshire, and was there defeated and captured on March 16. He was summarily tried and beheaded a few days later in his own Castle of Pontefract. According to one account Sir Robert de Holland was at this fight ; according to another he did not arrive in time. In any case he surrendered to the King immediately after the conflict, and escaped the penalty of death, but the whole of his great territorial possessions were confiscated by the Crown.

After the fall of the great Earl, and of his agent Robert, Lord Holland, Lancashire sank for a space into anarchy. The men crushed by the Hollands seven years earlier raised their heads again. 'Banastre's old associate, Sir William Bradshaw, formed a confederacy with Thomas de Banastre and others against the Hollands, who united their forces under Sir Richard de Holland. They attacked each other whenever they met, besieged one another's houses, overawed courts of law, and kept a great part of the country practically in a state of war for more than a year.' [1]

Signs of this wild state of things appear in the Court records. In 1324 Sir William de Bradeschagh (Bradshaw) accused Henry de Gylibrand of coming with Richard de Holland and Adam de Hindelaye on the Friday next before the Feast of St. John in the preceding year to Leyland with a hundred armed men, who attacked the complainant and carried off two of his horses. The troop then rode on to Preston, where Edward de Nevile and Gilbert Singleton, two of the King's Judges, were holding assizes, and so much terrified them by noise and clamour that they dared not proceed with business, nor did the complainant dare 'to defend his sentence in an assize of novel disseisin,' [2] whereby he suffered damage to the extent of ten marks. In 1330 the Prior of Lancaster complained that he had been seized and imprisoned by one of the Banastres and others. In 1334 Sir Richard de Holland laid a claim to a mill and two plough-lands at Aighton. The successful defence was (1) that there was only one plough-land at Aighton, (2) that the said Sir Richard had been convicted of felony. In the same year a man named Richard le Skimmer, parker or forest-keeper of Ightenhill, was prosecuted at a County Court held at Wigan on the charge of having ridden with thirty armed men to Prescot Church on the Sunday after Barnabas' Day in 1330, four years before, and having dragged from the church Richard de Holland, Thomas de Hale, and John Walthew. He would have beheaded the last-named then and there, had not Walthew

---

[1] *Victorian History of Lancashire*, ii. 201.

[2] *Assize of Novel Disseisin.*—An action to recover property of which a party had been disseised (dispossessed) after the last circuit of the judges. Abolished by 3 & 4 Will. 4, c 27 (1833) —Wharton, *Law Lexicon*

claimed the refuge of the Church. This vigorous parker was probably inflamed by some outrageous raiding in pursuit of deer, since the forest laws about this time were freely violated in Lancashire, and this was one great cause of fighting.

While affairs went thus rudely in Lancashire, Robert, Lord Holland, Chief of the family, languished for a while in successive prisons at Dover and York, until at last he was set free upon giving pledges of good behaviour. He must have been in poverty. In 1828, six years after Boroughbridge, in the second year of the reign of Edward III, the attainder of Thomas, Earl of Lancaster, was reversed, and his estates were restored to his brother and heir, Henry, Earl of Lancaster. About the same time the new King, with the assent of Parliament, directed that the estates of those who had joined Earl Thomas against the Despensers and the late King should also be restored ; and, among others, it was ordered that the possessions of Robert de Holland should be redelivered into his hands. The Earl of Lancaster opposed this restitution, and Holland addressed a petition to the King in Council. On October 7, in the same year, Holland was killed by adherents of that Earl. According to Dugdale he had ' incurred much hatred from the people for dealing unfaithfully with his lord, who, out of his great affection, had raised him from nothing, so that, in 1328, being taken in a wood near Henley Park, toward Windsor, he was beheaded on the nones of October, and his head was sent to Henry, Earl of Lancaster, then at Waltham Cross, in Essex, by one Sir Thomas Wyther, a knight, and some other private friends.'

The allegation seems to have been that Holland, in order to gain favour with the King and to save his estates and his life, had taken care not to arrive at Boroughbridge, with a strong division which he led, either at all, or, at least, until it was too late to avert defeat. If this be true—and it is all very doubtful—it is clear that he gained nothing from this infidelity but his life. He was imprisoned and involved in the ruin of his patron, and the estates of his kinsmen, John and Richard de Holland, were confiscated as well as his own. Mr. Croston says, in his book on Samlesbury Hall, that 'the charge of treachery had no foundation in truth, and was, in all probability, devised by the adherents of Earl Henry to secure his removal, and thereby prevent him from becoming repossessed of the manors which had been conferred upon him by Earl Thomas.' The dispatch of his head to Earl Henry has, however, an air of personal revenge which could hardly be entirely explained by a mere motive of interest. Eventually the patrimonial estates were restored to the family, but few, if any, of those granted by Earl Thomas were recovered.

Sir Robert, Lord Holland, in the day of his wealth and greatness, was not forgetful of the Church. He founded, at Upholland, in connection with the church, a chapel of St. Thomas the Martyr, a collegiate foundation of a Dean and Chaplains, or secular Canons. It was not a success, as is shown by the recitals in a later deed of June 10, 1319, which was executed by Walter, Bishop of Coventry and Lichfield, with the consent of Robert de Holland. The deed says, in Latin, that ' the said Chaplains (capellani) who for a short time were in agreement, have long and rashly (temere) abandoned the said place, and thus the religion or devotion which it was hoped would there be exercised for ever is dissolved and has ceased. We, considering that the college there ordained has been dispersed, and seeing that the divine worship in that place has been frustrated, and desiring that, for the increase of religion and divine worship, the state of the said place should be reformed, and having inspected the unproductiveness and situation of the place, it appears to be more convenient that religious

rather than secular men should abide there for ever.'
Evidently the strength of the monastic rule was necessary
to make religious men live in so sterile and remote a spot.

The deed therefore substituted for the former foundation
one of a Prior and twelve monks of the Order of St. Benedict,
'nigrum habitum gerentes.' Thomas de Banastre was
presented by Robert de Holland as first Prior. The only
information about this priory is that John de Barnaby
was Prior in 1350, when he and others were tried for a riot
and were acquitted. The monks chanted their masses for
more than two hundred years in remote Upholland, and
then came Henry VIII and Thomas Cromwell. At the
dissolution, in 1534, the place was granted to John Holcroft.
The gross income was then £61 3s. 4d. and the net income
£53 3s. 4d. The church was kept for a chapelry of Wigan,
and still remains. A few fragments of wall mark the site
of the other buildings.

The Sir Robert Holland who founded this priory and
was slain near Henley in 1328, left five sons and a daughter.
The eldest son, also named Robert, was for a time engaged,
like his brothers, in the French wars, and was summoned
to Parliament as Baron Holland from February 25, 1342,
to October 6, 1372.

This second Sir Robert de Holland, Baron Holland, took
part in 1347 in an affair which created a sensation at the
time. He and several other Lancashire gentlemen assisted
Sir Robert Dalton of that county to abduct with violence a
wealthy widow, whom Dalton wished to marry. Her name
was Margery, widow of a large landowner named Nicolas de
la Beche, and she subsequently had been married to Gerard
de l'Isle. The Lancashire gentlemen carried her off by
force from her manor house called Beaumes or Beams in
Berkshire, close to Reading. In the affray the lady's uncle,
Michael le Poyning, and another man were killed, and

several were wounded. The crime was the more outrageous, and was severely prosecuted, because it was committed ' within the verge of the marshalsea ' of the Duke of Clarence, the King's brother, who was acting as ' keeper of the realm ' while the King was in France, and was just then residing at Reading. The arrest of Dalton, Holland, and the rest was at once ordered, and they fled to wild Lancashire with the lady. There some of them took refuge at Upholland Hall, the house settled for life on the Lady Maud Holland, Robert Holland's widowed mother. She thus became implicated in the proceedings, but pleaded that the house was empty and that she was ignorant of this harbouring. On the arrival of the King's writ at Upholland the abductors fled farther north.

This crime of widow or heiress stealing was then very common. About the same time there was a famous case of the widow Lady de Boteler, who was carried off from her house in Lancashire with no more luggage, as she complained, than her ' smock and her kyrtle.' John of Gaunt issued a special proclamation in his duchy against lady-stealing, in which it was recited that the offence was more common in Lancashire than in any county, and that the ladies carried off were too apt to marry their ravishers. In that age, when land was wealth, a nobleman or gentleman could only increase his estate in one of two ways—by marrying an heiress or widow, or by obtaining a share in confiscated possessions of unsuccessful traitors who had been attainted for treason. This necessity, vital to those who would be great, vitiated motives both in marriage and in politics, just as, later, the prospect of the plunder of the vast estates of the monasteries vitiated the religious motive of English and German reformers. In later times, although marriage was still the pleasantest and the best way of gaining or increasing wealth or power, the long wars and plunder of France opened out new avenues and careers to English gentlemen, and, after that, came successively distribution of the monastic lands, increasing sale of wool to the manufacturing towns of Flanders, opening of the new world, and capture of bullion by sea-rovers from the Spaniards, and, later still, development of the British Empire, and other modes of earned or unearned income.   But before the middle of the fourteenth century the roads to wealth were scanty, and even less consistent than they now are with strict virtue.

Lady Maud Holland, *née* la Zouche, died in 1349, two years after the Beaumes affair, at the age of sixty-five, and the Manor of Upholland passed to her son Robert, second Lord Holland.   He died at the age of sixty-one, in the year 1373.   His son, also named Robert, died before him, and Upholland and other estates passed to the last mentioned Robert's daughter Maud.   This Maud de Holland, at the age of seventeen, married Sir John Lovell, K.G., afterwards Lord Lovell.[1]   The Manor of Upholland and other estates remained in that family until they were confiscated after the death of Francis, Viscount Lovell, one of Richard III's leading adherents, at the battle of Bosworth, in 1485.   The manor was thereupon granted by Henry VII to the first Earl of Derby.   On the death of the ninth Earl it passed to his daughter, Henrietta Maria, Countess of Ashburnham, who sold it in 1717 to Thomas Ashurst. His successor sold it to Sir Thomas Boothe, the ancestor of the Lords Skelmersdale.

Such was the fate of the eldest line of the Hollands, and

[1] Some of the estates, e.g. the Manor of Torrisholme, passed to Maud's uncle, John Holland, and when he died in 1456, without issue, went to his distant cousin, Henry Holland, Duke of Exeter, as next heir.   These must have been bound to go in tail male.   This Sir John Lovell died in 1408.   A long list of his manors in right of his wife Maud, daughter of Robert Holland, appear in the *Inquisitio post mortem.*   Most of them were in Leicestershire, Oxfordshire, and Wiltshire.

of their ancestral Manor of Upholland. Among other
branches from that stem were (1) that derived from Sir
Robert, Lord Holland's second son, Thomas, whence came
the Earls of Kent and Dukes of Exeter; (2) that
derived from the said Sir Robert's younger brother William
de Holland, whence came the Hollands of Denton, Clifton,
&c.; and (3) that derived from his great uncle, Richard de
Holland, whence came the Hollands of Sutton. What is
known of these lines will be stated in this book, but it is convenient to mention here, and get rid of, another short-lived
line, the Hollands of Euxton.

The Hollands who owned the Manor of Euxton bore for
their arms those of the race, azure semé with fleurs de lys,
a lion rampant guardant, argent, over all a bandlet gules.
They came from a younger brother of Thurstan de Holland,
namely, Adam de Holland, who was in possession of the
Manor of Euxton about 1250, apparently through marriage
with an heiress of the great landed family of the Bussells.
His eldest son was Robert, who married an heiress of the
Ellels. The pedigree of these Hollands of Euxton was as
follows :

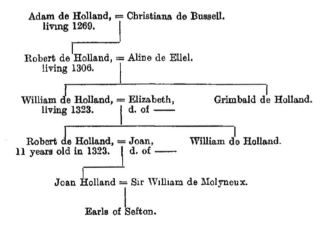

Adam de Holland, = Christiana de Bussell.
    living 1269.

Robert de Holland, = Aline de Ellel.
    living 1306.

William de Holland, = Elizabeth,   Grimbald de Holland.
    living 1323.   d. of ——

Robert de Holland, = Joan,   William de Holland.
11 years old in 1323.   d. of ——

Joan Holland = Sir William de Molyneux.

Earls of Sefton.

The first of the two Robert Hollands mentioned in this pedigree seems to have been rather a lawless character. In 1278 the Abbot of Leicester lodged a complaint that Robert de Holland of Euxton and others had seized his corn in the highway at Ellel, and in 1281 his own relative by marriage, William Bussel, complained that Robert de Holland had seized his cattle. His grandson, the second Robert, came to some violent end, since two men were pardoned in 1339 for their share in the death of Robert de Holland of Euxton. His daughter Joan became heiress, and carried the manor in marriage to Sir William de Molyneux of Sefton, a gentleman distinguished in the Edwardian Wars, the direct ancestor of the present Earls of Sefton.

But the story of the main line of the Hollands of Upholland must now be completed. Sir Robert, Lord Holland, he who was illegally beheaded near Henley-on-Thames, had, besides his eldest son Robert, four younger sons, Thomas, Otho, John, and Alan, and one daughter, Isabel de Holland.[1] At his death in 1328 his eldest son was sixteen, so was born in 1312. Isabel became involved in the fortunes of a remarkable man, John, Earl de Warenne, and Earl also of Surrey and Sussex. He was born in 1286 and was the last of a very great Norman family, the heads of which had taken a leading part in the affairs of England since the Conquest. The first of them had married Gundred, a daughter of William the Conqueror. The last Earl had acted with Lancaster and his allies of the feudal aristocracy against Piers de Gaveston, but afterwards had gone over to the side of the Court. His alliance was valuable, for he had wide domains north of the Trent with Conisborough Castle in Yorkshire for his central stronghold, the ruins of which still rise above the Don, and also great possessions in the south. To him belonged the

[1] John is doubtful. He only appears in the pedigree of the Devonshire Hollands.

towns and castles of Reigate in Surrey and Lewes in Sussex. In 1322 he acted against the Earl of Lancaster in Yorkshire, and was one of the peers who signed his death warrant at Pontefract.

In addition to his landed wealth the Earl de Warenne, towards the end of his life, was enriched, if the frequently incredible monk of St. Albans, Walsingham, is to be believed, by the discovery through the wizard doings of a Saracen physician of a great treasure hidden in the cave on his Bromfield estates in Herefordshire. This monk says in his Latin Chronicle : ' There came at that time a certain Saracen physician to the Earl de Warren, asking his leave to catch a certain Serpent in his Welsh estates, in a place called Bromfield. When, by incantations, he had caught the said Serpent, he declared that in a cavern, in a neighbouring place, where the Serpent had dwelt, there was a great treasure. Hearing which, some men of Hereford, by the advice of a certain Lombard, named Peter Picard, began to dig there, and finding that to be true which the Saracen had predicted, often met there at night, until, discovered by the servants of the Earl, they were taken and put in prison. The Earl, truly, made no small gain from this event.'

John, Earl de Warenne in 1307, when he was twenty, married a French lady, Jeanne, daughter of the Count de Barre. Their life was unhappy ; they both sued for divorce, but the law of the Church presented difficulties, and at first, at any rate, the attempt was not successful. There is no evidence that it ever was. They lived separated, and Earl de Warenne pursued his wild career. On the Monday before Ascension Day, in the year 1317, a kinsman and retainer of his carried off Alice, the wife of Thomas, Earl of Lancaster, from a manor house at Canford in Dorsetshire and, ostentatiously, at the head of an armed escort, conveyed

her to de Warenne at his castle of Reigate in Surrey.[1] The
lady was the heiress of the great Norman family of the
de Lacys, and had brought to the House of Lancaster
Pontefract Castle and wide domains in Yorkshire.[2]

It was alleged that this ravishing was connived at by the
Court who hated Thomas of Lancaster, and it was probably
done with the consent of the Countess Alice, who was accused
of a previous northern intrigue with de Warenne, when she
was at Pontefract, and he in his hunting domain at Conisborough.   The act was an audacious challenge by de Warenne
of the Earl of Lancaster, who was then at the height of his
power, and it led to a short private war between the Earls
of Lancaster and de Warenne in Yorkshire.   For his evil
living the Earl de Warenne was threatened with excommunication by the Archbishop of Canterbury, and actually
did incur a diocesan excommunication by the Bishop of
Chichester, which caused an affray between his men and
those of the Bishop.[3]   The Archbishop's proceedings were
intended, it seems, to make the Earl break off his connection
with Maud de Nerford, a lady of good family in Norfolk,
who lived with him for many years, and bore him six illegiti-

---

[1] The monk, Walsingham, gives an absurd and dream-like description of what
happened on the road near Farnham.   His object evidently was still further to
blacken the character of the Countess for the benefit of that popular hero, Thomas
of Lancaster.

[2] Pontefract Castle was afterwards acquired by John of Gaunt, Duke of Lancaster, through his marriage with Blanche, daughter of Henry, Earl of Lancaster.
So it passed to his son King Henry IV.

[3] The diocesan excommunication of a great man for a great crime happened now and then.   In the early twelfth century, for instance, William Duke
of Aquitaine carried off with violence the beautiful Viscountess de Chatelhérault,
and kept her immured in his castle at Poitiers.   Peter, Bishop of Poitiers,
thereon excommunicated him.   The Duke, with sword drawn, came furiously
into the cathedral while the Bishop was celebrating Mass, and commanded him
to withdraw the interdict.   Bishop Peter refused, and the Duke returned his
shining blade into the scabbard, with the words, ' Je ne t'aime pas assez pour
t'envoyer en Paradis.'

mate children, John, Edward, William, Joan, Katherine, and Isabel. In 1316 the Earl, in agreement with the King, made a deed of settlement of his lands north of the Trent, on himself for life, then on Maud de Nerford, if she survived him, for her life, with remainder to her sons by him and their heirs male, and in the event of the extinction of all these, then to the Crown. Maud died before the Earl. Her three sons survived him, but this settlement was set aside in favour of a new one which he made in 1346. Before this date Isabel de Holland was living with John, Earl de Warenne, as his recognised wife. His first wife, Jeanne de la Barre, was still, indeed, alive, for she survived him, and died in France in 1361. Perhaps the suit for divorce had, after all, been at last successful.[1] In any case, Isabel was recognised in the deed of 1346, and in the Earl's will of 1347, as, at least virtually, his wife. In the will, written in France, he calls her 'ma compaigne.' This is an expression which was then sometimes used in French wills, for wife. So, for instance, John of Gaunt in his will, also written in French, speaks of his first two wives as ' Blanche et Constance, mes très chéres compaignes.' On the other hand, both in the deed of 1346, and the will of 1347, Isabel is described by her own family name of 'Isabelle de Holande,' which would be unusual. On the whole the character and position of the fair Isabel must remain enigmatic.

The indenture in 1346 shows that the Earl, then sixty, and only a year from his death, still contemplated the possibility of having by Isabel a child, who would be the legitimate heir of his estates. Dugdale gives this deed as follows : It was provided that, ' If God should please to send him an heir by Isabel de Holland, then his wife,-

---

[1] Brayley, in his *History of Surrey*, says that the Earl did obtain the divorce. I know not on what authority. Dallaway, in his *History of Sussex*, denies it.

should the said heir be male or female, it should be joined in
marriage to some one of the blood royal unto whom the
King should think fittest, so that the whole inheritance of
the Earl with the name and arms of Warenne should be
preserved by the blood royal in the blood of the said Earl.
If he had no issue from the said Isabel, then his castles
and lands should, after his death, remain to the King to be
bestowed on one of his own sons on condition that the
name, honour and arms of Warenne should be for ever
maintained and kept.'

This settlement, apparently, like that of 1316, applied
to all his territories north of the Trent, but not to his
southern possessions. As the Earl left no child by Isabel
de Holland, the remainder over came into force, and, a few
days after the Earl's death, King Edward III made an
appointment by Letters Patent of these possessions in favour
of his fifth son, Edmund de Langley, then six years old.
Edmund was afterwards Duke of York, and this inheritance
was the foundation of the wealth and power of the House
of York, especially in Yorkshire, and so is of some importance
in English history.

In the following year the Earl de Warenne, then at Conisborough Castle, made his will, dated June 23, 1347, an
interesting document in many ways.[1] He appointed as
his executors the Archbishop of Canterbury, the Lady Maud
de Holland (the widow of Robert, Lord Holland), Sir Thomas
Holland, her second son, and eight other persons. He gave
instructions for the payment of his debts by the sale of
sufficient live-stock, and gave legacies to the shrine of St.
Thomas at Canterbury, and numerous other religious foundations. He left money legacies to his illegitimate children
by Maud de Nerford, and to William, one of the sons, who

[1] The will of 1347 is given in *Testamenta Eboriacensia*—Surtees Society, i.
41–5.

was Prior of Horton in Kent, his translation in French of
the Bible. He devised to Lady Maud Holland four horses
(jumentz) from his stud farm (haras) in Sussex. To Sir
Robert de Holland and Sir Otho de Holland he bequeathed
various specified parts of the metal trappings of his charger,
and he made a number of other legacies. To Isabel de
Holland, ' ma compaigne,' he left a ruby ring, the plate and
vestments of his chapel, and one-half of all his live-stock ;
and, after payment of debts and legacies, he made her
residuary legatee of his real and personal estate. This
bequest did not carry the land and castles north of Trent,
which had been settled by the deed of the preceding year,
nor any lands elsewhere, which the Earl could not devise
by will. Most of these, including the important Surrey
Castle of Reigate, went to Richard Fitz Alan, the son of his
sister Alice de Warenne, who had married the Earl of Arundel.
Apparently any territorial benefits to Isabel were cancelled
by a Royal Patent of December 12, 1347, seven months
after the Earl's death.[1]

This will shows that John, Earl de Warenne, was upon
excellent terms with the Hollands, since the whole family,
except John and Alan, appear in it either as legatees or
executors, and, inasmuch as the Archbishop of Canterbury,
the virtuous and aged Stratford, is an executor, it must be
supposed that the union of Isabel Holland with the Earl
was not disapproved by the Church, like that with Maud de
Nerford. Since Isabel's eldest brother was born in 1312,
she was probably about thirty, most enchanting age of
woman, in 1347, when the Earl died at about twice her age.
The sinful Earl, the beautiful Isabel, for she must have been
beautiful to please a man like him, the Saracen physician,
and other characters in the drama, would afford food for
imagination to a weaver of historical romance.

[1] See Dallaway's *History of Western Sussex*, ii. 130

John, last Earl de Warenne, and Surrey and Sussex, was buried, as in his will he desired, alone, under a raised tomb, near the High Altar, in the Abbey of Lewes. ' It is impossible,' says the modern historian of Sussex, ' from the remains of this distinguished edifice, to form any correct notion of its relative parts. The High Altar, before which so many of the noble family of De Warren reposed under splendid tombs, cannot be traced.'

These devastations by our vandals of the sixteenth and seventeenth centuries, are certainly an irreparable grief to the antiquary, and a cause of real regret to the lover of historical continuity. They call to remembrance the Elizabethan poet Webster's fine lines in his ' Duchess of Amalfi ' :

I do love these ancient ruins ;
We never tread upon them but we set
Our foot upon some reverent history ;
And, questionless, here, in this open court—
Which now lies naked to the injuries
Of stormy weather—some men lie interred,
Loved the Church so well, and gave so largely to it,
They thought it should have canopied their bones
Till Domesday ; but all things have their end ;
Churches and cities, which have diseases like to men.

It is not recorded what subsequent adventures befell the fair and successful Isabel, daughter of Robert, Lord Holland, and sister to Robert, Thomas, Otho, John, and Alan. That which happened to the line of her eldest brother, and to the ancestral manor, already has been narrated. The eventful history of the most famous cadet branch of the Hollands of Upholland continues through her second brother, Thomas, who rose in the wars oversea, made a great marriage, and became Earl of Kent.

The fortunes of this line will be narrated in the following

chapters. Of the other brothers, Otho and, perhaps, Alan left no posterity. There is said by one authority to have been a fourth brother, John, who married a lady called Eleanor Medsted, and founded a family who in lineal male descent held the manor of Weare near Topsham in Devonshire until the middle or end of the seventeenth century.

HOLLANDS, EARLS OF KENT AND HUNTINGDON, ETC.

Sir Robert de Holland = Maud, d. of Alan, Lord de
of Upholland, Lancashire, | la Zouche.
Lord Holland, illegally beheaded, October 1328.

Sir Thomas de Holland, = Joan Plantagenet, = 2ndlyEdwardPrince
K G., 1st Earl of Kent; b. | d. of Edmund Earl | of Wales, son of
before 1320, d. 1360, second | of Kent, and grand- | King Edward III
son. [1] | daughter of King
| Edward I.

King Richard II.

Thomas Holland, = Alice, d. of Fitz-   John de Holland, = Elizabeth, d.
K.G., 2nd Earl of | Alan, Earl of   K.G., Earl of Hunting- | of John of
Kent; b. 1350, d 1397. | Arundel.   don and Duke of | Gaunt, Duke
                                     Exeter; b. about 1352; | of Lancaster.
                                     illegally beheaded, 1400.

John Holland, = (1) Anne   (2) Beatrice,   (3) Anne,
K.G., 2nd Earl of | widow of   illegitimate,   d. of John
Huntingdon and | Edmund   d. of John I,   de Monta-
Duke of Exeter; | Mortimer,   King of Por-   cute, Earl
b. 1394, d. 1447. | Earl of   tugal; d.   of Salis-
              | March; d.   1439.   bury.
              | 1432.

Anne Holland = (1) John Lord
Nevill.
(2) Sir John
Nevill.

Thomas Holland, = Joan, d. of   Edmund, K.G , = Lucia, d. of
K G., 3rd Earl of | Ralph de   4th Earl of Kent; | Bernabo
Kent; b 1376; | Stafford.   b. 1384; killed in | Visconti of
d.s.p., illegally   France, 1408 s.p. | Milan.
beheaded, 1400.

——Alianora = Roger Mortimer, Earl of March.   Henry Holland, = Anne, d. of
——Joan = (1) Edmund of Langley, Duke of   3rd Duke of | Richard Plan-
                York.   Exeter; b.1430, | tagenet, Duke
            (2) Sir William de Willoughby, Lord   d., probably | of York, and
                d'Eresby.   murdered by | sister of King
            (3) Henry Scrope, Earl of Masham.   Yorkists, 1475. | Edward IV.
            (4) Henry Bromflete, Lord de Vesci.
——Margaret = (1) John de Beaufort, Earl of Som-
                erset son of John of Gaunt,   Anne Holland, d. unmarried.
                Duke of Lancaster.
            (2) Thomas, Duke of Clarence, son
                of King Henry IV.
——Eleanor = Thomas de Montacute, 4th Earl of
                Salisbury.
——Elizabeth = Sir John Nevill.
——Bridget, became a nun at Barking.

[1] Sir Thomas Holland, 1st Earl of Kent, also had two daughters: Joan, who married John, Duke of Brittany, and Maud
who married (1) Hugh, Lord Courtenay, (2) Waleran, Count of St. Pol.

CHAPTER II

THOMAS HOLLAND, EARL OF KENT

'Quell the Scot,' exclaims the lance,
'Bear me to the heart of France,'
Is the longing of the shield—
Tell thy name, thou trembling Field!
Field of death, where'er thou be
Groan thou with our victory.

W. WORDSWORTH.

Woman born to be controlled,
Stoops to the forward and the bold.

WALTER SCOTT.

THOMAS HOLLAND was born some time before 1320, and was a boy when his father came to his sudden and violent end. His first military experience seems to have been upon Edward III's expedition to Flanders in 1340, undertaken to assist his brother-in-law of Hainault and the citizens of Ghent and the other Flemish cities against the French. This campaign opened with the English naval victory off Sluys, which was, according to Froissart, 'a murderous and horrible' combat. After this Holland did some campaigning with the Spanish Christians against the Moors of Grenada, and with the Teutonic knights against the heathen in East Prussia. In 1342 he went with Sir John d'Artevelde to Bayonne, to defend the Gascon frontier. In 1344, together with his brother Otho, he was made one of the first members of the Order of the Garter. 'Forty knights,' says Froissart, 'were chosen, according to report esteemed the bravest in Christendom, who sealed and swore to maintain and keep the feast and ordinances which had been made.[1] On St. George's Day the grand inaugural ceremony took place at Windsor. 'The King made great preparations, and there were earls, barons, ladies and damsels most nobly entertained. Many knights came to them from beyond sea, from Flanders, Hainault and Brabant, but not one from France.'

Two years after this festival Thomas Holland went with the King, who was now claiming the French throne, into Normandy, and took part in the capture of Caen, now a flourishing and then, for those times, a populous and wealthy city, larger than any in England except London, and full of delicious plunder, says Froissart, 'fine draperies, rich citizens, and noble dames and damsels.' Here Holland made a splendid prize. The story is best told by Froissart in one of his most vigorous battle pictures. The Caen townsmen, absolutely confident in their valour and numbers, insisted upon marching out to fight the English, contrary to the advice of the Constable of France, the Count of Eu, who represented the French King there. Froissart says:

'So soon as these citizens of the town of Caen saw these English approach, who came on in three battalions, closely ranked, and perceived these banners and these pennons

---

[1] Froissart was wrong as to the number, forty. The first knights were twenty-six in number, and were listed in the following order :

1. King Edward
2. Edward, Prince of Wales.
3. Henry, Earl of Lancaster.
4. Thomas, Earl of Warwick.
5. Piers, de Greilly, Capital de Buch.
6. Ralph, Lord Stafford.
7. William, Earl of Salisbury.
8. Roger, Earl of March.
9. John, Lord Lisle.
10. Bartholomew, Lord Burgherst.
11. John, Lord Beauchamp
12. John, Lord Mohun of Dunster.
13. Hugh, Lord Courtenay.
14. Sir Thomas Holland.
15. John, Lord Gray of Codmore.
16. Sir Richard Fitzsimon.
17. Sir Miles Stapleton.
18. Sir Thomas Wale.
19. Sir Hugh Wrottesley.
20. Sir Nele Loring
21. Sir John Chandos.
22. Lord James Audley.
23. Sir Otho Holland.
24. Sir Henry Eam of Brabant.
25. Sir Sanchio d'Amberticourt.
26. Sir Walter Pareley.

flap and fly in the wind in great plenty, and heard these soldiers shout, which they were not accustomed to see nor to hear, so frightened and discomfited were they that all those in the world never have kept them back from flight, so that one and all they retreated towards their town without order, did the Constable wish it or not.

' Then could one see men shudder and be all dismayed, and this order of battle melt to nothing, for each man laboured to re-enter the town in safety. There was there great confusion, and many a man overturned and thrown on the ground, and they tumbled in heaps one on another, so scared were they. The Constable of France and the Count of Tancarville and other knights placed themselves on a gate at the foot of the draw-bridge,[1] for they saw that since their men fled, there was no resource at all, for these English were already entered and came among them and slew them at pleasure without mercy. Some knights and squires and others, who knew the way towards the castle went in that direction, and Robert de Warignies took them all in, for the castle is strong and great and stands advantageously. Those were in safety who could get there. The English, men at arms and archers, who were chasing the flying made great slaughter, for they gave quarter to no one, whence it happened that the Constable of France and the Count of Tancarville, who were on this gate at the foot of the draw-bridge, looked up and down the street and saw such great pestilence and tribulation that it was hideous to consider and imagine, and they thought that they should fall on this side into the hands of archers who would not know who they were.[2] While they looked down in great dread on these people slaying, they saw a gentleman, an

---

[1] I.e. at the drawn-up end.

[2] And would consequently kill them, not knowing their great ransom value if alive.

English knight, who had only one eye, who was called Sir Thomas Holland, and five or six good knights with him, which Sir Thomas they knew, for formerly they had seen him and been comrades with him in Granada and Prussia, and in other campaigns to which knights repair. So they were all comforted again when they saw him. So they called to him as he passed and said to him, "Sir Thomas, speak to us ! " When the knight heard himself named, he stopped short and asked, "Who are you, gentlemen, who know me ? " The said Lords named themselves and said, " We are such and such, come and speak to us here, and take us prisoners." When the said Sir Thomas Holland heard these words he was all joyous, both that he could save them, and for that he had, in taking them, a fine day's business, and a fine chance of good prisoners worth 100,000 " moutons." [1] So he withdrew as soon as he could all his troop that way, and he and sixteen of those with him, dismounted and went up to the top of the gate and found the aforesaid Lords and quite twenty-five knights with them, who were not safe from the slaying which they saw in the streets, and all yielded themselves at once and without delay to the said Sir Thomas, who took them and pledged them his prisoners ; and then left enough of his men to guard them, and mounted his horse and went into the streets, and that day prevented many cruelties and horrible deeds which would have been done, if he had not stood in the way, of his charity and knightly kindness. With the said Sir Thomas Holland were many knights of England, who prevented much mischief from being done, and saved many a beautiful citizeness and many a cloistered lady.'

Knights in these wars, when in good humour, sometimes did merciful acts of this kind, while the rank and file, as

---

[1] 'Moutons,' a French coin so called because it had a lamb stamped on it. It was equal in value to five English shillings of that period.

many tales in Froissart show, assumed, where they could, full licence to plunder and ravish. On the other hand, no quarter was given on either side to the rank and file of the other, whereas gentlemen were, when possible, saved from death, partly on account of a comradeship feeling and partly on account of their ransom value. But the wars for the English claim to the French succession were cruelly waged, and, while happy England as usual remained untouched, unhappy France was burnt and plundered and devastated without mercy.

Sir Thomas Holland sold the Constable of France to the King for 80,000 florins. The King afterwards, in England, committed the prisoner to the custody of Sir Otho Holland, the brother of Sir Thomas. Beltz, in his 'Memorials of the Order of the Garter,' says that the King delivered the Count of Eu ' by an indenture into the custody of Sir Otho Holand, under condition that the prisoner should not be admitted to leave England, or to bear arms publicly, until he should have paid his full ransom to the King.' It seems, notwithstanding, that Sir Otho took the Count with him to Calais, where he was seen at large and armed. Information thereof being given, Sir Otho was brought to the bar of the King's Bench before the Chancellor and other high personages, and, being unable to deny the charge, he put himself upon the King's favour, and was thereupon committed to the custody of the marshal.

After the taking of Caen, the English advanced to the gates of Paris, and burnt St. Germain, St. Cloud, Boulogne, and other villages in the environs. Then they marched north to the Beauvais country, plundering and burning as they went. The inhabitants of Poissy, having promised in the presence of the main army to pay a certain sum to save the town, then refused to pay it, and fell upon a small detachment which had been left behind to receive the ransom.

These English defended themselves gallantly, and sent to the army for succour. When the Kentish Lord Reginald de Cobham and Sir Thomas Holland, who commanded the rear-guard, heard this, they 'cried out "Treason! Treason!"' and returned to Poissy, where they found their countrymen still engaged with the townsmen. Almost all the inhabitants were then slain, the town was burnt, and the two castles razed to the ground.

A few days after this act of military punishment, on Saturday, August 26, 1346, Thomas Holland took part in the glorious battle of Crecy. He was in the division, or battalion, commanded by the Prince of Wales, then sixteen years old, together with the Earls of Warwick and Oxford, Sir Godfrey de Harcourt, Lord Reginald de Cobham, Lord Stafford, Lord Mauley, Lord Delaware, Sir John Chandos, Lord Bartholomew Burgherst, Lord Robert Neville, Lord Thomas Clifford, Lord Bouchier, Lord Latimer, and others. The division consisted of about 800 men at arms, 2000 archers, and 1000 Welshmen. There were two other battalions. 'They marched,' says Froissart, on the morning of the fight, ' in regular order to their ground, each lord under his own banner and pennon, and in the centre of his men.' The lion rampant, guardant, argent, on a field azure semé of fleurs de lys, which his father bore in the lists at Stepney, no doubt waved over Sir Thomas Holland. When the three divisions had been thus ranged in the early morning, they were visited by the King, riding on a small palfrey, with a white wand in his hand, and attended by his two marshals. He rode slowly through all the ranks, exhorting the men, ' to guard his honour and defend his right.' Then they ate a meal and heard a mass, and, in order to keep fresh, sat on the ground, placing their helmets and bows before them, and awaited the arrival of the French, who were coming in a disorderly manner by the road from Abbeville.

The brunt of the battle, so strikingly narrated by Froissart, fell upon the Prince's division, for here alone the French, under the Count d'Alençon, attacked in anything like regular order. Here there was hard fighting for a space. After this victory the siege of Calais began, and lasted almost a year. One day during the siege Sir Thomas Holland led a party of 2000 English out to forage. They were attacked by the French near St. Omer, and were driven in with the loss of 600 men.

Sir Thomas Holland made a very great marriage which affected, for good or evil, all the subsequent fortunes of this branch of the family. Edmund of Woodstock, Earl of Kent, was a younger son of King Edward I, and brother of King Edward II. He was amiable and popular, but came to a disastrous end. England was, for a while, during the minority of Edward III, ruled by Queen Isabella his mother, and her favourite, the Lord Mortimer. Against their rule conspired and rose the Earl of Lancaster, that same Henry of Lancaster to whom Robert de Holland's head had been sent in a basket. For a few days the Earl of Kent, the King's uncle, joined Lancaster, but almost immediately abandoned him. This action of incipient revolt was not forgiven by the Queen and Mortimer. Their agents, it is said, made Kent believe a story that his brother Edward II, although apparently buried, was not really dead, but alive, and shut up in Corfe Castle. Kent wrote letters to his dead brother, and these naturally came into the hands of the Government. They summoned a special, and packed, parliament to Winchester to try him ; he was convicted of high treason, and sentenced to death. He had to wait for four hours outside Winchester before anyone could be found who would take up the axe, and behead the uncle of the King. This happened in 1330, when Kent was twenty-nine years old. He left two sons and one daughter. The two sons were successively Earls of Kent, and died without issue. The second son, John, Earl of Kent, died December 27, 1852. Joan, the daughter, was two years old when her father lost his head. She grew up famous ' for her admirable beauty,' and men called her, after her father's title, the ' Fair Maid of Kent.' Her position was lofty, since she was a first cousin of Edward III, and, if her brothers died childless, the heir to great possessions.

When she was about twelve years old, Joan entered into a contract of marriage with Sir Thomas Holland, who was then about twenty-five. Their union was consummated before, apparently, the marriage was properly solemnised. Afterwards, while Holland was in Prussia, warring to aid the Teutonic Order against heathen Wends and Letts, Joan entered into a new contract of marriage with the eldest son of William de Montacute, Earl of Salisbury, who took her into his keeping, until his son should be old enough to complete the marriage.[1] Holland appealed to the Pope. A papal letter, dated May 3, 1347, was addressed from Rome to the Archbishops of Canterbury and York, and the Bishops of London and Norwich, on the petition of Thomas de Holland, Knight, stating that his wife, Joan, daughter of Edmund, Earl of Kent, to whom he was married upwards of eight years ago, was afterwards given in marriage to William, son of William de Montacute, Earl of Salisbury, during the absence from the realm of the said Thomas, then in Prussia, and that the said William, and Margaret, Joan's mother, opposed Thomas in recovering his conjugal rights. The cause was, at Holland's instance, brought before the Pope, and a suit of nullity of marriage against William and Margaret and Joan was ordered to be heard by Aymer,

---

[1] This Earl of Salisbury, the son, was born 1328, and succeeded to the title in 1344. He died 1387. He would therefore have only been a boy of about thirteen when, as was alleged, he received Joan in marriage before 1344.

Cardinal of St. Anastasia, but Joan was caused by William to be detained in England, and kept in custody. The Pope's letter directed that Joan should be set free, so that she might appoint a proctor and carry on the cause. Finally, Rome gave sentence in Sir Thomas Holland's favour, apparently on the ground that his was the earlier contract, and that its actual consummation had made it a virtual first marriage.[1] Salisbury released his claim and married another, and the high-born Beauty, now about twenty years old, became, whether with her will or against does not appear, fully Holland's wife, and she bore him children. Edward the Black Prince, her cousin, stood godfather to her eldest son, Thomas, afterwards second Earl of Kent of the Holland line.

In 1353 both of Joan's brothers were dead, and then Sir Thomas Holland obtained from the Crown a grant of 100 marks a year for life for the better support of this wife of the blood royal. Two years later possession was granted to him of the lands of her inheritance. Holland had been summoned several times to Parliament as a baron, under the title of Lord Holland, and, in 1360, a few months before his death, he was summoned under the title of Earl of Kent, which he had received, or assumed, in right of his wife.

After Crecy, Sir Thomas Holland held various military and administrative posts. In 1354 he was Lieutenant of the King in Brittany, during the minority of the Duke, and disposed of all the revenues of the Duchy. In 1356 he was Warden of the Channel Islands, and in 1359 he was appointed to be Captain and Lieutenant-Governor in Normandy. In September 1360, he received the lofty title of Captain and Lieutenant in France and Normandy. This

---

[1] By the law of the Roman Church a formal contract made a civil marriage. In Scotland this law continued after the Reformation, which is why runaway English couples went to Gretna Green.

D

office, like his title of Earl of Kent, he enjoyed but for a brief space, for he died on December 30 in that year, then being between forty and fifty years old, and was buried at the Grey Friars' Abbey at Stamford. He died possessed of a number of manors in the counties of Kent, Surrey, Essex, Suffolk, Buckingham, Worcester, Stafford, Hertford, Northampton, Derby, and York, mainly his wife's heritage.

Evidently this Thomas Holland was an able and trustworthy man of action, and had the personal charm which is also so important to success. Froissart calls him 'un gentil chevalier,' and, elsewhere ' le bon chevalier.' Another old chronicler says that he was a vigorous soldier, ' miles strenuus.' The Chandos Herald poetically styles him :

> Le bon Thomas de Holland
> Qui en lui eut proesse grand.

Still, the social world must have deemed Joan of Kent's marriage with Holland a bad *mésalliance* for a granddaughter of King Edward I, and first cousin of King Edward III. Holland certainly did not belong to the old feudal nobility, but only to a Lancashire Squire family, which had recently produced one distinguished, but unpopular man, Robert de Holland, who had come to a disastrous end. At her husband's death, Joan, Countess of Kent, was about thirty-three, and now perhaps in fullest ripeness of her glorious beauty. Not long afterwards she married her cousin, Edward Prince of Wales, who was then about thirty years old. They were within the prohibited degrees and therefore a dispensation had to be obtained from Rome. It was given on condition that the Prince founded a Chantry, which he did, in the crypt of Canterbury Cathedral. But how was it that the heir to the great throne of England had remained so long unmarried in those days of early marriages, notwithstanding that various high alliances had been discussed ? Some have said that, since he was a boy, the Black Prince had been passionately attached to this beautiful cousin of his, and that he had wished to marry her even before she married Thomas Holland, but was prevented by the dislike of his parents to the match. Certainly when the Prince returned from Poitiers, a hero of twenty-five, leading with high chivalry the French King captive, a beautiful woman at the passionate age of twenty-eight, playing her part amidst the magnificent festivities of Windsor, may well have found such a cousin irresistible.

Froissart, according to the Amiens MS., says that the Prince, before leaving for his Government of Aquitaine, in 1362, lived at his house at Berkhampstead with ' Madame la Princesse sa femme, qu'il avoit par amour prise a épouse et a compaigne de sa vollente sans le sceu du roy son pere. En avant la ditte dame etait mariée a ce bon chevalier monsigneur Thummas de Holland de qui elle avoit des biaus enfans.'

Froissart was an excellent authority, for he was in England at this time. But he must mean, not that the marriage ceremony was secret, but that the Prince had engaged himself to marry Joan without his father's previous knowledge. An excellent seventeenth-century English historian, who laboured hard at original sources of history,[1] says that in the year 1361, the object of the Prince of Wales' affection was ' that incomparable paragon of beauty the Lady Joan, commonly called the Fair Countess of Kent, at this time a widow, and yet neither in age much unequal to this great Prince, nor in virtue, or nobility, though a subject, unworthy of him. She was now in the thirty-third year of

[1] Joshua Barnes's *History of Edward III and the Black Prince*, printed at Cambridge, 1688, one of the most spirited histories of this period.

her age and the Prince in the thirty-first of his, he being
great grandchild of King Edward the First, and she grandchild to the said King by a second venture, he, the glory
of his sex for military performances and other princely
virtues, and she the flower of hers, for a discreet honorable
mind sweetened with all the delicacies of a most surprising
beauty. However 'tis said [1] the Prince only intended at
first to incline her to the love of a certain knight, a servant
of his, whom he designed to advance thereby ; but that
after certain denials with which he would not be put off,
she told him plainly "how when she was under ward she
had been disposed of by others ; but that now, being at
years of discretion and mistress of her own actions, she
would not cast herself beneath her rank ; but remembered
that she was of the blood royal of England, and therefore
resolved never to marry again but to a Prince for quality
and virtue like himself." '

What woman's son could resist such woman's wooing ?
The Black Prince did not resist the kindred Plantagenet
Beauty, obtained his father's consent, and the marriage
was celebrated with solemnity and splendour at Windsor
on October 16, 1361.[2]

The Duchy of Aquitaine had been secured to the English
Crown by the Treaty of Bretigny made with France in
1360. It was granted on feudal tenure, by Edward III to

---

[1] Said by John Hardyng (the early fifteenth-century chronicler) more concisely.
The gallant conversation in the text rests, alas, on slender evidence.

[2] Bernard Burke in his *Royal Descents* quotes a curious certificate given to the
Prince by Simon, Archbishop of Canterbury, dated October 9, 1361. (Harleian
MS. 6148) In this allusion is made to the Bull of Pope Innocent granting a
dispensation for the Prince's marriage he being within the prohibited degrees of
kindred and as being the godfather of Joan's eldest son, ' whereupon many
scandals may arise ' *Item*, ' she was afore contracted to Thomas Montacute, Earl of
Salisbury, after to Thomas Holland, knight, betwixt whom grew strife in that
cause before the Pope's Court, but judgment was given against the Earl, and she
remained wife to the knight, and the Earl, therewith content, married another
lady at Lambeth.'

his son, the Prince of Wales, by a Charter dated July 19, 1362, together with the title of Prince of Aquitaine. The Prince and Princess left England for their new principality at the beginning of February 1363. Immediately after Christmas, the good Queen Philippa, together with King Edward III and other princes of the royal family, had made a visit of five days to them at Berkhampstead, so that if the marriage had been against her own inclinations this admirable lady seems to have forgiven it. John Froissart came to Berkhampstead on this occasion in the Queen's retinue. He heard there an old knight, conversing with the ladies, say that in a certain ancient book it was predicted that the Prince of Wales would never be King of England, but the realm and crown should pass to the House of Lancaster.

The Queen was, no doubt, kind to the Holland children whom she found at Berkhampstead, two boys and two girls of remarkable beauty all under thirteen or fourteen years of age. Froissart, too, must have known these children well, and encouraged them with tales of chivalry and love.

Joan lived with the Prince until his death on Trinity Sunday, June 8, 1376, and she did the honours of his gay and splendid court at Bordeaux and Angoulême. She bore him two sons, Edward the eldest, born at Angoulême, February 1365, who died when he was seven, and Richard, born at Bordeaux in the year 1367, who became King Richard II. At the deposition of Richard, 1399, Henry of Lancaster alleged that Richard was not really the son of Edward Prince of Wales. He said that he himself had heard from several knights, who were at the Court of Bordeaux, that the Prince was uneasy about his wife's conduct, and that having for some years had no child by the Prince, she was anxious to have one because she knew that the King of England was vexed that she, who had given two sons to Sir Thomas Holland, had as yet given none to the Prince of Wales. The great unlikeness of Richard in every respect to his father was said also to be proof of this, but this is a weak argument. He was no more unlike than was the weak and gentle Henry VI to his undoubted and heroic sire. A slight mist of doubt, perhaps, hangs over the life of the Beauty of Kent, but Henry's accusation was, in all probability, quite untrue, and certainly to make it was more politic than chivalrous, since his cousin Joan was dead and could not reply or deny.[1]

That admirable author, so deeply versed in mediæval history and sentiment, Kenelm Digby, in his book, the ' Broadstone of Honour,' calls the Princess ' wise and excellent.' He is following a French chronicler, in relating how ' when Pedro the Cruel of Castile, upon flying to Angoulême, had prevailed upon the Prince of Wales to defend his cause, having presented him with a superb golden table, the Prince ordered that the present should be shown to the Princess, who was at the same time informed of his resolution in favour of the war. This ' wise and excellent woman ' says Digby, lamented in bitter terms the decision of the Prince, and exclaimed that she heartily wished that the table had never been presented, and that the wicked Pedro had never set foot in their Court.[2] When the words of the Princess were related to the Prince, ' I see well,' said he, ' that she wishes that I should be always by her side, and

---

[1] Lord Bacon in his *Historical Discourse* ascribes a ' light inconstancy ' to Joan Plantagenet, of which he says ' a tincture ' reappears in her son, Richard II. There is not much ground for attributing inconstancy to Joan more than to other beautiful women. How can they be entirely constant ?

[2] The golden table was at a later date sold by the Prince to Fitz-Alan of Arundel, then Bishop of Ely, for only 300 marks, and the Bishop left it by will to his episcopal successors, but, says an old historian, ' Time, Avarice, or Sacrilege, or some other Accident, have devoured the very table itself,' which is a pity. The chronicler calls it ' a wonderful, sumptuous and costly table, adorned with gold and precious stones.'

never leave her chamber ; but a Prince must be ready to
win worship and to expose himself to all kinds of dangers,
comme firent autrefois Roland, Olivier, Ogier, les quatres
fils Aimon, Charlemagne, le Grand Leon de Bourges, Jean de
Tournant, Lancelot, Tristan, Alexandre, Artus et Godefroy,
dont tous les romans racontent le courage, la valeur, et
l'intrepidite toute martiale et toute heroique ; et par St.
Georges, je rendray Espagne en droit heritier.'

This story calls up a vision rather of too fond a wife than
of the flirting and faithless princess solemnly suggested by
Henry IV to Parliament. The Prince did not venture to
consult his beautiful Princess until after he had made his
decision, for he knew too well what, notwithstanding the
table, she would think of Pedro.

The exact words of the Prince's splendid tirade, of which
Don Quixote would have highly approved, are, alas ! probably
the work of a romantic imagination; but, according to the
more exact Froissart, some of the Black Prince's men
counsellors advised him not to espouse the cause of Pedro,
a cruel tyrant, hated and just expelled by all classes of his
people, and whose opinions and actions were, says Froissart,
' durement rebelles a tous commandements de l'Eglise.'
The Prince said, in reply, that he knew of Pedro's crimes,
but that, if a bastard were elected to dethrone a legitimate
brother, it would imperil ' l'estat royal.' He warned Pedro,
however, that, if he replaced him on his throne, he should
expect him hereafter to reform his ways. No doubt, as
Froissart says, the Prince then at the height of his masculine
vigour, was really impelled by the desire for adventure and
glory. He was inspired by the romantic literature of the
age, just as modern Princes may be inspired to war by
scientific theories as to race, survival of the fittest, and so-
forth. The Father Possévih, a learned Jesuit of the sixteenth
century, used to complain that for the last five hundred years

the Princes of Europe had been infatuated by romances.
Men in those days, as now, took trouble to find just causes
for war, but they believed in their hearts that a good war
was its own justification.   All this happened in the autumn
of 1366.

Thomas Holland, first Earl of Kent, had by his wife
Joan Plantagenet two sons, Thomas and John, and two
daughters, Joan and Maud.   These two Holland girls were
young stars shining in the last and most glorious years of
that mediæval England which seemed to come to an end
with the deaths of Edward III and the Black Prince.   The
younger, Maud, was married about the year 1365, when she
was not more than ten, to the Earl of Devon's eldest son,
Hugh, Lord Courtenay, who was four or five years older.
He was grandson to the Earl of Devon who married Margaret
de Bohun ; their finely carved effigies are still to be seen
at Exeter Cathedral.   In 1367 this boy Hugh, together with
Maud's brother Thomas, second Earl of Kent, and others, was
knighted by the Black Prince before the battle of Vittoria
when the army was arrayed for battle.   Hugh Courtenay
died young, in 1373, and Maud was left a widow at about
eighteen.

Waleran of Luxembourg, Count of St. Pol, and Lord of
rich possessions in Picardy, was born in 1355, succeeded to
his father's title in 1371, and in the year 1375 was taken
prisoner by the English near Calais, and detained as a prisoner
in England until he could raise a huge ransom.   Here he
fell in love with the ravishing beauty of the young widow
Maud Holland.   Froissart relates how the young Earl was
kept prisoner for long ' in the fair castle of Windsor ; and
he had so courteous a keeper, that he might go and sport
and fly his birds between Windsor and Westminster ; he
was trusted on his faith.   The same season, the Princess,
mother of King Richard, lay at Windsor, and her daughter

with her, my Lady Maud, the fairest lady in all England ; the Earl of St. Pol and this young lady were in true amours together, each of other ; and sometimes they met together at dancing and carolling and other disports, till at last it was spied. And then the lady discovered to her mother how she loved ardently the young Earl of St. Pol ; then there was a marriage spoken of between the Earl and Lady Maud ; and so the Earl was set to his ransom to pay some six score thousand francs, so that when he married the Lady Maud, then he was to be abated three score thousand and the other three score thousand to pay. And when this covenant of marrying was made between the Earl and the Lady, the King of England suffered him to repass the sea to fetch his ransom, on his only promise to return again a year after.' The King of France detained St. Pol in prison a long time on some charge, but he at last got free and then came back with his ransom to England and married Lady Maud, and they went to live at the castle of Ham on the river Eure, which was lent to them by St. Pol's brother-in-law the Sire de Moriaume, till the French King's wrath should abate.

The eighteenth-century historian of France, Père Daniel, says politely of Maud the Fair, that she was ' une des plus belles personnes de l'Europe,' and of Waleran that ' c'etait un seigneur bien fait, adroit a tous les exercices du corps, enjoué dans la conversation, et qui par tous les beaux endroits mérita de plaire beaucoup a cette princesse.' The date of the marriage seems to have been somewhere about 1380. Waleran and Maud would each have been twenty-five or thereabouts. Froissart, a great connoisseur of appearances, must have known both of them well, for he lived in their country near Valenciennes and was working there at his history for about ten or twelve years after 1374, so that his evidence as to Maud's beauty is good.

The Count of St. Pol survived his wife and lived till 1417,

marrying secondly a daughter of the Duke de Barre. In
later years he became violent and cruel, and in one campaign
against insurgents in 1391, burned down a hundred and
twenty villages in Luxembourg. He had no son by Maud
the Fair, only one daughter who, like the Princess, her
grandmother, was named Jeanne. This valuable heiress,
for there were no children by the second marriage, was
married in 1402 to Antoine, second son of the Duke of
Burgundy, 'laquelle feste,' says Monstrelet, 'fut moult
notable, et y eut plusieurs princes et princesses avec très
noble chevelerie.' This marriage united the great St. Pol
possessions to the House of Burgundy. On the death of
his father, Antoine became Duke of Brabant. In 1407,
on the death of his mother, heiress of the Counts of Flanders,
the Duke of Brabant became Seigneur of the Flemish cities.
Antoine was killed at Agincourt, and when, in 1430, his
son, Duke Philip of Brabant died without leaving issue,
the whole of the St. Pol, Brabant, and Flemish possessions
went to swell the greatness of the main or elder line of the
Dukes of Burgundy. Thus Waleran de St. Pol and his
Countess, Maud, are links in history, for round the rich
Burgundian inheritance turned many a later war.

Maud Holland's form and beauty, like that of her brother
Lord Huntingdon, came no doubt from her maternal Plantagenet ancestry, rather than from the Lancastrian squires
of her paternal line. The tombs at Westminster Abbey,
and that of the Black Prince at Canterbury, studied com-
paratively, show that the beauty of the later Plantagenets
was mainly derived from the wife of Edward I, Eleanor of
Castile. Richard II is certainly a singular departure from
the type, seeing that both his parents were Plantagenets.
He has not the straight, or delicately aquiline, nose, the
finely moulded cheeks, and the small well-chiselled head.
But then neither, according to the monument at Canterbury,
had his cousin Henry IV, also a Plantagenet on both sides,

who dethroned him. Had it not been for the reformers of religion we should have had the exact likenesses of Thomas Holland, the first Earl of Kent, and of his wife Joan Plantagenet, from their monument in the Grey Friars at Stamford. As it is, we only have a full carved face surrounded by luxuriant hair, embossed on the vault of the Black Prince's Chantry at Canterbury, which is believed to represent the Fair Maid of Kent. There are no special praises of the beauty of Joan, elder sister of Maud, and perhaps she was more of a Holland. This Lady Joan, in her girlhood, adorned the Court of her step-father the Black Prince at Bordeaux, and was married very young in 1366 to John de Montfort, Duke of Brittany, who had previously been married to Mary, a daughter of King Edward III.

'The nuptials,' says Froissart, 'were celebrated with great pomp and magnificence in the good city of Nantes.' It was a fine marriage for Joan, but not a happy one. 'Duke John,' says a French historian, 'was a politic and war-like prince, but his great qualities were tarnished by his pride, cruelty and bad faith,' and he lived in perpetual turmoil. The battle of Auray, in 1364, where his rival Charles de Blois, supported by the French, was killed, made John master of the whole duchy, but in 1372 he was driven out for a while. In 1381 he allied himself with Charles VI of France, and so quarrelled with his previous English allies, who had to leave Brittany, but kept possession of Brest, and also detained from him his wife who was in England. In that year she was living at Byfleet in Surrey (spelt Byflete in old chronicles). Here, in the pleasant meadows by the River Wey, was a manor house belonging to the Crown where now stands the present manor house, portions of which are very ancient. The old house now belongs to Mrs. Rutson, whose mother was a Holland. John, Duke of Brittany, with the permission of his sovereign the French King, sent envoys to Richard II to ask, among other things, that his Duchess, the King's half-sister, should return to him.

Richard referred the matter to his council, who directed Bazvalen, the chief envoy, to repair to Byflete and convey to the Duchess the request of his master. The Duchess expressed her willingness to obey, and to depart for Brittany immediately, if the King and the Princess of Wales, her mother, would permit. Bazvalen then visited the Princess at Wallingford-on-Thames, and obtained her consent, and then the King allowed the departure of his sister. It was this same Bazvalen, a wise counsellor, who, a few years later, saved the life of Sir Olivier de Clisson, and the honour of his own master, in that dark affair in the Breton Castle of L'Hermine. The Duchess of Brittany died in 1386, and the Duke who married again, at the end of 1399.

This story must now pursue the adventures of the two brothers of Joan, Duchess of Brittany, and Maud, Countess of St. Pol—namely, Thomas Holland, second Earl of Kent, and John Holland, Earl of Huntingdon and finally Duke of Exeter. These two were, in 1360, the only living male descendants, save for their eldest uncle Robert and his son, of their grandfather Sir Robert, Lord Holland of Upholland in Lancashire. Alan Holland, one of their uncles, had died, according to some authorities, without leaving children, and the other uncle, Sir Otho Holland, K.G., had died on September 3, 1359, a few months before their father. He certainly left no children, and his estates went, under different entails, to his brothers Robert and Thomas. Otho had not been very fortunate. Some years after his trouble about the Count d'Eu, he accompanied his brother Thomas on a campaign in France in 1355, and was made prisoner together with Sir Thomas Beaumont in an action near Grandserre, in Dauphiny. He was ransomed, and was Governor of the Channel Islands in 1359, and died that autumn in Normandy.

CHAPTER III

THOMAS HOLLAND, SECOND EARL OF KENT, AND SIR JOHN HOLLAND

> .   .   .   .   .   Glories
> Of human greatness are but pleasing dreams
> And shadows soon decaying; on the stage
> Of my mortality, my youth hath acted
> Some scenes of vanity, drawn out at length
> By varied pleasures, sweetened with mixture,
> But tragical in issue.
>
> FORD—*Broken Heart.,*

THOMAS HOLLAND, second Earl of Kent, was ten years old when his father died at the end of 1360. His brother John was a year or two younger. Men began life early in those days. At the age of about thirteen, Thomas was married to Alice Fitzalan, the daughter of Richard, Earl of Arundel, one of the old Norman-sprung nobility, and of his wife Maud, who was second daughter of Henry, Earl of Lancaster, and so descended from King Henry III. Young Thomas Holland went to France in the train of his step-father, the Black Prince. In 1366, when he was sixteen, he went with the Prince's army into Spain in the attempt to overthrow Enrique, who had usurped Don Pedro's throne, and he received knighthood at his hands, under the walls of Vittoria, on March 18, ' after the trumpets had sounded for marshalling the host.'

An English historian of the seventeenth century says that the Prince's army arranged themselves in the pre-ordained order ' in a moment,' at the sound of the trumpets,

' they were all so practised and expert in war. Surely it was a gallant sight to behold the brightness of their arms, to observe the stateliness of their barbed horses, to view the rich banners and streamers embroidered and beaten with arms, both in colours and metal, and waving with a delightful terror in the wind.'

The sun of Spain never shone upon array more beautiful, for it was a great army, and the chivalry of England and Aquitaine were there. The Prince of Wales was in the centre, on one wing was the King of Majorca, another was commanded by the Duke of Lancaster, then twenty-seven, with the great Captain, Sir John Chandos, as the Chief of his Staff. Three hundred young men were made knights on the field. The Black Prince knighted Don Pedro, his stepson, young Thomas Holland, the three sons of the Earl of Devon, Hugh, Philip, and Denis Courtenay, of whom the eldest, Hugh, was already married to Maud Holland, the lovely child-sister of Thomas Holland. He knighted also William de Molyneux of that Lancashire family and other youths. Others were knighted by the Duke of Lancaster, Chandos, and other chief leaders. An English victory at Vittoria was, however, to be deferred till a later age. Neither side were anxious to fight as both were awaiting reinforcements, and though there were some sharp encounters, the decisive battle did not take place for about three weeks, and was then fought on April 3, upon the plain of Najara. It was a grand fight, greater than that of Poitiers, between two great armies. The Castilians, with their French allies had the larger numbers ; they counted, it is said, a hundred thousand men, but the Prince's force was much better trained and disciplined and won by superior arrow-fire and tactics. Spanish slingers were no match for English bowmen. The victory was decisive and the loss of the English-Gascon force was small compared with that of the foe. Thomas Holland is mentioned as fighting this day close to his step-father the Black Prince.

In 1373 the young Earl of Kent was in the army with which John, Duke of Lancaster, marched right through France from Calais to Bordeaux, dreadfully ravaging on the way the Somme Valley and all the country round Noyon and Laon, and Soissons and Rheims, and the region of the Loire, ' killing and ransoming the people, wasting the country and firing the towns wherever he came,' says the old writer. There was hardly any fighting, but the English lost almost all their horses and many of their men through sickness and fatigue.

In 1374 and 1375 the Earl of Kent was still in the French wars. In the latter year he was made a Knight of the Garter, and accompanied the Earl of Cambridge, son of the Duke of York, into Brittany with 3000 archers and 2000 men-at-arms. When King Edward died in 1377, the Earl of Kent was in full manhood, about twenty-seven years old. In 1381 took place the rising caused by the poll tax in Kent and Essex. Joan, the widow Princess of Wales, was caught in the Tower by the Kentish rebels and treated with some rudeness. It was alleged that the two Hollands felt themselves so unpopular that when young King Richard rode to Smithfield to parley with Wat Tyler, they dropped out of his train and would not face the music of the mob. The subsequent punishment of the Kentish insurgents was entrusted to the Earl of Kent and was cruelly severe. In 1385 he accompanied the King's great expedition into Scotland.

Thomas, Earl of Kent, and his brother John Holland, as half-brothers of King Richard, were constantly at Court, and they were accused of exercising a bad influence upon Richard. A monkish chronicler of the time, Walsingham, was evidently one of their best haters ; but then the Court party were accused of sympathy with the Lollards, who were, indeed, religious radicals not at all deserving sympathy, and their political opponents were the old aristocratic and more religiously conservative Englishmen. No doubt, also, the Hollands were still, notwithstanding their mother's rank, considered by the feudal party to be adventurers and upstarts. Holinshed wrote in Tudor days and based his statements mainly on the chronicles of the monk Walsingham and other ecclesiastics, but to some extent, perhaps, on tradition. He says that the people at the time of the arrest and death of the Duke of Gloucester and Arundel, accused John Holland, Earl of Huntingdon, 'as one of the chief authors of all the mischief . . . having trained up the King in vice and evil customs from his youth.'

He also says of Richard, 'He was seemly of shape and favour, and of nature good enough, if the wickedness and naughty demeanour of such as were about him had not altered it.' The learned modern historian, Bishop Stubbs, follows in the same line. The good Bishop of Oxford did not, by temperament, or character, or way of life, at all resemble the Hollands, and was not well qualified to understand or imagine them. He says in his 'Constitutional History' (ii. p. 464) :

'Richard was most unfortunate in his surroundings ; in his two half-brothers, the Hollands, he had companions of the worst sort, violent, dissipated, and cruel.'

Again he says :

'Capable of energetic and resolute action upon occasion, Richard was habitually idle, too conscious, perhaps, that when the occasion arose he would be able to meet it. The Hollands were willing that the tutelage should last as long as they could wield his power and reap advantage of his inactivity.'

This may have been so, though blame of this kind seems to attach more in Richard's earliest days to his guardian uncles, but some of the contemporary evidence as to the character and motives of the Hollands must be taken with much caution. It is a bad thing for kings to inherit crowns in early boyhood. No doubt Richard was exposed to great flatteries and temptations. He was vacillating, inconstant, and easily influenced, childish and artistic in temperament, with no fixed convictions and no steadfast policy, the kind of man who will do anything to avoid a bad quarter of an hour. His Court was voluptuous and extravagant, even the most obsequious Parliament of his reign complained of the number of ' bishops and ladies ' who lived in it. In this Court the Hollands were certainly not immaculate any more than were the Guises, Beauforts, Rohans, and Rochefoucaulds in the Court of Louis XIII.

One must judge them in connection with their own age and not by the test of modern moral standards. The end of the fourteenth century was not a morally good period. There was, indeed, much true religion existing. Was not Mother Julian at this very time receiving her revelations of divine love in her cell at Norwich ? Doubtless there was many a good parish priest like him described by Chaucer, and there was certainly among the English and other European common people more deep and true religious feeling than there is now. The exquisite religious art is a witness, for then, as now, artists delineated that which they saw in the faces all around them. The ideal was high, though lives often fell far short of it. If men were immoral, they were not hypocritical, and they knew how to repent. Ecclesiastical government was certainly demoralised and secularised by long prosperity and power ; it was in many places corrupted by avarice, sensuality and worldly pursuits and pleasures, and it was discredited by the long papal schism. All this never reached a lower depth (except, perhaps, under Alexander VI) than when, a few years later, John XXIII was Pope. The tide of Catholic

fervour was still ebbing from the high point which it reached
when it broke upon the walls of Jerusalem, and did not
begin to flow again till the sixteenth century. Religion
was loosely associated with her ever-uneasy companion
Morality, and the way in which the marriage jurisdiction
of the ecclesiastical lawyers at Rome was then exercised,
was the reverse of salutary. Morals were lax, not only
in royal and aristocratic, but also, if one may at all
credit Chaucer and more prosaic records, in bourgeois circles.
Then again, the old Saxon ferocity and barbarism in
the English, and the aristocratic contempt of the Norman
families for plebeian life had not yet softened down
into the later civilisation. English and French gentlemen
treated each other courteously enough, but other classes
in France were mercilessly dealt with by the invaders.
The story revealed in French chronicles is really dreadful. Towns and villages were usually plundered, directly
or by way of ransom, and often burnt, and their inhabitants
were frequently slain and ravished. The kind of warfare
is described in a letter from Sir John Wingfield to ' a certain
noble lord then in England,' dated from Bordeaux, December 22, 1855, giving an account of the Prince of Wales' campaign that year. Here is one passage. ' So then we marched
through the seigniory of Thoulouse, and took many good
towns before we came to Carcassonne, which is greater
and stronger and fairer than York. But as well this as
all other towns in the country which we took were burned,
plundered and destroyed.' Or again, ' Then he (the Prince)
went into the country of Estarac wherein he took many
towns and wasted and ravaged all the country.' Imagine
the details of this process. The object was, says Sir John,
to destroy the revenues of the French King.[1] The fact

---

[1] Sir John's two letters, very interesting, are quoted in Guthrie's *History of England* (1747).

was that the English were then a hard and fierce race, little as yet softened by civilisation. The historian Froude, describing them as they were a little later, calls them 'a sturdy high-hearted race, sound in body and fierce in spirit and furnished with thews and sinews which, under the stimulus of those great " shins of beef," their common diet, were the wonder of the age. . . . Again and again a few thousands of them carried dismay into the heart of France. . . . Invariably, by friend and foe alike, the English are described as the fiercest people in all Europe (the " English wild beasts " Benvenuto Cellini called them), and this great physical power they owed to the profuse abundance in which they lived, and the soldiery training in which every man of them was bred from childhood.'

This training was not likely to make gentlemen of the mild and well-ordered mentality dear to constitutional historians of the Liberal school. Then again, no doubt, the long absences of gentlemen in foreign wars had, like the Crusades, bad effects on domestic morality. There is evidence that the level of morals and religion had declined both in England and France between the thirteenth century and the fifteenth. All these things had a deteriorating effect on English character, except with regard to valour in fighting, a constant quality throughout all English history, and this influence was felt for two centuries to come.

On the other side of the account one must admire the strong individuality of men of these times, not yet flattened out by the steam-roller of democratic civilisation. The French historian and statesmen, Guizot, said in one of his lectures that there is a political advantage in studying the Middle Ages. ' Our time may be characterised by a certain weakness, a certain softness in minds and manners. Individual wills and convictions want energy and confidence, obey a general impulse, and yield to an exterior necessity.

Whether it be for resistance or for action, no one has a great idea of his own force, or any confidence in his own thought. Individuality, in a word, the intimate and personal energy of man, is weak and timid. Amidst the progress of general liberty many men seem to have lost the noble and powerful sentiment of their own liberty. Such was not the Middle Age, the social condition was then deplorable ' (and yet, perhaps, not, after all, so unhappy) 'but in many men individuality was strong and will energetic, the moral nature of men appeared here and there, in all its grandeur and with all its power.' In fact men were not yet so much ' civilised ' as later, nor so far removed from the northern barbarian. Shakespeare lived before the change to modern civilisation had well set in, and he found in men around him models for his vigorous and passionate historical characters. Poets who wrote such speeches now would be copying from Shakespeare and not from life, which is why this kind of writing seems unreal.

As to the Hollands, they were as vigorous, and probably not worse than, the other lords of their time whose position or wealth exposed them to the higher temptations. But they were usually on the unpopular and losing side, and this has made historians, who, on the contrary, are usually on the popular and winning side, write them down as specially bad men.

John Holland was rather a favourite with the experienced Froissart, who knew a man of character when he came across one. We had much better take the opinion of such men of the world as Sir John Froissart, who knew John Holland very well at Richard's Court,[1] or John de Wavrin, seigneur of

---

[1] Froissart lived in England between 1361 and 1366 and must have often seen the second Earl of Kent and Sir John Holland as boys, and he met them as men (unless John had already started for Palestine) at Richard's Court on his last visit to England in the summer of 1391, twenty-seven years later.

Forestel, who knew men who remembered him, than of the monk, Walsingham, gloomily writing in the cloisters of St. Albans, or of the virtuous and learned Bishop Stubbs, writing in the nineteenth century in an Oxford library to show how the popular English Constitution developed notwithstanding the assaults of the malignant. Walsingham was prejudiced by anti-Lollardism, and Stubbs by the imagination of progress. The constitutional and economic histories written in the later nineteenth century, however meritorious, must have been an ungrateful offering to the muse of History when she remembered her Herodotus and Thucydides, her Livy and Plutarch and Tacitus, her Froissart and de Commines, her Gibbon and her Macaulay. For it is doubtful whether to the mind of a muse, being a woman, any degree of conscientious labour and scientific accuracy and 'sound' political views, can compensate for the absence of dramatic and personal interest.

John Holland was, it must be owned, of a violent temper in youth, and not tenderly scrupulous in action when older. In 1372, when he was about twenty, he went on a military expedition against the Scots. In 1381 he was made Chief Justice of Chester, and after that was seldom out of some great employment. In 1382 he was sent with Sir Simon de Burley and other men of quality to bring into England Anne, daughter to the Emperor Charles IV, whom Richard had espoused by proxy. They met the Princess at Calais and brought her across the sea to Dover, where they stayed for two days. Thence they escorted her over Barham Downs to Canterbury, where they were received in state by the Earl of Buckingham and others, and thence rode on to London and the impatient Richard.

In the following year, 1383, the Duke of Lancaster was anxious to obtain men, ships and money for an expedition to assert his wife's claim to the throne of Castile. This was delayed by a rival expedition. Urban, the Italian Pope whom the English supported against his rival 'Pope' Clement at Avignon, preached a crusade against the Clementines, among whom were the King of France and the Count of Flanders. The English willingly took up this quarrel and a force crossed the sea under the very unfit command of the Bishop of Norwich, who was a Despenser. These crusaders slew some nine thousand Flemings near Dunkirk, and assisted by the jealous 'Gantois' laid siege to Ypres, then a formidable industrial rival to Ghent.

Upon the advance of a large French army from Arras, the English had to raise the siege and retire to Calais, and the entire expedition failed, rather to the satisfaction of the Duke of Lancaster and his friends, who wished for the rival Spanish expedition. They now attempted to make peace with the French in order to facilitate this object. In the following November, the Duke of Lancaster, his son, Henry of Derby, Sir John Holland, Sir John Cobham, Sir John Marmion and others were sent to meet the Dukes of Burgundy and Berry and other French lords at Wissant, between Calais and Boulogne, to try to arrange a peace or truce. The Count of Flanders gave the company a banquet in a pavilion made of Bruges cloth erected near the sea, and proceedings were agreeable and friendly, but the French asked too much, even for Calais itself, and the negotiations broke down.

In the year 1384, rumour connected John Holland's name with a deed of violence. There was an Irish Carmelite Friar who had begun to hatch an accusation of treason against the Duke of Lancaster, whose daughter, Elizabeth, John Holland married two years later. Walsingham of St. Albans, the monkish chronicler, alleges that John Holland murdered this Friar Latimer in prison with his own hands, assisted by Sir Henry Green, in a shockingly cruel manner.

Walsingham is the sole authority for this highly improbable story, which later historians have repeated. He was evidently inspired by a violent dislike for the Hollands and their set. Beltz, the author of ' Memorials of the Order of the Garter,' justly observes, ' The horror with which the Lollard heresy had inspired him is evident at every mention of its fautors, to whom the Duke of Lancaster is known to have extended his protection.' Walsingham's credit in this matter is not increased by his transmission of the legend that, as Friar John Latimer's corpse was dragged through the streets, buds and leaves broke out from the wood of the hurdle to which it was bound, and that a blind man who touched it was restored to sight. It is quite unnecessary to believe the unlikely story that the King's half-brother put to death a miserable Irish Friar with his own hands.

In the year 1384 both the Earl of Kent and his brother Sir John Holland were Knights of the Garter. The wardrobe accounts show that they, and other Knights of the Order, received in that year ' robes of cloth in violet colour, embroidered with garters, furred with miniver, and lined with scarlet.'

In 1385 John Holland accompanied the King, who was now eighteen years old, in an expedition against the Scots. These incessant foes, aided by a strong contingent of their French allies, had invaded Northumberland, and were burning and destroying. The English made great preparations for an expedition against Scotland both by land and sea. ' The King took the field,' says Froissart, ' accompanied by his uncles, the Earls of Cambridge and Buckingham, and his brothers, Sir Thomas and Sir John Holland. There were also the Earls of Salisbury and Arundel, the young Earl of Pembroke, the young Lord de Spencer, the Earl of Stafford, and so many barons and knights that they amounted to full forty thousand lances, without counting those of the Duke of Lancaster, the Earl of Northumberland, the Earl of Nottingham, the Lord Lacy, the Lord Neville and other barons of the marches, who were in pursuit of the French and the Scots, to the number of two thousand lances and fifteen hundred archers. The King and the lords who attended him had also full fifty thousand archers, without including the varlets.' Sir John Holland had in his pay and command 100 men-at-arms and 160 archers. The Earl of Stafford brought 120 men-at-arms and 180 archers. His son Ralph Stafford had seven men and twelve archers. By such contingents, great and small, the feudal army was made up. The Scots and their French allies, who immensely disliked the food, drink, manners, language, and climate of the rude north, prudently retired into Scotland upon approach of this formidable host, and afterwards the English invaded Scotland, devastated the better part of it as far north as Aberdeen, and burned Edinburgh and Dunfermline and Dundee. But before that, when, on his advance northward, Richard was in Yorkshire at the beginning of August, a terrible thing happened in the English host which, as Froissart says, ' caused a mortal hatred between different lords,' and, as Thomas Walsingham says, ' clouded all public and private joy.' It would be a very great pity to relate this story in other words than those used by Froissart, whose way of relation recalls scenes in Homer's ' Iliad.' He had known the Hollands as boys when he was in England in the early sixties, and he doubtless obtained the details of this story on the best authority.

' Round about St. John of Beverley in the diocese of York, were lodged the King of England, and great plenty of the earls, barons and knights of his kingdom, for each lodged the nearest they could to him, and especially his two uncles and his two brothers, Sir Thomas de Holland,

Earl of Kent, and Sir John de Holland were there with a
beautiful company of men-at-arms.   In the retinue of the
King was a knight of Bohemia, who was come to visit the
Queen of England, and, for love of the Queen, the King
and the lords entertained him well.   The knight was named
Sir Nicles ; a gay and handsome knight he was after the
German fashion.   And it chanced that in a horse camp in
the fields outside a village near Beverley, two squires of Sir
John de Holland, the brother of the King, had words about
lodgings with Sir Nicles and followed him and made him
great displeasure.   Upon this, two archers of Ralph de
Stafford, son of Earl de Stafford, began to take the part of
the knight, because he was a foreigner, and blamed the
squires, saying, " You are wrong to insult this knight.   Do
you know that he belongs to my lady the Queen and her
country ?   You ought to give him a preference over our-
selves."   " Ah," said one of the squires, " thou rascal, dost
thou wish to talk ?   What the devil hast thou to do with
it if I blame his follies ? "   " What have I to do with it ? "
said the archer.   " I have plenty to do with it, for he is a
comrade of my master's and I'll not stand his being blamed
or insulted."   " And if I thought, rascal," said the squire,
" that thou wouldest help him against me, I would run this
sword through thy body."   And as he spoke, he made as
though he would strike him.   The archer stepped back,
for he held his bow all ready, drew a good arrow and let fly
at the squire, and sent the arrow right through his breast
and heart and killed him dead.

' The other squire, when he saw his comrade thus served,
fled.   Sir Nicles was already gone back to his lodging.
The archers returned to their master and told him their
adventure.   Sir Ralph said they had done ill.   " By my
faith," replied the archer, " Sir, it had to be so if I wished
not to be killed, and I had rather I killed him than that

he killed me." "Come, come!" said Sir Ralph. "Don't go where they can find you. I will arrange peace with Sir John de Holland, through my lord, my father, or others." The archer answered and said, "Very well, Sir."

'News came to Sir John de Holland that one of the archers of Sir Ralph de Stafford had slain one of his squires, the one whom he loved best in all the world, and they told him that it had been the fault of Sir Nicles, this foreign knight. When Sir John de Holland heard what had happened, he was furiously enraged and said, "Never will I drink or eat till this be avenged." Forthwith, he got on his horse, and made his men mount also, and went from his lodging, and by now it was late in the evening, and he made inquiry where this Sir Nicles was lodged. They told him they thought he was lodged in the rear-guard with the Earl of Devonshire and the Earl of Stafford and their people. Sir John de Holland took this road and began to ride about at hazard to find this Sir Nicles. As he and his men rode between hedges and bushes along a very narrow lane where those who encountered could not turn aside, Sir Ralph de Stafford and Sir John de Holland met each other, and when they saw each other, each asked in passing, "And who is there?" "I am Stafford." And "I am Holland." Then said Sir John de Holland, who was still in his fury, "Stafford, Stafford! I was looking for thee! Thy people have killed my squire whom I loved well." And thereupon he thrust out with a Bordeaux sword which he held unsheathed and naked. His thrust pierced the body of Sir Ralph de Stafford, and laid him dead, which was a great pity. And then he passed on and knew not yet whom he had slain, but he knew well that he had slain someone. Then were the men of Sir Ralph de Stafford much enraged when they saw their master dead, and began to shout, "Ah

Holland, Holland! You have slain the son of the Earl of
Stafford! Evil tidings will they be to his father when he
shall know it!" Some of the men of Sir John de Holland
heard this and said to their master, "Sir, you have slain
Sir Ralph de Stafford!" "All the better," said Sir John.
"I would rather have killed him than one of less degree,
for so I have the better avenged my boy."

'Then went Sir John Holland to the town of St. John
of Beverley, and took sanctuary, and departed not thence,
for well he knew that he should have great trouble in the
army from the friends of the knight for his death, and he
knew not what his brother, the King of England, would say
of it. So to avoid all these dangers, he shut himself up in
the sanctuary.

'News came to the Earl of Stafford that his son was
slain by a great misadventure. "Slain!" said the Earl.
"And who killed him?"

'Those who had been there said, "My lord, it was the
King's brother, Sir John de Holland," and they told him
how it was and why. Those who loved his son, for many
there were, and they were fine, young, bold and enterprising
knights, were wroth beyond measure, and he called
together all his friends to take counsel what he should
do and how he should avenge himself. But the wisest
and best advised of his counsellors held him back, and
told him that on the morrow they should lay this before
the King of England, and require that he should do law
and justice.

'So passed the night, and in the morning Sir Ralph de
Stafford was buried in a church of a village thereby, and
there were there present all those of his kindred, lords and
knights that were in this army.

'After the funeral, the Earl of Stafford and full sixty
of his lineage and that of his son, mounted their horses and

came to the King, who was already informed of this adventure ; they found the King and his uncles and great plenty
of other lords with him.   The Earl of Stafford, when he was
come before the King, knelt, and then said with weeping,
and in great anguish of heart : " King, thou art King of all
England, and thou hast solemnly sworn to maintain right
in the realm, and to do justice, and thou knowest how thy
brother without cause or reason has slain my son and heir.
I require that thou do me right and justice, or else thou shalt
have no worse enemy than me, and I will thee to know that
the death of my son touches me so near that, were I not
unwilling to break and ruin the expedition on which we are,
and to receive more harm than honour by the trouble which
I should bring into our host, it should be paid for and avenged
so highly that men would talk of it in England for a hundred
years to come.   But now I will refrain so long as we be
on this expedition to Scotland, for I will not rejoice our
enemies by my grief."

' " Earl of Stafford," replied the King, " be assured
that I will maintain justice and right to the highest limit
that the lords of my realm can deem possible, and that not
for any brother will I fail to do so."   Then answered the
kinsmen of the Earl of Stafford, " Sir, you have spoken well
and great thanks to you."

' The Earl of Stafford went through the expedition to
Scotland, and during all that time he seemed to have forgotten the death of his son, wherein all the lords thought
he showed great wisdom.'   So far Froissart.

John Holland was aged about thirty-three when this
happened.   His unpremeditated deed of chance fury in
that dark lane near Beverley was attended by disastrous
consequences years later, and was one of the causes which
indirectly contributed to the downfall and murder of

Richard II.   On such chances or destinies do things depend.
If the honest archers had not overheard the squires banter-
ing with youthful spirits the possibly fantastic German
knight, many things might have happened otherwise than
they did.

The King at first declared that his brother must expiate
the crime by the extreme rigour of the law.   Ralph Stafford
had been a favourite at the Court, having been bred up with
the King from childhood.   He was also a great friend of
the Queen's, and was on his way to speak with her about the
affair when, by ill-fortune, he met Holland in the dark lane
near Beverley.

The Princess of Wales, the mother both of Richard
and of John Holland, was at Wallingford on the Thames.
She heard that the King had vowed that John should suffer
death, and sent to him a messenger imploring him to have
mercy on his brother, but finding that her prayer availed
not, she fell into such grief that she died within five days.
Her body was wrapt in cere cloth and enclosed in a lead
coffin, and was kept till the King's return from Scotland
and then was buried, not by the side of her more glorious
second husband, the Black Prince, in Canterbury Cathedral,
but by that of her first husband, Sir Thomas Holland, Earl
of Kent, in the Abbey of the Grey Friars at Stamford.   Their
monument, like hundreds of the most interesting monuments
in England, perished with the Abbey at the Reformation.
Such was the end of the singular life of the Fair Maid of
Kent.

Her will began thus :

' In the year of Our Lord 1385 and of the reign of my
dear son, Richard King of England and France the ninth,
at my castle of Wallingford in the diocese of Salisbury the ·
7th of August ; I Joan, Princess of Wales, Duchess of Corn-

wall, Countess of Chester and Lady Wake ; [1] etc.   My body
to be buried in my Chapel at Stamford near the monument
of my late lord and husband the Earl of Kent ; To my dear
son, the King, my new bed of red velvet embroidered with
ostrich feathers of silver and herds of leopards of gold with
boughs and leaves issuing out of their mouths ; To my dear
son, Thomas Earl of Kent, my bed of red camak paied with
red and rays of gold ; To my dear son John Holland a bed
of red camak ; To—etc.'

Her executors were the Bishops of London and
Winchester, Lord Cobham, Sir William de Beauchamp, Sir
William de Nevill, Sir Simon de Burley, Sir Lewis de Clifford,
Sir Richard de Sturry and six others, two of whom were
her ' dear chaplains.'   The Princess was at her death about
fifty-seven years old.   She had returned to England with
her sick husband in 1873, and had been a widow since he
died at Westminster on June 8, 1876.

King Richard, after all, proved swiftly placable.   The
Duke of Lancaster and other lords mediated between the
Staffords, the Hollands, and the King.   An agreement was,
at last, arrived at that John should go through a public
ceremonial symbolic of penitence and remorse, and should
also ' find three priests to celebrate divine service every
day, to the world's end, for the soul of him, the said Ralph,
in some such place as the King should appoint.'   Whereupon the King appointed that two of the priests should
perform this at the very place where Ralph Stafford was
slain, and the third in some place near to it.   It was, however, afterwards arranged that all the masses should be
said at Langley in Hertfordshire, in the Church of the ' Friars
Preachers,' where young Stafford's body was finally interred.
This mode of expiation was then not uncommon.   So

---

[1] Edward III had made Sir Thomas Holland Baron Wake of Lydel.   Joan's
mother was Margaret, heiress of Lord Wake of Lydel in Cumberland.

Shakespeare makes Henry V say in his meditation on the eve of the battle of Agincourt :

> Not to-day, O Lord !
> O ! not to-day, think not upon the fault
> My father made in compassing the crown.
> I Richard's body have interred new ;
> And on it have bestow'd more contrite tears
> Than from it issued forced drops of blood :
> Five hundred poor I have in yearly pay,
> Who twice a-day their wither'd hands hold up
> Toward heaven, to pardon blood ; and I have built
> Two chantries, where the sad and solemn priests
> Sing still for Richard's soul.

The monastic chronicler, Malvern, gives an account in Latin of the ceremonial act of penitence performed, no doubt prudently but reluctantly, by John Holland.   It was at Windsor Castle.   ' John Holland, clothed in mourning, entered to the King, between the Archbishop of Canterbury and the Bishop of London, and thrice bowed to the ground on his knees and arms, before he came to him, then, raising himself on his knees, and extending his arms upwards, weeping and humbly seeking mercy from the King, and beseeching forgiveness for that rashly and indiscreetly he had committed such a crime contrary to prohibition.   Some of those who stood around wept on seeing this.   At the third prostration the said Bishops knelt before the King with him.   Then the King, somewhat moved by the prayers of the nobles who were present, and chiefly by those of Earls Stafford and Warwick, whom above all the Lord John Holland had offended, pardoned him for that which he had done.'   It was the kind of carefully arranged, and somewhat Byzantine, ceremonial, which Richard II enjoyed above all things.

After this enforced forgiveness, the Earl of Stafford, deprived of the hope of his House, departed on a pilgrimage to Jerusalem, and died, in 1387, on his way home, in the Island of Rhodes. His body was brought home to England by John Hinkley, his squire, and buried with those of his ancestors before the high altar of Stone, in Staffordshire. John Holland, on the other hand, pursued his wild career. He was so quickly restored to full royal favour that a few months later he was sent with John of Gaunt, Duke of Lancaster, to treat with the Earl of Flanders touching certain differences then pending between the English and the Flemings, and also to treat of peace with the French. In the earlier half of the same year, 1386, John Holland married Elizabeth, second daughter of the Duke of Lancaster, and sister to Henry of Bolingbroke, Earl of Derby. This was the second marriage with the royal family made by the Hollands. Elizabeth of Lancaster was on her father's side granddaughter of Edward III, and on both sides was a descendant from Henry III. But notwithstanding these successes the crime at Beverley pursued John Holland to the disastrous end of his life. He had slain a distinguished member of the ring of the great Norman-descended families, and he was never forgiven.

Blanche, daughter of Henry, Duke of Lancaster, the mother of Elizabeth, was the heiress who brought the vast Lancaster possessions to John of Gaunt. She was not only the greatest heiress but one of the most delightful women of her time. Froissart, an excellent judge in these things, says of this Blanche : ' I never saw two such noble dames, so good, liberal and courteous as this lady and the late Queen of England (Philippa), nor ever shall, were I to live a thousand years, which is impossible.' Blanche of Lancaster died of the ' Black Death ' pestilence in 1369,

still a young woman.   A French contemporary poet wrote
of her charmingly :

> Elle morut jeune et jolie,
> Environ de vingt et deux ans,
> Gaie, lie, friche, esbatans,
> Douce, simple, d'umble semblance,
> La bonne dame ôt à nom Blanche.[1]

The poet was wrong as to the twenty-two years.   She
died, in 1369, at twenty-eight years of age, but left her
children quite young, Henry, Philippa, and Elizabeth.   John
of Gaunt, soon afterwards, in 1371, married his second wife,
the Princess Constance of Castile.   Philippa and Elizabeth
were placed under the charge of Katherine, wife of Sir
Hugh Swynford, as a governess and duenna.   This Katherine
was the daughter of a Hainault gentleman who came over
to the Court of England with Queen Philippa.   Katherine
was very beautiful and seductive and knew the ways of
the Court.   In the inscription on the once existing monument
of John of Lancaster in St. Paul's Cathedral she was described as 'eximià pulchritudine feminam.'   Froissart calls
her 'une dame qui scavoit moult de toutes honneurs.'   She
was made a Lady of the Order of the Garter in 1387.   The
Duke of Lancaster, all his life, was notoriously pervious
to feminine seductions.   Katherine Swynford, while her
husband was in France, and during the Duke's marriage
to Constance of Castile, became his mistress and bore to
him three sons, the Beauforts, and two daughters.   After
the death of Constance, the Duke, then fifty-six years of
age, married Katherine, who was ten years younger, and
their offspring were declared legitimate both by Act of
Parliament and by a Bull of Pope Boniface IX.

Philippa and Elizabeth, the daughters of the good Blanche,

---

[1] From *Le Joli Buisson de Jonèce.*

F

were thus brought up in immoral surroundings. Elizabeth was betrothed in childhood to a young boy, the Earl of Pembroke. When she was old enough she was brought to the royal Court to acquire the manners of the day. Here John Holland made ardent love to her, and in 1386, soon after the Stafford affair, they were married, hurriedly, it seems, and without much ceremony, with a view, it was alleged, to the saving of honour.[1] Elizabeth was about twenty-two and John Holland about thirty-four when this marriage took place. It was as important in the relationships and history of the Hollands as that which Thomas Holland had made with the Fair Maid of Kent.

The sister of Blanche, the mother of Elizabeth, her aunt Maud of Lancaster, had married for her first husband Ralph de Stafford, the victim of the encounter at Beverley, so that John Holland married the niece of the wife of the man whom he had killed a few months earlier.

During this period the elder Holland brother, Thomas, Earl of Kent, had advanced in his mundane career. After his return to England, during the truce in the endless French war, he received a money grant from the Crown. In 1378 he acted as a Commissioner in awarding certain damages between the English and the Scots, and in the same year he was made Marshal of England. In 1381 he was sent as an Ambassador to Flanders to treat of the marriage between Richard II and Anne, the Emperor's sister. After his mother's death in 1386, he obtained numerous manors of her inheritance. He was

---

[1] A contemporary monastic chronicler, Malvern, gives some details as to this, which show the story circulating at the time. He is the only authority, and the gossip about a distant and suspected Court current in provincial monasteries must be received with caution. But John Holland's passionate and hasty character, and the level of morals in John of Gaunt's house, makes this story probable enough.

now a wealthy Earl, and his wife, Alice Fitz-Alan, daughter of the ninth Earl of the noble and ancient House of Arundel, bore a large family of beautiful children, of whom more hereafter. Through his daughters he was the ancestor of many kings and great nobles, down to the present day.

CHAPTER IV

Faire sheilds, gay steedes, bright armes, be my delight,
These be the riches fit for an advent'rous knight.
SPENSER.

JOHN HOLLAND'S life was more filled with adventure than
that of his elder brother, Thomas, Earl of Kent. The Duke
of Lancaster's second wife, Constance, was the elder daughter
of King Pedro ' The Cruel,' of Castile and Leon, who had
been dethroned by his illegitimate half-brother, Enrique.
Pedro recovered the throne in 1367 after the Black Prince's
victory over Enrique at Najara, but, a year later, was over-
thrown again by Enrique, and slain by that brother's own
hand. Pedro's two daughters fled to the Black Prince's
Court at Bordeaux, and there Lancaster met and married
Constance. Enrique's son, John, supported by the French,
was now King of Castile. For some years the Duke of
Lancaster had called himself King of Castile in right of his
wife, daughter of a legitimate sovereign whose throne had
been usurped by a bastard line. He now proposed to set
forth for Spain at the head of a fleet and army to vindicate
the claim. For political reasons he was glad to leave
England for a space, and King Richard was delighted
to get rid of at least one powerful uncle. Government support was therefore given to this expedition.
Parliament voted a supply, and, in July 1386, Lancaster
sailed from Plymouth with a force of men-at-arms and

archers. Sir John Holland had good reasons of his own
for leaving England for a while, and he was appointed
to be Constable of this army. The Marshal was Sir Thomas
Moreaux, who was married, according to Froissart, to an
illegitimate daughter of the Duke. The Duchess of Lancaster
went in the Duke's ship with her own daughter Catherine
and the Duke's two daughters by his first marriage, Elizabeth, now the wife of John Holland, and Philippa, the elder
sister, a girl still unwed.

'It was,' says Froissart, 'the month of May' (it really
was July) 'when they embarked, and they had the usual
fine weather of that pleasant season.' They sailed near
enough to the French shores to be seen, 'and a fine sight
it was, for there were upwards of two hundred sail. It
was delightful to observe the galleys, which had men-at-
arms on board, coast the shores in search of adventures as
they heard the French fleet was at sea.' So it had been, but
had retired into Havre. The Duke resolved to put into
Brest in order to relieve the castle, where an English garrison
was being blockaded by a Breton force. 'The weather,'
says Froissart, 'was now delightful, and the sea so calm
that it was a pleasure to be on it ; the fleet advanced with
an easy sail, and arrived at the mouth of Brest harbour,
where, waiting for the tide, they entered in safety. The
clarions and trumpets sounded sweetly from the barges
and the castle.' A spirited encounter, in which no one was
much hurt, followed, and the besiegers evacuated their
positions and retired up country. The Duke, Sir John
Holland, and some other knights, went into the castle, with
their ladies, and had refreshments. On the next day they
set sail for Corunna, where they cast anchor five days later.
'It was a fine sight,' Froissart continues, 'to view all the
ships and galleys enter the port, laden with men-at-arms,
with trumpets and clarions sounding.' A defiant reply

was blown by trumpets and clarions from the castle, then by chance occupied by a force of French knights who had come to assist the Castilian King, and happened to be passing on a pilgrimage to San Iago of Compostella. The English landed, and the Duke sent the ships back to England, for he wished all the world to know, he said, ' that I will never recross the sea to England, until I be master of Castile, or die in the attempt.' The army lodged in huts covered with leaves and remained before Corunna for nearly a month ' amusing themselves, for the chief lords had brought hounds for their pastime, and hawks for the ladies. They had also mills to grind their corn, and ovens to bake, for they never willingly go to war in foreign countries without carrying things of that kind with them.'

One day the French garrison in Corunna surprised a party of three hundred English foraging archers, and killed two hundred of them. The Duke and Sir John Holland, the Constable, sharply reprimanded Sir Thomas Moreaux the Marshal for letting foragers go so near the enemy without a protecting guard of men-at-arms. Sir Thomas replied that ' they had been caught, to be sure, this once, though they had foraged ten times before without any interruption.' ' Sir Thomas,' said the Duke, ' be more cautious in future ; for such things may fall out in one day or hour, as may not happen again in a century.'

At the end of a month the army abandoned the siege of Corunna, and marched in three battalions to San Iago of Compostella. The Marshal led the van of 300 lances and 700 archers ; next marched the Duke with 400 spears, accompanied by all the ladies. The rear was composed of 400 lances and 700 archers, accompanied by the Constable, Sir John Holland. San Iago surrendered, on a threat of total destruction if it did not, and became Lancaster's headquarters. The Duke and his ladies lodged in the Abbey,

Sir John Holland and Sir Thomas Moreaux in the town,
and the rest in houses or extemporised huts. There was
plenty of meat, and so much strong wine that the English
archers ' were for the greater part of their time in bed drunk,
and very often, by drinking too much new wine, they had
fevers, and in the morning such headaches as to prevent
them from doing anything the rest of the day.' The English
fought no battles, but took two or three towns, and
devastated the country, as did also the French who had come
to assist the King of Castile. The King of Portugal was
friendly to the English, and arranged to meet the Duke of
Lancaster on the Portuguese frontier. The Duke and Sir
John Holland rode to the place appointed, at the head of
300 spears and 600 archers. The King gave a dinner to the
Duke in a pavilion covered with leaves. ' The Bishops of
Coimbra and Oporto and Braganza were seated at the King's
table with the Duke, and a little below him were Sir John
Holland and Sir Henry Beaumont. There were many
minstrels, and this festivity lasted till night.' The King
was clothed in white lined with crimson, with a red cross
of St. George. The next day the Duke gave a return dinner
in his pavilion to the King. The apartments were hung
with cloth and covered with carpets just as if ' the King
had been at Lisbon or the Duke in London.' It was settled
that they should attack the usurper of Castile, early in March,
with their united forces, and then they talked about a
marriage for the King, who was still unwed. The Duke
said, ' Sir King, I have at San Iago two girls, and I will
give you the choice to take which of them shall please you
best. Send thither your Council and I will return her with
them.' ' Many thanks,' said the King, ' you offer me more
than I ask. I will leave my cousin, Catherine of Castile, but
I demand your daughter Philippa in marriage.' Two days
later the Duke gave a still more glorious banquet to the

King. 'His apartments,' says Froissart, 'were decorated with the richest tapestry, with his arms emblazoned upon it, and as splendidly ornamented, as if he had been at Hertford, Leicester, or at any of his mansions in England, which very much astonished the Portuguese.'

On the Duke's return to San Iago the Duchess asked him many questions about the Portuguese King as to whose character, health, strength, and appearance the Duke gave a favourable report. 'Well, and what was done in regard to the marriage?' said the Duchess. 'I have given him one of my daughters.' 'Which?' asked the Duchess. 'I offered him the choice of Catherine or Philippa, for which he thanked me much, and fixed on Philippa.' 'He is right,' said the Duchess, 'for my daughter Catherine is too young for him.' There must have been much talk about all this among the ladies at San Iago, and Elizabeth Holland may have felt a touch of jealousy that, in the result of too easy a surrender, she was only the wife of King Richard's half-brother while her own sister Philippa was to be a reigning queen.

After this came some more warfare, in the course of which Sir John Holland took by storm a Galician town called Ribadeo, where 1500 unfortunate townsmen, whose only offence was that they had refused to surrender, were slaughtered by the English, and much booty was gained.

Thereafter the Archbishop of Braganza arrived at San Iago to marry the Lady Philippa for the King of Portugal by way of proxy. The ceremony was performed, 'and the Archbishop of Braganza' (says the ever-delightful Froissart) 'and the Lady Philippa were courteously laid beside each other, on a bed, as married persons should be.' On the morrow she mounted her palfrey, as did also her damsels and her bastard sister, Lady Moreaux. Sir John Holland

and Sir Thomas Percy escorted her to Oporto with 100
spears and 200 archers.   There were banquetings, music
and dancing, and a grand tournament, in which Sir John
Holland won the stranger's prize.   The last words that the
King, who was much pleased with Philippa, said to Holland
were that he was ready to invade Castile with the Duke.
'That is good news indeed,' said the Duke when Holland
repeated this to him.

The Duke soon took the field and captured a town of importance called by Froissart Entenca (the modern Betanzos,
probably).   At Valladolid, among the French who had come
to aid the King of Castile, was a knight famous for his
prowess in battles and in tournaments, Sir Reginald de
Roye.   The following story must be quoted in full from
Froissart, for it is very characteristic both of those times, in
which war and tournaments were different forms of the most
popular game, and also of that writer.   Froissart says :

'During the stay of the Duke of Lancaster in Entenca,
a herald arrived from Valladolid, who demanded where Sir
John Holland was lodged.   On being shown thither, he
found Sir John within, and, bending his knee, presented
him a letter, saying, " Sir, I am a herald-at-arms, whom Sir
Reginald de Roye sends hither : he salutes you by me, and
you will be pleased to read this letter."   Sir John answered,
he would willingly do so.   Having opened it, he read that
Sir Reginald de Roye entreated him, for the love of his
mistress, that he would deliver him from his vow, by tilting
with him three courses with the lance, three attacks with
the sword, three with the battle-axe, and three with the
dagger ; and that if he chose to come to Valladolid, he had
provided him an escort of sixty spears ; but, if it were more
agreeable to him to remain in Entenca, he desired he would
obtain from the Duke of Lancaster a passport for himself
and thirty companions.

'When Sir John Holland had perused the letter, he smiled, and, looking at the herald, said, " Friend, thou art welcome ; for thou hast brought me what pleases me much, and I accept the challenge. Thou wilt remain in my lodging, with my people, and, in the course of to-morrow, thou shalt have my answer, whether the tilts are to be in Galicia or Castile." The herald replied, " God grant it." He remained in Sir John's lodgings, where he was made comfortable ; and Sir John went to the Duke of Lancaster, whom he found in conversation with the Marshal, and showed the letter the herald had brought. " Well," said the Duke, " and have you accepted it ? " " Yes, by my faith have I ; and why not ? I love nothing better than fighting, and the knight entreats me to indulge him : consider, therefore, where you would choose it should take place." The Duke mused a while, and then said, " It shall be performed in this town : have a passport made out in what terms you please, and I will seal it." " It is well said," replied Sir John ; " and I will, in God's name, soon make out the passport."

'The passport was fairly written and sealed for thirty knights and squires to come and return ; and Sir John Holland, when he delivered it to the herald, presented him with a handsome mantle lined with minever and with twelve nobles. The herald took leave and returned to Valladolid, where he related what had passed, and showed his presents.

'News of this tournament was carried to Oporto, where the King of Portugal kept his court. " In the name of God," said the King, " I will be present at it, and so shall my queen and the ladies." " Many thanks," replied the Duchess of Lancaster ; " for I shall be accompanied by the King and Queen when I return." It was not long after this conversation that the King of Portugal, the Queen, the Duchess with her daughter and the ladies of the court,

set out for Entenca in grand array.   The Duke of Lancaster,
when they were near at hand. mounted his horse, and,
attended by a numerous company, went to meet them.
When the King and Duke met, they embraced each other
most kindly, and entered the town together, where their
lodgings were as well prepared as they could be in such a
place, though they were not so magnificent as if they had
been at Paris.

'Three days after the arrival of the King of Portugal,
came Sir Reginald de Roye, handsomely accompanied by
knights and squires, to the amount of six score horse.   They
were all properly lodged ; for the Duke had given his officers
strict orders they should be well taken care of.   On the
morrow, Sir John Holland and Sir Reginald de Roye
armed themselves, and rode into a spacious close, well
sanded, where the tilts were to be performed.   Scaffolds
were erected for the ladies, the King, the Duke, and the
many English lords who had come to witness the combat ;
for none had staid at home.

'The two knights, who were to perform this deed of
arms, entered the lists so well armed and equipped that
nothing was wanting.   Their spears, battle-axes and swords,
were brought them ; and each, being mounted on the best
of horses, placed himself about a bow-shot distant from
the other, but at times they pranced about on their horses
most gallantly, for they knew every eye to be upon them.

'All being now arranged for their combat, which was to
include everything except pushing it to extremity, though
no one could foresee what mischief might happen, nor how
it would end ; for they were to tilt with pointed lances, then
with swords, which were so sharp that scarcely a helmet
could resist their strokes ; and these were to be succeeded
by battle-axes and daggers, each so well tempered that
nothing could withstand them.   Now, consider the perils

those run who engage in such combats to exalt their honour, for one unlucky stroke puts an end to the business.

'Having braced their targets and examined each other through the visors of their helmets, they spurred on their horses spear in hand. Though they allowed their horses to gallop as they pleased, they advanced on as straight a line as if it had been drawn with a cord, and hit each other on the visors with such force that Sir Reginald's lance was shivered into four pieces, which flew to a greater height than they could have been thrown. All present allowed this to be gallantly done. Sir John Holland struck Sir Reginald likewise on the visor, but not with the same success, and I will tell you why. Sir Reginald had but lightly laced on his helmet, so that it was held by one thong only, which broke at the blow, and the helmet flew over his head, leaving Sir Reginald bare-headed. Each passed the other, and Sir John Holland bore his lance without halting. The spectators cried out that it was a fine course. The knights returned to their stations, when Sir Reginald's helmet was fitted on again and another lance given to him ; Sir John grasped his own, which was not broken. When ready, they set off full gallop, for they had excellent horses under them which they well knew how to manage, and again struck each other on the helmets, so that sparks of fire came from them, but chiefly from Sir John Holland's. He received a very severe blow, for this time the lance did not break ; neither did Sir John's, which hit the visor of his adversary without much effect, passing through, and leaving it on the crupper of the horse, and Sir Reginald was once more bare-headed. "Ha ! " cried the English to the French, "he does not fight fair : why is not his helmet as well buckled on as Sir John Holland's ? We say he is playing tricks : tell him to put himself on an equal footing with his adversary." "Hold your tongues ! " said the Duke, "and let them alone : in arms, every one takes what advantage he can : if Sir John think there is any advantage in thus fastening on the helmet, he may do the same. But for my part, were I in their situations, I would lace my helmet as tight as possible ; and, if one hundred were asked their opinions, there would be four-score of my way of thinking." The English, on this, were silent, and never again interfered. The ladies declared they had nobly jousted ; and they were much praised by the King of Portugal, who said to Sir John Fernando, " In our country, they do not tilt so well, nor so gallantly : what say you, Sir John ? " " By my faith, sir," replied he, " they do tilt well ; and formerly I saw as good jousts before your brother, when we were at Elvas to oppose the King of Castile, between this Frenchman and Sir William Windsor ; but I never heard that his helmet was tighter laced then than it is now."

' The King on this turned from Sir John to observe the knights, who were about to begin their third course. Sir John and Sir Reginald eyed each other, to see if any advantage were to be gained, for their horses were so excellent that they could manage them as they pleased, and, sticking spurs into them, hit their helmets so sharply that they struck fire, and the shafts of their lances were broken. Sir Reginald was again unhelmed, for he could never avoid this happening, and they passed each other without falling. All now declared they had well jousted ; though the English, excepting the Duke of Lancaster, blamed greatly Sir Reginald ; but he said, " he considered that man as wise who in combat knows how to seize his vantage. Know," added he, addressing himself to Sir Thomas Percy and Sir Thomas Morcaux, " that Sir Reginald de Roye is not now to be taught how to tilt : he is better skilled than Sir John Holland, though he has borne himself well."

' After the courses of the lance, they fought three rounds

with swords, battle-axes, and daggers, without either of
them being wounded. The French carried off Sir Reginald
to his lodgings, and the English did the same to Sir John
Holland.'

The Duke then entertained at dinner all the French
visitors ; the Duchess sat beside him, and next to her Sir
Reginald de Roye. After dinner, the Duchess said to the
French knights, with tears in her eyes, that she marvelled
much that gentlemen like themselves could fight for the
claim of a bastard against her claim as rightful heiress. Sir
Reginald bowed, and said, ' Madam, we know that what
you have said is true ; but our lord, the King of France,
holds a different opinion from yours, and, as we are his
liegemen, we must make war for him, and go whitherso-
ever he may send us, for we cannot disobey him.' At these
words Sir John Holland and Sir Thomas Percy handed
the lady to her chamber ; wine and spices were brought,
and then the French knights took leave, mounted their
horses and rode to Valladolid.

After the tournament, the Duke and the King of Portugal
had a conference, and settled plans of operation. The
King was to enter Castile while the Duke continued to
subdue Galicia, and they were not to join forces unless the
enemy showed inclination to battle. The reason was partly
one of forage supplies, but also because the armies might
easily quarrel, ' for the English are hasty and proud, and
the Portuguese hot and impetuous, easily angered, and
not soon pacified.' But if a battle against the common
foe were imminent they would agree very well for the time,
' like Gascons,' says Froissart, or, as we perhaps should say,
like the Irish. The English captured a town or two, but
the campaigning had no appreciable results, the weather
was hot, and the men began to grumble in good old English
fashion. One said—' We should have done more if he had

not brought women who only wish to remain quiet, and
for one day that they are inclined to travel they will repose
fifteen. What the devil! What business had the Duke
to bring his wife and daughters with him, since he came
here for conquest? It was quite unreasonable, for it has
been a great hindrance to him.' Others said that Spain
was not nearly so pleasant a country to make war in as
France, 'where there are plenty of large villages, a fair
country, fine provender, ponds, rich pastures, and good
wines, and a climate fairly temperate; but here everything
is the reverse.' There was also much sickness in the army,
due in part to excessive drinking, by men brought up on
good ale, of the hard and hot Spanish wines. The horses
were in bad condition and died, and so did very many of
the men. The Duke himself was unwell. The enemy,
under the guidance of a wary antagonist, the Frenchman
Bertrand du Guesclin, who had been made Constable of
Castile, kept in the towns and castles most of which they
held, harassed the English in small encounters, and offered
no large battle. This was also the successful policy of
du Guesclin in France.

Sir John Holland saw the army daily wasting away,
and heard the bitter complaint of the men. They used,
says Froissart, words such as these : ' Ah, my lord of Lancaster, why have you brought us to Castile? Accursed
be the voyage! He does not, it seems, wish that any Englishman should ever again quit his country to serve him. He
seems resolved to kick against the pricks. He will have
his men guard the country he has won; but when they shall
all be dead, who will then guard it? He shows poor knowledge of war, for why, when he saw that no enemy came to
fight him, did he not retreat into Portugal, or elsewhere,
to avoid the losses he must now suffer? For we shall all die
of this cursed disease, and without having struck a blow.'

Sir John Holland, adds Froissart, ' was much hurt on hearing such language, for the honour of the Duke whose daughter he had married, and he determined to speak with him on the matter, which, from his situation, he could do more easily than any one else.'

He said to the Duke : ' My lord, you must at once change your plans, for your army is all sick. If an assault should now be made upon you, you could not meet it, for your men are all worn down and discontented, and their horses dead. High and low are so discouraged that you must not expect any service from them.' ' What can I do ? ' said the Duke feebly. ' I wish to have advice.' Thereupon Holland advised him to disband his army and let the men go where they would, and go himself to Portugal. The question then rose how the individuals in the army could get back to England. They had no ships, and the way through Spain and France was beset by enemies. There was nothing for it but to send envoys to the usurping King of Castile, and humbly crave that he would allow the remnants of the English host to pass through his territories, and would also obtain permission from his ally, the French king, that they might pass through his. The King of Castile graciously consented, in order to get rid of the English as soon and as cheaply as possible. Many of those who then set forth in scattered bands died on the way ; and although the actual fighting in Spain had not been much, not half of the 1500 men-at-arms and 4000 archers, who had sailed from Plymouth in such gallant array, ever saw the shores of Old England again. It was an inglorious end to an ambitious expedition. Holland and his wife were the last to leave the Duke, who returned for a while to San Iago, where he had to endure the merry jests of French pilgrims on his discomfiture, and then went to Oporto, and finally by sea to Bayonne. John Holland, leading a troop in some order, visited the King of

Castile, who received him politely and gave him handsome mules for his journey, and he picked up some English who had been detained by sickness in Castilian towns. He rode across the Black Prince's famous battle-field of Najara, crossed the Pyrenees, after an interview with the King of Navarre, by the pass of Roncesvalles, and rode on to Bayonne, where he and his Countess remained for a time. He was home in England by St. George's Day, April 23, 1388, because he was at the Garter Banquet at Windsor. The Duke of Lancaster wrote repeatedly to England from Bayonne and Bordeaux asking for a new army with which to renew his Spanish venture, but in vain. 'Those,' says Froissart, 'who had returned from Castile gave such accounts as discouraged others from going thither. They said, "The voyage was so long, a war with France would be much more advantageous. France has a rich country and temperate climate, with fine rivers ; but Castile has nothing but rocks and high mountains, a sharp air, muddy rivers, bad meat, and wines so hot and harsh there is no drinking them. The inhabitants are poor and filthy, badly clothed and lodged, and quite different in their manners to us, so that it would be folly to go there. When you enter a large city or town you expect to find everything ; but you will meet with nothing but wines, lard, and empty coffers. It is quite the contrary in France ; for there we have many times found in the cities and towns, when the fortune of war delivered them into our hands, such wealth and riches as astonished us. It is such a war as this we ought to attend to, and not a war with Castile or Portugal, where there is nothing but poverty and loss to be suffered.'

Such was the talk of the returned English, and no doubt their grumblings still further diminished the fast waning popularity of the royal house with which John Holland was so closely connected. None paid any attention now

G

to the once glorious Duke of Lancaster, at Bordeaux, and his concerns. Not long afterwards, however, the quarrel about the Castilian throne was amicably compromised by the marriage of his daughter, the Lady Catherine, to the son and heir of the King of Castile. Thus one sister of Elizabeth Holland had become reigning Queen of Portugal and the other Queen-to-be of Spain. The Duke of Lancaster's expedition had failed, had cost two or three thousand English lives, and had caused great misery to people in Galicia and Castile ; but, then, he had made two excellent matches for his daughters.

CHAPTER V

VICISSITUDES OF FORTUNE

'And yet time hath its revolutions; there must be a period and an end to all things temporal—*finis rerum*—an end of names and dignities, and why not of De Vere? For where is Bohun? Where is Mowbray? Where is Mortimer? Nay, which is more and most of all, where is Plantagenet? They are entombed in the urns and sepulchres of mortality. And yet let the name and dignity of De Vere stand so long as it pleaseth God.'—CHIEF JUSTICE CREW *in the Earldom of Oxford Judgment, temp. Charles II*

SIR JOHN HOLLAND went to Spain in the summer of 1386, and returned home before the end of April 1388. Fierce political storms meanwhile swept over England. King Richard, in 1385, gave the dukedom of Gloucester to his uncle Thomas, and that of York to his uncle Edmund. He raised Michael de la Pole to be Earl of Suffolk, and conferred upon a far more high-born courtier, Robert De Vere, the offensively high-sounding title of Duke of Ireland, much to the irritation of the royal dukes. The Duke of Gloucester reformed the opposition party against the new favourites. Behind him were great lords of the Norman caste : Thomas de Mowbray, Earl of Nottingham, Thomas Beauchamp, Earl of Warwick, and Richard Fitz-Alan, Earl of Arundel, who was related to the Hollands, for his sister, Alice, had married the second Earl of Kent. These proud warrior nobles were backed by powerful Churchmen; Courtenay, Archbishop of Canterbury, first cousin on the materna side to Henry of Bolingbroke, William of Wykeham, Bishop of Winchester, a moderate and prudent man, and Thomas

Fitz-Alan, brother of Lord Arundel, then Bishop of Ely, and later Archbishop of York, and finally Archbishop of Canterbury, one of the most ambitious politicians of his time. These prelates supported Gloucester and his aristocratic allies, who were religious conservatives, while the Court party were deemed to be tainted by the doctrines of the Lollard preachers, men of Saxon breed, who not only were violent heretics in religion, but advocated the temporal spoliation of the Church.

Parliament met in October 1386, was asked to vote supplies for a French expedition, and demanded that the King should first dismiss his Chancellor and Treasurer. Richard replied that he would not dismiss a kitchen scullion to please Parliament. The Duke of Gloucester and Bishop Arundel told him that, if he alienated himself from his people and would not be governed by the laws and by the advice of the Lords, the said Lords might, with the assent of the Commons, lawfully deprive him of his crown and confer it upon some near kinsman of the royal line. For want of means of resistance, Richard gave way, and the Earl of Suffolk was impeached by the Commons and sentenced to imprisonment. Gloucester's party then placed the King, who was now twenty, under the tutelage of certain Commissioners, who were to receive all the revenues of the Crown and to control all the expenditure. It was an early attempt at the system of Cabinet government which was perfected in the eighteenth century.

In August 1387, however, Richard obtained from the judges a unanimous and obviously correct opinion that the instrument which he had signed under force and constraint, appointing this commission, was illegal. Gloucester, Nottingham, and Arundel marched from Essex on London at the head of 40,000 men, and were joined at Waltham Cross by that discreet and time-observing son of the Duke

of Lancaster, Henry Bolingbroke, Earl of Derby. Gloucester
and his friends entered London, and, in the Parliament held
early in 1388, known by those whom it savagely oppressed
as the 'Merciless,' and by its admirers as the 'Wonderful,'
appealed of treason the Archbishop of York, the Duke of
Ireland, the Earl of Suffolk, the Chief Justice Tressilian,
Sir Nicholas Brember, Mayor of London, and others. The
appellants were Gloucester, Henry of Bolingbroke, Arundel,
Warwick, and Nottingham.

The Duke of Ireland raised some troops in the west, but
was defeated at Radcote Bridge by Gloucester and Henry
of Bolingbroke, and fled beyond the seas, only to die at
Louvain in Brabant, gored by a wild boar. The Earl of
Suffolk fled to France, and the judges who had given the
opinion as to the commission were sentenced to the horrible
doom of exile for life in Ireland. The Chief Justice and
the Mayor of London and five other leading courtiers, gentlemen of distinction, were hung. Sir Simon Burley, K.G.,
falsely accused of a plot to deliver Dover Castle to the French,
was beheaded on May 5, 1388. This gentleman had been
a kind of tutor or guardian of Richard in his childhood.
Froissart says of him, ' God have mercy on his soul ! To
write of his shameful death right sore displeaseth me, howbeit,
I must needs do it to follow the history. Greatly I complain
of his death, for, when I was young, I found him a gentle
knight, sage and wise.' Henry, Earl of Derby, tried hard
to save Burley's life, and quarrelled with his uncle of
Gloucester over this ; for, says Holinshed, the Duke ' being
a sore and right severe man, might not by any means be
removed from his opinion and purpose, if he once resolved
on any matter.'

By these evil deeds the Court party was crushed, and,
for a year, Gloucester reigned supreme in his nephew's
kingdom. In May 1389, however, Richard succeeded in

effecting a mild counter-revolution. He dismissed from his Council Gloucester and his friends, and held his own for some years with the support of a middle party. Thomas Arundel, now Archbishop of York, ceased to be Chancellor, and was replaced by the moderate William of Wykeham. In 1391 Arundel again received the Great Seal, and in 1396 was made Archbishop of Canterbury.

Affairs were nominally managed for the indolent and pleasure-loving King by his uncle the Duke of York, but the real manager at this time seems to have been the astute Henry of Bolingbroke, Earl of Derby, who made himself very popular by his personal charm and by his use of power.

The Court's headquarters were mainly at this time at the royal palace at Eltham, near London, in the delightful county of Kent, and it was as magnificent as those times allowed. The King was young, fond of luxury and pageantry, and, as John Gower testifies in verse and John Froissart in prose, he was, like Charles I and other unfortunate kings, a discerning patron of art and literature.

'I was in his court,' says Sir John Froissart, 'more than a quarter of a year together, and he made me good cheer because that in my youth, I was clerk and servant to the noble King Edward III, his grandfather, and with my lady Philippa of Hainault, Queen of England, his grandmother, and when I departed from him it was at Windsor, and at my departing the King sent me by a knight of his called Sir John Golofer, a goblet of silver and gilt weighing two marks of silver, and within it a hundred nobles, by the which I am as yet the better and shall be as long as I live, wherefore I am bound to pray to God for his soul, and with much sorrow I write of his death.'

The greatest poet of those days, Geoffrey Chaucer, also belonged to the Court. In May 1398 he was employed by the King on urgent and secret business in the kingdom, and in October 1398 received an annual grant of wine from the Port of London. As John Holland was then virtual First Minister, this shows that he must have liked and trusted the poet.[1] A Court of which Chaucer and well-experienced John Froissart approved—he must have seen and heard much there of the Hollands—had no doubt merits and charms. Holinshed says of Richard, ' He kept the greatest port and maintained the most plentiful house that ever any King of England did either before his time or after. For there resorted daily to his Court about ten thousand persons. They had meat and drink there allowed them. In his kitchen there were three hundred servitors. Of ladies, chamberlains, there were about three hundred at least. They wore gorgeous and costly apparel.' This way of life was distasteful to the bourgeoisie, who, with some justice, thought that good money was being wasted, though the taxation was probably the lightest in Europe, and to the rude country lords, who deemed it frenchified and effeminate. But it was a delightful court in which the Hollands lived, too delightful to last long in a still rough and feudal England. It was the most refined and civilised that England had until the charming early years of Charles I, for that of the virgin Elizabeth, though showy, was fundamentally coarse and parvenu.

John Holland pursued a successful career. Immediately after his return, at request of the Commons in Parliament, in 1388, he was made Earl of Huntingdon. For the brother of a king, he arrived late at a peerage ; the honour had probably been deferred by the Stafford affair. We have

---

[1] Chaucer on the occasion of his secret mission received a letter of protection, which he asked for on the ground that he was afraid of being molested by his rivals and enemies. Besides the wine he had a grant of £20 a year from Richard. After Richard's fall Henry IV continued these allowances, although the poet had accidentally lost the letters patent which conferred them.

an account of this creation by the monastic chronicler, Malvern. He says :

' The second day of June, the King, sitting in full Parliament, and all the temporal and spiritual lòrds standing round him, the Earl of Bolingbroke and the Earl of Salisbury brought my lord John Holland, brother of the King, apparelled as an Earl into Parliament, and Thomas Hobell, Esquire, carried the sword of the said Lord John Holland, and the King took the sword, and touched the said Lord John Holland and named him Earl of Huntingdon, and also gave him two thousand marks a year for the maintenance and support of his rank.'

Also he received manors in several counties, mainly in Devon, Somerset, and Cornwall, and he obtained the forfeited house which had belonged to the Earl of Suffolk in Thames Street, London, and bore the curious name of ' The New June,' though he seems to have usually lodged in another house in the same locality called ' Cold Harbour.' He was appointed Admiral of the King's fleet from the Thames westward, and Governor of Brest in Brittany, the land where his late sister Joan had been Duchess. He maintained his prowess in the lists, and in 1390 went to a famous tournament in France. Three French gentlemen had undertaken to hold the lists for thirty days round about Whitsuntide against all comers. They were Huntingdon's old antagonist in Spain, Reginald de Roye, the young Boucicault, and the seigneur de St. Pye. The challengers announced they would pitch their tents close to Calais, and it was the opinion of the Earl of Huntingdon, Sir John Golofer, Sir William Clifton, Sir William Clynton, and other gentlemen whom Froissart names, and many other knights and squires, that this was a challenge to England, and that they should take part in this sport; for, said they, ' Surely the knights of France have done well, and like good companions, and we shall not fail them at their business.' So the Earl of Huntingdon, with over sixty knights and squires, passed the sea and lodged at Calais.

It was, says Froissart, 'at the entering in of the jolly, fresh, lively month of May,' that the three young French knights came from Boulogne to the Abbey of St. Inglevert, and in a fair plain between that place and Calais, set up three light green pavilions, and at the entrance to each pavilion each knight hung up two shields with his arms. On May 21, the tournament began before a large audience from Calais and all the country round, with all the sound and bustle and colour which Chaucer describes in his 'Knight's Tale.' The rule was, that each visitor could run six courses, selecting which of the French knights he pleased, for each. John Froissart no doubt was there, for it was near his country, and he would not have missed such a gathering and sight for all the world, and he describes every course that was run for four days with the utmost minuteness.[1] It will be enough here to report shortly the feats of the Earl of Huntingdon, who opened the proceedings. John Holland was now a man of about thirty-eight, of noble appearance, tall, and at the maximum of his physical strength. He first sent his squire to touch the shield of Boucicault, who, ready mounted and armed, rode out of his pavilion. The two knights regarded each other, drew apart for a space, then 'spurred their horses and came together rudely.' Boucicault struck the English Earl on the shield, but the spear-head glided off and did no harm, and so they passed and turned and rested at their distances ; 'this course was greatly praised.'

---

[1] Froissart's wealth of detail, equal to any modern reporter's account of a prize fight, is here too much even for the leisurely Lord Berners, who has to omit many of the finer points in his translation. The eighteenth-century translator Johnes abbreviates it still more. Froissart, regarded as a historian, has, luckily for us, no artistic sense of proportion relatively to supposed importance of events

In the second course they met without damage to either side, and in the third their horses swerved, and they failed to meet. ' The Earl of Huntingdon, who had great desire to joust and was somewhat chafed, came to his place and awaited Boucicault, but Boucicault would not take his spear, and showed that he would run no more that day against the Earl.' Then Huntingdon sent his squire to touch the shield of St. Pye, who came out of his pavilion, and ' when the Earl saw that he was ready, he spurred his horse, and St. Pye likewise ; they couched their spears, but at the meeting their horses crossed, and the Earl was unhelmed. Then he returned to his squires and ' was rehelmed and took again his spear,' and St. Pye his, and then they ran again and ' met each other with their spears in the midst of their shields ' so that each of them was nearly carried out of the saddle, but by the grip of their legs saved themselves and so returned and took breath. ' Sir John Holland, who had great desire to do honourably, took again his spear and spurred his horse, and when the Lord of St. Pye saw him coming, he dashed forth his horse to encounter him ; each struck the other on the helmet so that the fire flashed out, in which the Lord of St. Pye was unhelmed, and so they passed forth and came to their own places. This course was greatly praised ; and both French and English said that those three lords, the Earl of Huntingdon, Sir Boucicault, and the Lord of St. Pye, had done well their devoirs, without any damage to each other. Again the Earl desired, for love of his lady, to have another course, but he was refused ; then he went out of the rank to give place to others, for he had run all of his six courses well and valiantly, so that he had laud and honour of all parties.' Huntingdon had not, however, touched the shield of Reginald de Roye, perhaps he was dissatisfied with that device of an unlaced helmet which he had experienced in Spain, or perhaps, having tested de

Roye's strength before, he did not care, so near to Dover,
to risk his dignity as brother to the King. But if he had
been allowed his request for one extra course he would,
perhaps, have run it against de Roye. In the rest of that
day, however, and on the three following days, Sir Reginald
met several English knights and had decidedly the better
of most of them, for, says Froissart, ' he was one of the best
jousters in the realm of France ; also he lived in amours
with a young lady which availed him in all his business,'
by increasing his spirit and daring, as such amours ever do.
On the third day he ran no less than five courses against
Sir John Arundel, who was ' young and fresh, a jolly dancer
and singer,' with very even results, lover meeting lover.
This Arundel sounds like the Young Squire in Chaucer's
' Prologue ' :

> Singing he was, or fluting all the day,
> He was as fresh as is the month of May.

On the fourth day Reginald de Roye sent a Bohemian knight
of the Queen's retinue clean off his horse in the second course,
and almost left him for dead. Possibly this was ' Sir Nicles '
who was concerned in the affair at Beverley five years earlier.
' The Englishmen,' says Froissart, ' were not displeased,'
because the German had ridden his first course against
Boucicault unfairly, which had caused much talk and com-
motion. By the rules of the game, the Bohemian knight
had forfeited his horse and arms, if Boucicault had chosen
to press his right. As it was, he was adjudged to lose his
option as to antagonist, and the umpires selected for his
second course the formidable de Roye, and after this
encounter, for good cause, the unnerved and unpopular
German ran no more. When their courses had all been run,
the Earl of Huntingdon and the other Englishmen took
courteous leave, thanking the French gentlemen for the

noble sport they had given, crossed to Dover, and rode up
to London by the old Roman highway, not forgetting to pay
their devoirs at St. Thomas' shrine in Canterbury. Here,
also, John Holland must have looked at the new and
beautiful monument and effigy of his step-father, the Black
Prince, to the right of the shrine, with helmet, sword,
gauntlets, and surcoat hung above it.

In radiant May weather and the gay air of Kent, this
gallant company rode in merry groups, between fresh green
woods and pastures dotted with sheep and white with
flowering thorn, meadows golden with buttercups, and
through old villages with admiring folk at doors and
windows, while the levels of the sea, the Medway, and the
Thames gleamed to their right all the fifty miles from the
top of Boughton Hill to London. The three French knights
stayed on the fair green plain by St. Inglevert for the residue
of their thirty days' challenge, and then rode over the chalk
downs to Boulogne, and by the water meadows of the Somme
through Abbeville and Amiens, and so leisurely to Paris,
'to see the King and the Duke of Touraine and other lords
that were at Paris at that time, who made them great cheer,
as reason required, for they had valiantly borne themselves
whereby they achieved great honour of the King and all
the realm of France.'

This same year Huntingdon appeared in a grand tournament held at Smithfield, which was attended by gentlemen
from France, Germany, and Flanders. Anyone who had
been in the then fashionable East End of London on the
Sunday after Michaelmas, might have seen, about 3 P.M.,
issuing out of the Tower, threescore coursers apparelled for
the jousts, and on each a squire riding at a soft pace, and
next threescore ladies mounted sideways on fair palfreys,
and richly apparelled, each leading by a silver chain a knight
ready equipped for the tournament. 'Thus they came

riding along the streets of London with a great number
of trumpets and other minstrels, and so came to Smithfield,
where the Queen of England and other ladies and damsels
were ready in chambers richly adorned to see the jousts,
and the King was with the Queen.' Count Waleran de
St. Pol, brother-in-law of the Hollands, on the first day won
the prize for the visitors, and the Earl of Huntingdon that
for the English challengers. On the second day the Count
of Ostrevant won for the visitors and Sir Hugh Spencer
for the challengers. Banquets and balls were given by
the King, the Duke of Lancaster, and the Bishop of London,
and at the end of this festive week there were great entertainments at Windsor.

Huntingdon was one of those sent in 1392 to treat of
peace at Amiens, and in 1394 he was made Lord Great
Chamberlain of England. In this year died Queen
Anne, whose good-humoured plain face may be seen on
her tomb at Westminster. King Richard, says Froissart,
was inconsolable, but soon afterwards, he adds, the light-
hearted King 'took the road for Wales, and hunted all
the way to forget the loss of his queen." His uncles of
York and Gloucester were with him, and so were his half-
brothers Kent and Huntingdon, and other lords in great
array.

In this same year, 1394, Huntingdon obtained a licence
to travel abroad for two years. In June of this year, the
Pope granted a plenary indulgence of sins to John Holland,
Earl of Huntingdon, going with some persons in his company
to fight against the Turks and other enemies of Christ.
He went on a pilgrimage to Jerusalem and Saint Catherine
of Mount Sinai, induced by love of travel, and thinking,
possibly, that his past life required religious expiation.
According to Froissart, he passed through Paris on his
way out, and was there handsomely received by the French

King, and heard that there was to be a war in Hungary between the King of that country and the Turks under Sultan Bajazet, to which many French knights were going, among them famous Sir Reginald de Roye, his old antagonist in Spain. Holland told his French friends that he would not fail to be there, and that he would return from Jerusalem through Hungary. Whether he actually did so, there is no record, but as he was at Eltham Palace in 1395, on the occasion of the visit of Robert the Hermit to King Richard, he would not have had time for a campaign in Hungary. A pilgrimage to Jerusalem and Sinai then took the best part of a year to accomplish.[1]

When English and French gentlemen were not engaged in fighting each other, they frequently went on such crusades in order to keep their hand in, and to make up accounts with Heaven. Chaucer's knight, a contemporary of John Holland, had been, says his creator, in Turkey, Spain, Prussia, Russia, Lithuania, fighting against various infidels, whereas his son, the young squire, had only as yet been in Flanders, Artois, and Picardy, like many of our young squires in the days of George V. Thus Henry of Derby went in 1394, with a thousand English knights and squires and their followers, to assist the noble and glorious Order of Teutonic Knights to fight against the stubborn heathen of Lithuania. The Hungarian war ended in .complete victory for the Sultan Bajazet at Nicopolis, and most of the numerous and gallant French gentlemen who fought on the Christian side were slain or captured.

John Holland two years later contemplated an Italian expedition. In 1396 Boniface IX, the Pope whom the English supported, wrote to the Archbishops of Canterbury and York concerning 'the purpose of John Holland, Earl of Huntingdon, the King's brother, to come into Italy

---

[1] Dates even make it doubtful whether Holland went to Jerusalem after all.

and other parts for the extermination of heretics, rebels, and usurpers of cities and lands of the Pope and the Roman Church,' as the Pope had learned from the Earl's letters and messengers. He directed the Archbishops to give to the Earl for that purpose, a grant from ecclesiastical first-fruits in their provinces. This crusade was directed against adherents of the anti-pope. Penitents who joined in the expedition were to have the 'usual Holy Land indulgence and remission of sins.' Huntingdon had probably been in Rome on his way to or from Palestine, and had there made the acquaintance of the Pope. In March 1397, Pope Boniface appointed the Earl of Huntingdon to be 'Gonfalonier of the Holy Roman Church,' and Captain-General of all men-at-arms fighting in that service. If the Earl had taken up this appointment, he might have had some fine adventures, and might also have avoided a great disaster, as he said himself in the last hour of his life. Unhappily his attention was distracted by home politics.

When he returned from his Eastern travels, new storms darkened the sky. His father-in-law, the Duke of Lancaster, had violently quarrelled with his younger brother, the Duke of Gloucester. Lancaster, after the death of his second wife, King Pedro's daughter, married Katherine Swynford, his former mistress and mother by him of the Beauforts. The Duke of York cared little, but the Duke and Duchess of Gloucester were furious, and the Duchess Eleanor, who came of the proud race of Bohun, refused to give to her new sister-in-law the social precedence to which Katherine was now entitled as legitimate wife of an elder brother. The Countess of Derby, another de Bohun, and the Countess of Arundel, very great ladies both by birth and marriage, were also indignant. Then, the unpopularity of the King was increasing, and his quarrel with his uncle of Gloucester threatened to burst into new flame.

The great question of the day was that of peace or war with France. King Richard loved peace and hated war; all his earliest memories were of France; in tastes and character he was more French than English. His tastes were artistic, not warlike. Little cared he that almost all the Edwardian conquests had been lost. His uncle, John of Lancaster, also desired peace, because, according to Froissart, he thought that continued war would lead to French invasions of the domains of his son-in-law, the King of Castile. The amiable Duke of York was also pacific. He preferred sport to war. But Thomas, Duke of Gloucester, was entirely set upon war and re-conquest, and he headed a formidable party. Froissart says:

'Many thought that the Commonalty of England were more inclined to war than peace, for in the time of the good King Edward and his son, the Prince of Wales, they had so many victories over the French, and so great conquests and so much money from ransoms, and payments by towns and countries, that they were become marvellously rich, and many, who were no gentlemen by birth, by their daring and valiant adventures, won so much gold and silver that they became noble, and rose to great honour, and so such as followed after would fain follow the same life. . . .

'The Duke of Gloucester and divers other lords, knights, and squires were of the same opinion as the Commons, and desired war rather than peace to sustain their estates. The King and the Duke of Lancaster would fain have had peace; howbeit, they would not displease the Commons of England.'

Young men with fortunes to make, and older men with fortunes to mend, and they who loved war for its own sake, and the mercantile class who wished to see French gold and silver once more roll into England and send up prices, were all for the Duke of Gloucester. In the long war, the

English had plunder and glory, the French defeat, misery, and spoliation. Richard II, by wishing to make peace with France, came against the presentiment of a young and vigorous nation instinctively conscious that its eventual mission was to annex and rule a large portion of this planet. James II was dethroned long after not, perhaps, more because he was a Roman Catholic, than because he wished to keep peace with France, now our friend, but then our great rival. Men in the eighteenth century sympathised with this view. Guthrie in his History published in 1747 says of the reign of Edward IV : ' The generous wines of France and Italy flowed round the English board and drowned every sentiment of that public jealousy of France, which ought to be the ruling passion of every English King.' Richard, the Hollands, and their friends were the more civilised people, but Gloucester was on the line of the future, for the main line of English history is the pursuit of dominion.

The English used to say that ' so long as we hold Calais, we have the key of France under our girdle.' Precisely because the French wished to recover Calais, the negotiations broke down, and those held in May 1393 at Leulinghen in Flanders between the royal Dukes of Lancaster, Gloucester, Burgundy, and Berri, also failed to arrange more than a four years' truce. The French complained that Gloucester was so mysterious that it was impossible to understand what he really intended or wanted.

At this time appeared ' Robert the Hermit,' originally a squire of Normandy, and by surname le Menuot, about fifty years old, who, on his return from Palestine, had seen at sea a vision commanding him to exhort the French and English kings to make peace, and to denounce Heaven's judgment upon those who continued to make war. He was well received by the French King, but the

H

English war party said that his vision was a trick of the French, whom they always accused of duplicity and sublety. Robert the Hermit was sent on to England by the French King, with the Count of St. Pol, in 1395, and had an audience at Eltham of King Richard, with whom were the Duke of Lancaster and the Earls of Huntingdon and Salisbury. The King sent Robert on to Essex to preach peace to his stubborn uncle of Gloucester, who had prevented its conclusion at Amiens and Leulinghen. The Hermit, by his own invitation, stayed for two days with the Duke and Duchess at Pleshy Castle. The Duke condescended to explain to him at length the reasons for war against the perfidious French, who had, he said, failed to observe the conditions of the peace made at Bretigny in 1360. The Hermit, in reply, reminded the Duke of the Crucified, said that the duty of Christians was to forgive offences, and told the Duke that those who opposed peace would dearly answer for it in this life or in the next.

'How know you that ? ' asked the surly Duke.

' Sir,' replied the Hermit, ' all that I say cometh by divine inspiration, by a vision that came to me as I returned from Syria upon the sea near the island of Rhodes.'

Afterwards, King Richard made Robert the Hermit ' good cheer at Windsor, for love that the French King had sent him, and because he was wise and eloquent, and of sweet words and honest.' At his departing he gave him great gifts, and so did the Dukes of Lancaster and York and the Earls of Huntingdon and Salisbury. It is to the credit of John Holland that he was kind to good Robert the Hermit. Both of the Hermit's hosts, the Duke who desired war, and the King who desired peace, came to violent ends, so that the ways of Heaven, as ever, remain mysterious.

The political quarrel was brought to a head by Richard's

second marriage, in October 1396, with Isabelle, daughter of King Charles of France, a child only eight years old, and by the more permanent treaty with France which accompanied it. The Earls of Nottingham and Rutland went to Paris in the spring of 1396 to inspect the little Princess and discuss the matter with the French Court. On their return they rode so fast to give news to the impatient Richard that they came from Sandwich to Windsor in a day and a half. Then the French King sent over the Count of St. Pol, whose wife was Huntingdon's lovely sister, Maud Holland, to treat secretly of the marriage and peace. St. Pol found the King in his palace on Eltham's pleasant hill, and with him the Duke of Lancaster and the Earls of Kent and Huntingdon. It was an inner family circle. Richard told St. Pol that he, himself, was all for peace with France, but could not act alone, that his brothers, the Hollands, and his uncles of Lancaster and York, were also inclined thereto ; ' but,' he added, ' I have another uncle, the Duke of Gloucester, who is a right perilous and marvellous man.' He said that Gloucester was so secretive that no one could tell what he intended, but that he had with him the Londoners and many lords and knights, and that, in order to prevent peace with France, he would probably raise a rebellion, and in that event he, Richard, would lose his realm. St. Pol replied, ' Sir, if you suffer this, they will destroy you. It is said in France that the Duke of Gloucester intends nothing but to prevent peace and renew the war again, and that, little by little, he draws the hearts of the young men to his side, for they desire war rather than peace, so that the ancient wise men, if war begins to stir, would not be heard or believed; therefore, sir, provide rather betimes than too late ; it were better you had them in danger than they you.' St. Pol advised the King to keep Gloucester soothed by fair words and gifts until the marriage was completed, and thereupon the French King would aid him to suppress any rebellion. The Earl of Huntingdon said, 'Sir, my fair brother of St. Pol hath showed you the truth, therefore take good advice in this matter.' Richard said to St. Pol, 'In God's name, you say well, and so will I do.'

It was arranged that the Kings of France and England should confer at St. Omer, and Richard and his retinue soon travelled down the famous old road to Dover and across the Channel. Terms of peace were discussed, but Richard cared little what they might be, so that he might have his little Princess. He showed much more interest, it was noticed, in the arrangements for the ritual of the marriage than in the terms of peace. However, he had to return to England to obtain the assent of Parliament ; but was soon back at Calais for the marriage, which was a most brilliant and artistic affair. The Duke of Gloucester was reluctantly there by the King's request, but he was rude and taciturn with the French. Froissart gives an account of the marriage banquet, at which the Duke of Burgundy, a 'merry man,' made jests in daring French style which diverted the company. One of the guests was Mademoiselle Jeanne de St. Pol, then about fifteen, the daughter of Maud Holland, Countess de St. Pol, and half-niece of the King. The French King said jestingly that he wished his daughter Isabelle were the age of our fair cousin here, for then she would be a better match for the King of England.' Isabelle was, indeed, much too young, since it was important to obtain a direct heir to the throne as soon as possible.

The King and Queen and wedding guests returned to Eltham, receiving great entertainments and gifts by the way, especially from the Archbishop and city of Canterbury. The Earl of Huntingdon had already given his little half-sister-in-law a 'fermaillet' (?) set with a great diamond in the middle, three fine rubies, and three great pearls, said to be worth 18,000 francs, and at Eltham he also gave her a gold chain a foot and a half long. The Duke of Gloucester also, sulkily and reluctantly, no doubt, gave some handsome jewellery.[1]

These family transactions were the last in which Thomas Holland, second Earl of Kent, was engaged. He died in the following year, 1397, on April 25, and thus escaped the revolution which brought about the temporary fall of the Hollands. He was buried at Bourne, or Brunne, in Lincolnshire, a small priory of eleven canons, which had been founded by a Lord de Wake in the twelfth century, and which he had himself endowed with an alien priory. The inquisition made after his death shows that he left very large landed possessions scattered over many parts of England, more especially in Yorkshire, Lincolnshire, Essex, and Kent. He left two sons, Thomas and Edmund,[2] and six daughters. His eldest son, Thomas, who now became third Earl of Kent of the Holland line, was a gallant and promising youth.

The young Earl married Joan Stafford, daughter of the Ralph de Stafford, whom his uncle, John Holland, had slain in 1386. This, unless it was a pure love affair, shows that the Stafford feud did not extend so strongly to the Kent branch of the Hollands.

The Duke of Gloucester could not forgive the truce and marriage alliance with France. He was a rough and rude warrior, thoroughly despised his unwarlike and artistic,

---

[1] An interesting inventory of all these gifts is extant, made when the girl was sent back to France after the death of Richard. By treaty she was to keep all her personal possessions.

[2] The second Earl of Kent had also two other sons who died young. There is extant a record of the banquet given at Oxford when one of them, Richard Holland, took his degree or something of that kind in February 1395. It cost £67, a great sum in those days.

and pleasure-loving and frenchified nephew, and firmly adhered to the claim of his house to the throne of France. It was a great opportunity, he said, to invade France now that so many of the flower of the French nobility had perished in the war of 1396 against the Turks, and he undertook to raise 6000 men-at-arms and 100,000 archers in England for that purpose. He thought war with France the true policy, because plunder of so wealthy a country made the English rich, and, on the other hand, peace made them indolent and enervated. Money raised by taxes, he said, instead of being used for war with France, which brought rich returns, was squandered by the Court, and went God knows where. The King talked about expeditions to subdue Ireland, but there was no gain in that, for ' the Irish are a wicked people with a poor country, and he who should conquer it one year would lose it the next.' ' Lackingay, Lackingay,' the Duke said to his confidential retainer, ' all you have just heard me say, know to be the truth.'

When Richard II, in the summer of 1397, gave up Brest to its rightful owner (and his own brother-in-law), the Duke of Brittany, who came to England that July, for 120,000 francs in gold, the Duke of Gloucester said to him before others, ' Your Grace ought to put your body in great pain to win a stronghold or town by feat of arms before you take upon you to sell and deliver a town gotten by the man-hood and strong hand and policy of your noble ancestors.' Richard, who was usually, says Froissart, ' humble and meek towards the Duke,' said sharply, ' What is that you say, uncle ? ' Gloucester repeated his words, and Richard said passionately, ' Think you that I am a fool or a merchant to sell my land ? No, by St. John the Baptist, no ! But my cousin, the Duke of Brittany, having paid the sums for which the town and haven of Brest were engaged to me, reason and good conscience required that I should restore it.'[1] Richard's displeasure was increased by the rude manners of this uncle, who appeared at Court when he was not invited, and did not attend when he was summoned, and showed his contempt in every possible way. The King heard that Gloucester talked of putting the crown once more in commission by force, and had said that the Earls of Arundel and Warwick and many barons and prelates were ready to uphold him in this enterprise. The Duke of Gloucester was undoubtedly stirring up the Londoners on the subject of Customs duties, and wasteful expenditure of the receipts on idle feasts and dances. They sent a deputation to Eltham with a petition on this subject.

At this time the Dukes of Lancaster and York, well aware of the storm rising in London and elsewhere, thought well to dissemble their opposition to their imperious younger brother of Gloucester, and came seldom to Court, so that Richard was left almost alone with the Hollands and their close allies. Froissart says that 'there were none of the King's servants but feared the Duke of Gloucester, and would gladly that he had been dead, they cared not how.' When the Duke did come to the Court, he regarded these elegant young men with fierce, contemptuous, and menacing looks. Sir Thomas Percy resigned his post as seneschal because he thought it dangerous to hold office about the King, and others told Richard that it was a perilous thing to serve him, and that they were running the risk of being put to death by Gloucester like Sir Simon Burley and others nine years earlier. John Holland, Earl of Huntingdon,

---

[1] The Duke's remark was provoked by seeing soldiers of the Brest garrison back in England with no wages and out of work. Brest had been granted by the Duke of Brittany to the King of England in 1378, to hold against the French, the Duke receiving £1000 and the rents from some crown manors in Wiltshire. The castle was to be given back to the Duke or his heirs after the war was ended unless the Duke died heirless. Thus it was hardly a case of paying off a mortgage, but neither was it the case of the sale of something which belonged absolutely to the English Crown. The documents in Rymer's *Fœdera* show how the matter stood.

leader of the King's party, shared these alarms and took advantage of them. He knew that Gloucester's most intimate adviser was a certain gentleman (probably the above-named Lackingay) who had formerly been in the household of the Earl of Stafford, and directly attached to the young Ralph Stafford whom he had slain in that encounter in the dark lane near Beverley. He knew also that he had never been forgiven that offence by the great ring of Norman families. Richard now heard of an elaborate plot. The Duke of Gloucester, it was said, had arranged a meeting at Arundel Castle between himself and the Earls of Arundel and Warwick, Arundel's brother, Fitz-Alan, Archbishop of Canterbury, the Abbot of St. Albans, the Prior of Westminster, and others. They did meet at Arundel, swore faith to each other, heard mass celebrated by the Archbishop, and resolved to take and imprison the King and the Dukes of Lancaster and York, and to hang, draw, and quarter the other lords of the Council, including, no doubt, the two Hollands. This was to be done in August. But the Earl of Nottingham, Earl Marshal, who had married Arundel's daughter, and, in the affairs of 1387–1388, had been one leader of the Gloucester party, revealed their whole plot to the King. Now Huntingdon decided to strike.

Richard was at Westminster signing documents on July 11. A day or two later he dined, says Holinshed, ' at the house of his brother, the Earl of Huntingdon, in the street behind All Hallows Church, upon the banks of the River Thames, which was a right fair and stately house.' This thrilling dinner, full of youth and fiery emotion, took place on July 12 or 13, 1397. The Duke of Gloucester and the Earls of Arundel and Warwick had been invited, and the intention had been to arrest them then and there. But only Warwick had come to London, and he was arrested that day at the Chancellor's house near Temple Bar.

Gloucester had excused himself on the ground of health, and Arundel had sent no excuse, but had gone to his castle at Reigate. So the leaders of the Court party dined without these guests at Lord Huntingdon's that morning. Holinshed says :

'After dinner the King gave his Council to understand the matter, by whose advice it was agreed that the King should assemble forthwith what power he might conveniently make of men and archers, and straightway take horse, accompanied with his brother, the Earl of Huntingdon, and the Earl Marshal. Hereupon at six o'clock in the afternoon, just the hour when they used to go to supper, the King mounted on horseback and rode his way, whereof the Londoners had great marvel.'

The King and his friends probably supped and had a long sleep or rest at Havering-atte-Bower, a royal hunting lodge in the wooded country of which Epping and Hainault forests are remains, between London and Pleshy, about twenty miles from the latter. Havering-atte-Bower stands on charmingly undulated rising ground, whence is a wide prospect south-east, with an occasional gleam of the distant Thames and the Kentish hills beyond. Very early in the July morning, they rode on through slumberous Essex villages, and at last came in sight of the great Norman tower built high upon the ancient, perhaps British, mound which still exists at Pleshy. A wide park or sporting domain was at that time attached to the castle. The King then bade Lord Huntingdon ride on fast and tell the Duke that the King was coming to speak with him. Holinshed continues :

'The Earl with ten persons in his company . . . came to the house, and entering into the court, asked if the Duke were at home, and, understanding by a gentlewoman who made him answer, that the Duke and Duchess were yet in bed, he besought her to go to the Duke and show him that the King was coming at hand to speak with him ; and forthwith came the King with a competent number of men-at-arms, and a great company of archers, riding into the base court, his trumpets sounding before him. The Duke herewith came down into the base court, where the King was, having no other apparel upon him but his shirt and a cloak or mantle cast about his shoulders, and with humble reverence said his Grace was welcome, asking of the lords how it chanced they came so early and sent him no word of their coming. The King herewith courteously requested him to go and make him ready and appoint his horses to be saddled, for that he must needs ride with him a little way and confer with him of business. The Duke went up again into his chamber and put upon him his clothes, and the King, alighting from his horse, fell in talk with the Duchess and her ladies. The Earl of Huntingdon and divers others followed the Duke into the hall, and there stayed for him until he had put on his raiment. And within a little they came forth again all together into the base court, where the King was delighting with the Duchess in pleasant talk, whom he willed now to return to her lodging again, for he might stay no longer, and so took his horse again, and the Duke likewise. But shortly after that the King and all his company were gone forth of the gate of the base court, he commanded the Earl Marshal to apprehend the Duke, which incontinently was done.'

Froissart gives a somewhat different version of this incident. He says :

'One day the King in manner as going a'hunting rode from Havering atte Bower, twenty miles from London, in Essex, and within twenty miles of Pleshy, where the Duke of Gloucester held his house. After dinner the King departed from Havering with a small company and came to Pleshy about five o'clock ; the weather was fair and hot.[1] So the

---

[1] Froissart may have heard of five o'clock and have mistaken 5 A.M. for 5 P.M.

King came suddenly thither about the time that the Duke of Gloucester had supped. For he was but a small eater, nor eat never long at dinner nor at supper. When he heard of the King's coming, he went to meet him in the middle of the court, and so did the Duchess and her children, and they welcomed the King, and the King entered the hall, and so into a chamber. Then a board was spread for the King's supper. The King sat not long and said at his first coming, " Fair uncle, cause five or six horses of yours to be saddled, for I will pray you to ride with me to London, as to-morrow the Londoners will be before us. And there will also be mine uncles of Lancaster and York, with divers other noblemen. For upon the Londoners' requests I will be ordered according to your counsel. And command your steward to follow you with your train to London, where they shall find you." The Duke, who thought no evil, lightly agreed to the King. And when the King had supped and risen, everything was ready. The King then took leave of the Duchess and her children, and leapt on horseback, and the Duke with him, accompanied by only seven servants, three squires, and four yeomen. So they rode a great pace, and the King talked by the way with his uncle and he with him, and they took the way of Bondeley to avoid Brentwood and the London common highway, and so approached to Stratford by the River of Thames. When the King came near to the ambush which he had laid, then he rode from his uncle a great pace and left him somewhat behind him. Then suddenly the Earl Marshal with his band came galloping after the Duke and overtook him and said, " Sir, I arrest you in the King's name." The Duke saw well he was betrayed and began to call after the King. I cannot tell whether the King heard him or not, but he turned not, but rode forth faster than he did before.'

Froissart says, in a later passage, that the arrest was

effected between ten and eleven o'clock at night. A ship was lying ready in the neighbouring Thames; the Duke was placed in it and carried off to Calais, where Nottingham was Governor.

Holinshed was a careful and conscientious historian, and his story must be based upon some written contemporary record which he considered to be trustworthy.[1] Otherwise, he would not have departed from the story in Froissart's Chronicle, which was before him. As a rule, when there are two versions, Holinshed gives both. On the other hand, Froissart's story is also circumstantial, and he was living and well informed. He had been for three months in England at Richard's Court only three years earlier, and must have had correspondents there who told him, though perhaps with some misunderstanding, how things happened. The two versions, using probabilities, might be reconciled in the following way.

It was important, from the view of Huntingdon and his friends, that the descent upon Pleshy should be so effected that no one, seeing the movements of the King, should ride on fast ahead and warn the Duke. Otherwise the Duke would have probably left the castle and raised the country, and there would have been that fatal business, a 'coup d'état manqué,' as when Charles I tried to arrest the five members. It was all-important that the arrests of Gloucester, Arundel, and Warwick should nearly coincide. It is therefore natural that, as Holinshed says, the ride to Pleshy should have been made by night. But they had not to ride from 6 P.M. till 5 or 6 A.M. to cover less than forty miles, so that, as Froissart says, they did probably break the journey at Havering-atte-Bower, though not to dine, but to sup and sleep awhile. This also had the advantage that

---

[1] The contemporary Walsingham merely says that Gloucester was arrested by force at Pleshy and sent to Calais

to go in the evening to a royal hunting lodge gave a good answer to awkward questions, since there was the appearance of an intention to hunt next day.   In the next place, it was important that the arrest of the Duke should not be known by the public before he was safely lodged on board ship on his way to Calais, because Essex and London swarmed with his adherents, and there might have been an attempt at rescue.   Probably, therefore, the arrest was made, not as Holinshed says, just outside Pleshy in the morning, but as Froissart says, late that night at Stratford near the river and the waiting ship.   The party would naturally avoid travelling along the crowded high road and in broad daylight.   Very likely they were back at Havering by ten o'clock in the morning, dined and supped there, and waited till dark, with careful watch of the Duke, who must have known by then that he was virtually a prisoner, and then joined the high road at Romford.   Havering is about two miles north of Romford, and some twenty miles from Pleshy by the lesser roads.   It is not clear what place Froissart means by 'Bondeley,' but the King's party may have travelled to Havering by way of Ongar, avoiding, as he says, Brentwood and the great road.

In any case, it is clear that the Duke was drawn from his Essex stronghold by a well-acted lie in the mouth of the King, supported by visible force, and was arrested by his old and faithless political follower, the Earl of Nottingham, the unworthy object, as 'banished Norfolk,' of some of the most beautiful lines of Shakespeare.

The Earl of Arundel was arrested on the evening of July 16, by the Earls of Kent and Rutland.   He was induced to give himself up by a promise made to his brother, the Archbishop of Canterbury, that the Earl should suffer no bodily harm, at least so it is said by a dubious authority. Warwick had been already arrested.   Thus the three leaders of the opposition were safe in custody, to the consternation of their rebel party, which was so strong in and around the City of London. It was not known who else of those who had taken part in Gloucester's movement ten years earlier might not be arrested. On July 15, a Royal Proclamation was addressed to the Sheriffs of London and Middlesex to allay these fears. It ran:

'We have had arrested and detained in safe custody, Thomas, Duke of Gloucester, Richard, Earl of Arundel, and Thomas, Earl of Warwick; on account of the very many extortions, oppressions, and other misdeeds perpetrated by them against Us and Our People, and for the peace and security of our People.' The Sheriffs were directed to inform their counties that the arrests had been made, not only with the assent of the Earls of Rutland, Kent, and Huntingdon, the Earl Marshal, and the Earls of Somerset and Salisbury, 'but also with the assent of our most dear uncles, John, Duke of Acquitaine and Lancaster, and Edmund, Duke of York, and our most dear cousin, Henry, Earl of Derby,' and that no one who had been implicated in the rebellious movements of Gloucester, Arundel, and Warwick would, if they remained quiet, be molested. There were, however, assemblings in Sussex, where Arundel was a great landholder, and on July 28, an order was sent to the Justices of the Peace in that county to arrest agitators.

John Holland, Earl of Huntingdon, was, no doubt, the soul of all these vigorous proceedings. With good right, apart, that is, from Christian morality, he struck his foes when they were nearly, but not quite, ready to strike him. Like Stafford's honest archer who shot his favourite squire, he would much rather they died than he should. Mediæval politics in their ethics resembled modern war. Gloucester and his allies would certainly have given no more quarter to the Hollands than the Hollands gave to them. Nine

years earlier, these fierce partisans enforced the unjust
death of the brave and virtuous Sir Simon Burley, who was
a friend of Huntingdon's mother, had been made a Knight
of the Garter by Edward III, had served the Black Prince
in war and peace, and had been a tutor to Richard in his
childhood. Then the good Queen Anne, daughter of the
proudest house in Europe, an Emperor's sister, was, it is
said, three hours with Gloucester entreating mercy for her
friend in vain, and Gloucester told King Richard that ' if
he wished to be king this must be done.' Richard II consented to the death of Burley for the same reason that
Charles I deplorably consented to that of the Earl of Strafford,
weakness in face of force. No doubt this Thomas, Duke
of Gloucester, was, as Polydore Virgil says, ' vir ferocissimus
et praecipitis ingenii.' He deserved well to expiate, by
his own death, his deliberate and cold-blooded terrorist
crime in causing on a false charge the death of Sir Simon
Burley, his fellow Knight of the Garter, and the intimate
and trusted friend of his heroic brother, Edward, Prince
of Wales.

These arrests were followed by a gathering of the
Royalists at Nottingham. Here were appointed certain
Lords Appellant to impeach Gloucester, Arundel, and
Warwick, and the Archbishop of Canterbury, the other
Fitz-Alan. The Lords Appellant were Rutland, Hunting-
don, Kent, Somerset, Salisbury, Despenser, and Scrope.

After the middle of August, the Court was at Woodstock,
near Oxford. Thence on the 17th, the King directed William
Rickhill to go to Calais, and hear what the Duke of Gloucester
wished to say.

It was now, probably, that Gloucester's doom was sealed.
On the 26th a circular was sent to Sheriffs directing that the
magnates, knights, and other gentlemen of each county
should meet the King at Kingston-on-Thames on the Monday

after the Exaltation of the Holy Cross, very early in the morning, ' sufficiently armed,' in order to ride with him to Westminster to open Parliament.

On August 28 the Court was at Westminster. By a letter that day the King informed the Sheriffs that the Duke of Lancaster was allowed to bring up for the meeting of Parliament, 300 men-at-arms and 600 archers, the Duke of York to bring 100 men-at-arms and 200 archers, and the Earl of Derby to bring 200 men-at-arms and 400 archers. It looks as though these royal princes were apprehensive, and had made terms as to conditions on which they would attend Parliament.

Parliament was opened on September 17, and the Bishop of Exeter began by a speech highly extolling the pure monarchic principle. He took for his text from the prophet Ezekiel the words, ' Rex unus erit omnibus,' and proved conclusively by many authorities that ' by any other means than one sole king no realm could be well governed.'

The Opposition were dismayed and thrown out by the loss of their leaders, and power for the time rested with the King, his lords and their retainers, and his force of paid Cheshire archers. Parliament was assembled in a large wooden shed especially built for the purpose in Palace Yard, open at both ends and surrounded by the Cheshire men, who sometimes threateningly drew their arrows ready to fly, ' ad pugnam arcubus tensis sagittas ad aures tendentes.' The Commons, as they have usually done in English history, faithfully carried out the behests of those who held real power. Sir John Bushy, a courtier, was elected Speaker. On September 20 the Commons impeached of high treason Thomas Arundel, Archbishop of Canterbury, brother of Richard, Earl of Arundel. The charges did not allege treasonable conspiracy at the present, as to which probably no sufficient evidence could be obtained, but related to the

transactions of 1387 and 1388.   The Archbishop was accused
of having instigated, aided and abetted Gloucester, Arundel,
and Warwick in their violent and armed usurpation of royal
prerogative in 1387, their creation of the Commission to
which the King's powers had been transferred, and their
execution without the King's real consent, of Sir Simon
Burley and Sir John Barnes.   The Archbishop was at once
convicted, and, by the King's decision, sentenced to banishment for life from England.   By subsequent papal decree,
obtained at the instance of the English Government, he was
translated from Canterbury to the remote and barbarous
diocese of St. Andrews in Scotland, a purely derisory appointment, since, at that time, Scotland, out of opposition to the
English, adhered to the anti-pope.

On the next day, September 21, the eight lords who
formed the inner Council—Rutland, Kent, Huntingdon,
Salisbury, Somerset, Nottingham, Despenser, and Scrope—
brought their appeal of treason, on the same heads, against
the great Richard, Earl of Arundel, Warenne, and Surrey.
He was tried by a commission of peers presided over by
the Duke of Lancaster.   The proceedings had the speed
of a court martial.   Arundel was accused of those proceedings ten years earlier for which he had received a formal
pardon.   Henry, Earl of Derby, gave evidence of one
treasonable saying of his, and the King himself deposed
to another.   Arundel pleaded his general and particular
pardon, but this plea was overruled on the ground that
the King, when he signed it, was acting under armed constraint.   Arundel's defence was drowned by shouts of
' Traitor,' and the Duke of Lancaster pronounced sentence
of death.   Arrangements for his execution had already
been made on Tower Hill, and he was led straight from
Westminster Hall through London to the scaffold.   Holinshed says : ' There went with him to see the execution done,

six great lords, of whom there were three Earls—Nottingham, who had married his daughter, Kent, that was his sister's son, and Huntingdon—being mounted on great horses, with a great company of armed men, and the fierce bands of the Cheshire men furnished with axes, swords, bows and arrows, marching before and behind him.[1] When he should depart the palace, he desired that his hands might be loosed to dispose of such money as he had in his purse, betwixt that place and Charing Cross. This was permitted, and so he gave such money as he had in his purse with his own hands, but his arms were still bound behind him. When they came to Tower Hill the noblemen that were about moved him right earnestly to acknowledge his treason against the King. But he in no wise would do so, but reiterated that he was never traitor in word or deed, and herewith, perceiving the Earls of Nottingham and Kent, that stood by with other noblemen busy to further the execution, being of kin and allied to him, he spake to them and said, "Truly it would have beseemed you both rather to have been absent than here at this business. But the time will come e'er it be long, when as many shall marvel at your misfortunes as do now at mine." After this, forgiving the executioner, he besought him not to torment him long, but to strike off his head at one blow, and feeling the edge of the sword, whether it was sharp enough, he said, "It is very keen; do that thou hast to do quickly." And so kneeling down, the executioner struck off his head with one blow.'

His body was buried together with his head in the Church of the Augustine Friars in Bread Street. Thomas of Walsingham says that Arundel 'flinched not at all, neither when he underwent the sad sentence of death, nor when he passed

---

[1] Walsingham says : ' Praecessit eum et sequebatur satis ferialis turba Cestriensium armata securibus, gladiis, arcubus et sagittis.' Holinshed closely follows Walsingham in this narrative.

from the place of judgment to the place of punishment, nor when, with bowed head, he offered himself to the stroke, but, changing not the colour of his face, he no more grew pale than if he were invited to a banquet.' It was a death worthy of a son of the Normans and of the warrior who, ten years earlier, defeated off Kent the invading fleets of France and Flanders. Of all the processions that have passed through the London streets, this was surely one of the strangest. Was any other Englishman ever escorted to his death by his nephew and his son-in-law ? ' The words of dying men enforce attention like deep harmony.' Those of Arundel must have sounded then and afterwards in the minds of Huntingdon, Kent, and Nottingham, and his prediction was fulfilled. Kent and Huntingdon came to the same death, and Nottingham died in exile.

In those fierce days and long afterwards, politics was a war-game played not as now with mere salaries and dignities; but with the lives and whole fortunes of men at stake. Ten years earlier, Arundel had caused death and exile to be inflicted upon men at least as virtuous as himself. But Arundel was on the popular side, and among the people soon arose the incredible legend that the light-hearted Richard was haunted by horrible dreams in which the Earl of Arundel appeared to him in dreadful and menacing aspect.

On September 21, the day of Arundel's execution, a royal direction was given to the Earl Marshal, Lord Nottingham, to bring the Duke of Gloucester up for trial. On the 24th an answer was received from Calais that the Duke had died there in prison. He was then declared by Parliament to be a traitor, and his property was confiscated to the King. All men believed that, as was afterwards proved, Gloucester had been secretly strangled or smothered in prison to avoid the spectacle of an uncle doomed to death and publicly executed at the behest of a royal nephew.

On October 6 a royal order was sent to the two Arch-bishops that they should direct all the clergy of their dioceses to offer up public prayers for the repose of the soul of Thomas, Duke of Gloucester, who—said the missive—had been appealed of treason, and, before he died, had confessed his guilt. On the 14th a direction was given to the Earl Marshal as Governor of Calais, to deliver the dead body of the Duke to the King's Clerk, Richard Maudelyn, to be brought home and buried in Westminster Abbey. But on October 31, the King, from Westminster, wrote to Eleanor, Duchess of Gloucester, that the body was not to be taken to the Abbey, but to Bermondsey Priory, there to await further orders. Probably demonstrations were feared. Eventually it was taken to Pleshy, and there interred in the Collegiate Church which the Duke had founded in 1393. Later, in the reign of Henry IV, the coffin was removed to Westminster and placed in a low floor sepulchre in the Chapel of Edward the Confessor between the shrine and the tomb of Edward III. A richly imaged brass which covered it disappeared so late as the eighteenth century.[1]

The third accused magnate, Thomas, Earl of Warwick, was tried on September 28. He was not put to death, but his estates were confiscated, and he was sentenced to life imprisonment in the Isle of Man. He saved his life by confessing to the treasonable intents of himself and his allies.

Richard, Earl of Arundel, by his will, dated December 5, 1375, founded the collegiate church at Arundel, which his son afterwards built. Among other bequests in this will, the Earl bequeathed 'to my very dear sister of Hereford my cup with hearts, and to my very dear sister of Kent my cup with trefoils, that is to say, if they be kind (*naturelles*)

---

[1] One would like to know how this valuable brass disappeared. It was still there in 1707, for there is a picture of it in Sandford's *Genealogical History*, published in that year. Who robbed the Abbey and despoiled the dead after that late date ?

and such as they ought in reason in aid and furtherance of my will,' otherwise they may have 'none of my aforesaid bequest.' It looks as though the Earl did not place much confidence in either very dear sister.

Now came a great creation of titles for the ruling set. The King first declared that Henry, Earl of Derby, and Thomas Mowbray, Earl of Nottingham, had 'loyally used themselves towards the King in coming (in 1388) from the Duke of Gloucester and the Earl of Arundel and Warwick, traitorously assembled, in defence of the King.' Then, ' On Saturday in Michaelmas week the King, sitting there, crowned in his royal majesty and holding in his hand the royal sceptre, created his cousin, Henry of Lancaster and Earl of Derby, to be Duke of Hereford, and gave to him the charter of his creation, which was read in open Parliament. And thereupon the King girded the Duke with a sword and set over his head a cap of honour and dignity of a Duke and received of him his homage.'[1] With the same ceremonial, the Earl of Rutland, the Duke of York's son, was made Duke of Albermarle, John Holland, Earl of Huntingdon, was made Duke of Exeter, and his nephew, Thomas Holland, third Earl of Kent, was made Duke of Surrey, and the Earl of Nottingham was made Duke of Norfolk.[2] John Beaufort, Earl of Somerset, was created Marquis of Dorset, with use of a circlet instead of a cap. Lord Despenser was made Earl of Gloucester, and Lord Scrope, Earl of Wiltshire. The estates of the vanquished were distributed among the victors. A substantial part of the Earl of Arundel's wide estates was granted to Thomas Holland, the new Duke of Surrey, who also got Warwick

---

[1] Tower records

[2] According to a contemporary Latin annalist, the people (*vulgares*) derisively called the new Dukes ' non duces sed dukettos,' ' not dukes but dukelets.'— *Annales Rich* ii p. 223. Holinshed says that these creations were made at Christmas, at Lichfield, where the King kept the feast, but he seems mistaken in this.

Castle, with a special grant of the valuable tapestry there, representing the combat of Sir Guy with the Dragon. Other portions of the Arundel and Warwick spoils went to the new Dukes of Exeter and Norfolk. The Duke of Norfolk obtained from the estates of his late father-in-law Lewes town and castle. To John Holland, Duke of Exeter, were assigned the castle, manor, lordship, and town of Arundel, with lands in Sussex and other counties, and with all the goods, vessels, and utensils in the said castle.[1] He also obtained Reigate Castle. The Hollands were thus placed on a far finer landed basis than they had ever had before. The Duke of Exeter was also given charge of the late Earl of Arundel's son and heir. The boy after a time escaped with the aid of one William Scott, and fled oversea to join his uncle, the exiled and deposed Archbishop Fitz-Alan of Canterbury, at Utrecht or Cologne. He came back to England two years later with that prelate and Henry of Bolingbroke and enjoyed a fearful revenge against the destroyer of his father.

The Earl of Kent probably chose the title of Surrey for his dukedom because he had received a large part of the Arundel estates in that county which had once belonged to the lover of Isabel de Holland, the famous John, Earl de Warenne and Surrey. John Holland, no doubt chose the title of Duke of Exeter because he aimed at being a magnate of the south-west. He already had large estates in Devonshire, Cornwall, and Sussex by grants from the Crown, and had built a great house on the river Dart, about twenty miles from Exeter. When created Duke, he was also made Governor of Exeter Castle. These western possessions, with a short interval of sequestration, continued in the hands of the Hollands till the end of the War of the Roses.

[1] Pat. 21 Ric. II, p. 143.

After the Michaelmas proceedings at Westminster, Parliament was adjourned, to meet again at Shrewsbury in the middle of February 1398, on the day after the feast of St. Hilary. A special summons to attend was sent to the King's Viceroy in Ireland, Roger de Mortimer, Earl of March, husband of Alianora Holland of Kent, and heir-presumptive to the Crown, who was so soon to die in an obscure skirmish in the west. Shrewsbury was a well-chosen place of meeting, for there Parliament would be under the influence of the King's wild but loyal subjects in Cheshire, Lancashire, and Wales. When it met, one or two measures were passed reversing the proceedings or declarations of the ' Merciless Parliament ' of 1388. Before it broke up, Parliament voted a subsidy on wool to the Crown, and a Commission of twelve peers and commoners, including the two Hollands, was appointed to ' examine and answer certain petitions to the King ' with which this particular Parliament had not had time to deal, and, generally, to wind up incompleted business. Some historians seem to have vastly exaggerated the constitutional or unconstitutional import of this procedure.

For a space after the well-designed and efficient stroke of state of 1397, Richard seemed all-powerful.

' In those days,' says Froissart, ' there was none so great in England that durst speak against anything the King did. He had a Council to his liking, who exhorted him to do what he list ; he kept in his wages two thousand archers, who watched over him day and night.' Froissart also says that Richard had confidence only in his brother, the Earl of Huntingdon—now Duke of Exeter—and the Earls of Rutland and Salisbury. It was the supreme hour of John Holland, chief organiser and promoter of the whole recent well-managed blow against the leaders of the high aristocratic ring, who were supported by the London middle class. Now, however, took place an event pregnant with the downfall of the new régime, the famous quarrel between the new Dukes of Hereford and Norfolk.

On January 25, 1398, Henry of Bolingbroke, now Duke of Hereford, 'humbly kneeling on his knees before the King,' in public audience, craved and received pardon for his offences of 1387 and 1388. As he had already, at Westminster, been exonerated, and had even received a dukedom, this ceremonial was an unnecessary as well as a dangerous humiliation to inflict upon a proud man of the blood royal, but Richard enjoyed this kind of rite, which John Holland also underwent in 1386. The ceremony probably had to do with the Norfolk affair. In the Parliament at Shrewsbury Hereford accused Norfolk of having said to him as they rode together, in December last on the road from Windsor to London, that the King indeed used fair words, but intended to destroy or exile them and others when a favourable opportunity came. Hereford and Norfolk, who (as Derby and Nottingham) had supported the Duke of Gloucester against the King in 1387, and the King against Gloucester in 1397, had certainly every reason to distrust both Richard and each other. The Duke of Norfolk denied the allegation, and challenged Hereford to ordeal by battle. The King, after a later hearing at Windsor, decreed that this sensational encounter should take place on Gosford Green, in the very centre of England, near Coventry, on April 29, 1398.

The Duke of Albemarle, says Holinshed, as High Constable, and Thomas Holland, Duke of Surrey, appointed to act as Earl Marshal, since the actual Earl Marshal was a combatant, ' entered into the lists with a great company of men apparelled in silk, embroidered with silver, every man having a tipped staff to keep the field in order. About the hour of prime the Duke of Hereford came to the barriers of the lists mounted on a white courser, barded with green and blue velvet embroidered sumptuously with swans and antelopes of goldsmith's work, armed at all points. The Constable and Marshal came to the barriers, demanding who he was. He answered, 'I am Henry of Lancaster, Duke of Hereford, who am come hither to do mine endeavour against Thomas Mowbray, Duke of Norfolk, as a traitor untrue to God, the King, the realm, and me.' Then he swore upon the Gospels that his cause was just, made the sign of the cross on his horse, sheathed his naked sword, drew down his visor, entered the lists, descended from his horse, sat down in a chair of green velvet at one end of the lists, and awaited his adversary. 'Soon after him entered the King in great triumph, accompanied with all the peers of the realm, and in his company was the Earl of St. Pol, who was come out of France in post to see this challenge performed.' After a proclamation for the maintenance of order during the combat, a herald cried, 'Behold here Henry of Lancaster, Duke of Hereford, appellant, who is entered into the lists royal to do his devoir against Thomas Mowbray, Duke of Norfolk, defendant, upon pain to be found false and recreant.'

'The Duke of Norfolk hovered on horseback at the entry of the lists, his horse being barded with crimson velvet, embroidered richly with lions of silver and mulberry trees, and when he had made his oath before the Constable and Marshal that his quarrel was just and true, he entered the field manfully, saying aloud, "God aid him that hath the right," and sat him down in his chair, which was of crimson velvet.'

The young Duke of Surrey measured their spears to see that they were of equal length, handed one himself to Hereford, and sent the other across the lists by a knight to Norfolk. Then the herald commanded the champions to mount and prepare for battle, and their chairs were removed.

Now the two dukes had their spears in rest and had begun to advance to the encounter, when the King, who sat in a lofty seat, threw down his truncheon, and the heralds shouted to arrest the fight. The two dukes sat again in their chairs two mortal hours while the King consulted with his Council, and then Sir John Bushy read out the royal decision, which must have come as a huge disappointment to the multitude which had assembled to see so fine a fight, including, according to Holinshed, ten thousand men-at-arms, and no doubt all the fashion and beauty of the wealthy Midlands.

Richard pronounced judgment before trial. Norfolk was to go into exile for life, Hereford for ten years, which the King afterwards reduced to six. This policy Richard adopted, Froissart says, upon the advice of John Holland, Duke of Exeter, who thought that in this way the King would be rid of two powerful and dangerous subjects, and that the life sentence upon Norfolk would please the people, because Norfolk was unpopular, while the sentence upon the adored Bolingbroke would not be severe enough to give rise to much displeasure. In fact, Bolingbroke's admirers said that it would not hurt him much ; he could well amuse himself abroad, where he had many friends, and he could make long visits to his sisters, the Queens of Castile and Portugal.

Froissart remarks that the news of the proposed combat between the Earl of Derby and the Earl Marshal, 'made a great noise in foreign parts ; for it was to be for life or death, and before the King and the great barons of England.' It was spoken of variously. Some said, 'Let them fight it out ! These English knights are too arrogant, and in a short time will cut each other's throats. They are the most perverse nation under the sun, and their island is inhabited by the proudest people.' But others, more wise, said, 'The King of England does not show great sense, nor is he well advised when, for foolish words not deserving notice,

he permits two such valiant lords of his kindred thus to engage in mortal combat. He ought to have said, when he first heard the charge, ' You, Earl of Derby, and you, Earl Marshal, are my near relations. I command, therefore, that you harbour no hatred against each other, but live like friends and cousins that you are. Should your stay in this country become tiresome, travel into foreign parts, to Hungary or elsewhere, to seek for deeds of arms and adventure.'

Hereford after the sentence looked melancholy, but seemed to accept his fortune resignedly. The day in October 1398 that he mounted his horse to ride down to Dover, there was great popular demonstration in his favour. ' Forty thousand men,' says Froissart, ' were in the streets bitterly lamenting his departure, and the leading citizens rode with him as far as Dartford.' ' A wonder it was to see,' says Holinshed, ' what number of people ran after him in every town and street where he came, before he took to sea, lamenting and bewailing his departure, as who should say that, when he departed, the only shield, defence, and comfort of the Commonwealth was gone.' One can imagine the scenes in the old streets of Rochester, Canterbury, and Dover. Henry was well received at Paris by the French King and the royal dukes. He was a widower, and dallied with the thought of marrying the fair Marie, daughter of the Duke of Berri, but Richard used diplomatic means to avert this alliance, sending over the Earl of Salisbury for that purpose. The Duke of Exeter was now appointed Governor of Calais in succession to the banished Norfolk, and the rumour at once spread that this was a preliminary step to the surrender of Calais to the French.

During the winter 1398–9, the Court was mainly at Westminster. About Christmas, John of Gaunt, Duke of Lancaster, ended his unsatisfactory life and career. He was buried with his first wife in St. Paul's Cathedral under a great monument which was destroyed in the fire of 1666. Richard, whose extravagant Court always needed more means of support, who was unwilling to summon a Parliament and ask for a subsidy, and who had already exhausted the patience of all classes of his subjects by various feudal and commercial exactions, now took possession of the revenues of the vast Lancaster estates on the ground that they belonged to the Crown so long as the exile of the successor to them should continue. The Duke of Exeter must have advised this fatal step against his brother-in-law, and he received some grants from the revenues. Froissart remarks that, if, after the death of the old Duke of Lancaster, Richard had at once recalled Henry from exile, placed him in possession of his estates, recognised him as the greatest person in England after himself, and had promised to take his advice in all things, he would have done well, and would have averted his doom. But those who know from modern experience how strong is the passion of power will not be surprised that such was not the advice given to the King by John Holland, Duke of Exeter.

Richard fatuously chose to leave England for a military expedition into Ireland at the very moment when he had desperately injured and offended his skilful, powerful, and exiled cousin, the darling of the Londoners and most popular of English nobles. Before he departed he enjoyed the last great festivity of his reign. The glorious Banquet of the Knights of the Order of the Garter at Windsor Castle on the day of St. George, April 23, 1399, marks the culmination of the fortune of the Lancastrian Hollands. It was Richard's custom to hold this festivity every year. Ladies were honorary members, and appeared in robes of uniform colour and pattern supplied by the royal wardrobe, and were called Ladies of the Order. The Countesses of Kent and Derby were new companions in 1388, and, in 1389, the third Duchess of Lancaster (Katherine Swynford) and the Countess of Huntingdon, her step-daughter.

This year the banquet of St. George's Day was celebrated with great splendour and noble company. The knights present, all apparelled in robes of scarlet, were King Richard, the Dukes of York, Bavaria, Brittany, Guelders, Surrey, Exeter, and Albemarle, the Marquess of Dorset, the Earls of Northumberland, Salisbury, Worcester, Gloucester, and Wiltshire, the Count of Ostravant, Sirs William Beauchamp, Peter Courtenay, John de Bourchier, William Arundel, Simon Felbrigge, and Henry Percy. The ladies were Queen Isabel of England, a child of twelve, Queen Philippa of Portugal, Henry Bolingbroke's sister, the Duchess of Guelders, and those of York, Ireland, and Exeter; the Marchioness of Dorset, and Alice, Dowager Countess of Kent, the perilous Constance, Lady Despenser, who was Albemarle's sister, the Countesses of Oxford, Salisbury, Westmoreland, and Gloucester; the Ladies Mohun, Poyninges, Beauchamp, Fitzwalter, Gommenys, Blanche Braddeston, Agnes Arundel, de Roos, de Courcy, and de Trivet.

The violently victorious Hollands were present in force. The Dukes of Exeter and Surrey represented the men of the clan; among the women the Duchess of York was Surrey's sister, the beautiful Joan Holland, and the Marchioness of Dorset (before and later known as the Countess of Somerset) was another sister, Margaret Holland. Joan and Margaret were now between twenty and thirty years old, in full flower of beauty, fair daughters of the house of Kent. Their mother, Alice, Countess of Kent, born Fitz-Alan, was also there, notwithstanding the recent execution of her brother, Lord Arundel.

At the annual banquet of the Order there was occasionally missing a knight who had sat in the Hall at Windsor on the previous year, and had been subsequently put to death at the instance of some of his brethren.   So Sir Simon Burley, the Earl of Arundel, the Duke of Gloucester had disappeared. On the present occasion, two knights, the Dukes of Lancaster and Norfolk, were in exile, and the Earl of Warwick was captive in the Isle of Man.   Some of those present may have had the sense of a distant gathering storm.   But if, at the splendid feast in Windsor Hall on St. George's Day, 1399, there had been present a seer endowed with second sight, as at that famous supper before the French Revolution, his predictions would have cast gloom and horror over the brilliant, triumphant assembly, and chilled the blood of April dancing through their veins.   Five months later, the gentle-minded, cultivated, and charming King, little more than thirty years of age, who sat at the centre of the table, was deposed from the throne ; nine months later, he and the brave and powerful Exeter, the young, chivalrous Surrey, the poetic and accomplished Earl of Salisbury, the Earls of Gloucester and Wiltshire, all lay slain in their graves.   The Duke of Brittany had ended his stormy career and changing fortunes before the close of the year.   Four years later, on July 21, 1403, another famous knight present at this feast, Sir Henry Percy, the gallant 'Harry Hotspur,' was slain as he furiously ranged that bloody field ' in the plain near Shrewsbury,' attempting to reach and kill the usurping Bolingbroke.   His head was fixed on a gate of York, and the four quarters of his body on gates of London, Bristol, Newcastle, and Chester.

This doom-preceding banquet was on April 23.   On the 16th King Richard had signed his will, written in choice Latin.   It contained thoughts on life and death, an expression of religious faith, and the most detailed and minute directions for the ritual of his funeral at Westminster Abbey.   He bequeathed £10,000 to his nephew the Duke of Surrey, and 30,000 marks to his brother the Duke of Exeter, both of whom were among the executors appointed by the will. The King was at Bristol on April 27, back at Westminster Palace on the 29th, and on May 29 he was at Milford Haven, and a few days later he sailed for Ireland on the expedition intended to crush the Irish, who had lately defeated and slain Roger Mortimer, Earl of March, his Viceroy and heir-presumptive. The Dukes of Surrey and Exeter were with him. The latter brought 140 men-at-arms and 500 archers.

On July 4 the new Duke of Lancaster landed with a few followers in Yorkshire, and in two or three weeks was at the head of an army of 60,000 men, and in possession of almost every part of the kingdom. The force which the honest but helpless Duke of York gathered to oppose his brother's son, melted away, as also did the troops which Richard hastily brought back from Ireland. Richard found himself exactly in the position of James II nearly three centuries later, suddenly abandoned by everyone and impotent. Even one of his recent Lords Appellant, the Earl of Rutland, now Duke of Albe-marle, a cousin whom Richard 'loved beyond measure,' betrayed him, as John Churchill betrayed his benefactor.

The Earl of Wiltshire, K.G., was beheaded on July 30. The Hollands remained almost alone at Richard's side. The Duke of Exeter seemed the best negotiator, since his wife was sister to Henry of Lancaster. He left Richard at Conway, and went with his nephew, the Duke of Surrey, to Henry at Chester to ask his intentions. Henry detained them there for a few days until he had secured the person of King Richard at Flint Castle. According to De Wavrin's account, he then sent for the Duke of Exeter and said to him, ' Brother-in-law, it would be well that you should return to Calais, the government of which shall not be taken from you unless we learn that there is something in you which we do not know at present. And there we charge you to remain until we shall have arranged with my Lord the King about those matters which you and I discussed the other day.   And, on your life, take care not to let anyone of the French party enter, and speak to none, by letters or otherwise, until we let you know.'

The Duke of Exeter, adds this chronicler, ' without showing sign of grief, took leave of the Duke, for well he understood how things were. He left the fair town of Chester, and rode so much that, without going to see his wife, he came to Dover, whence he set out to sea, and came to Calais ; but know ye that sorrow and sadness were so great in him that no one could express it, which grief and displeasure he had to endure, for there was nothing else to be had for the present ; so he was forced to dissemble.'

Certainly John Holland, fallen so swiftly from his estate as the most powerful man in England, and full of fears for the future, must have ridden gloomily down that Dover road which he had traversed so gaily on his way to and from King Richard's wedding, and to and from the grand tournament at St. Inglevert.   If de Wavrin is correct, it was a bold stroke of confidence to let him go to Calais, seeing how close-allied the Richardian party was with the French Government.   But Henry moved cautiously and advisedly, and no doubt felt secure of the allegiance of the Calais garrison.

The Duke of Exeter was soon back in London for one of the most eventful meetings of Parliament in English history. Parliament met in September 1399 to receive the forced resignation of Richard and sanction the succession of Henry. There was a passionate and stormy scene. Sir John Bagot, then a prisoner in the Tower, was brought to the bar, and made a declaration that it was by the advice and instigation of the Duke of Albemarle that the lords were arrested by the King, and that the Duke of Gloucester was murdered at Calais by the order of the Duke of Norfolk. Albemarle rose and denied the charge, and offered to vindicate his innocence by combat. Lord Fitzwalter and twenty other lords jumped up to accept the challenge. The Duke of Surrey, young Thomas Holland, rose and said that anything which Albemarle had done was by constraint, and offered to vindicate him in fight. There was a furious scene. All these challengers flung down their hoods by way of token, and the hoods were delivered to the Constable and Marshal to be kept.

Henry IV was crowned, and the first Parliament of the new reign met on October 14. It resolved on the 17th that the late advisers of the deposed King should be put in prison. The Duke of Surrey was sent to the Tower, and afterwards to Wallingford; the Duke of Exeter was imprisoned in Hertford Castle; Albemarle, Gloucester, and Salisbury were confined elsewhere. The accused lords were brought before Parliament on October 29. Albemarle again denied connivance in Gloucester's murder; Surrey pleaded that in 1397 he had been too young to take a real part in these affairs; Exeter also denied connivance. He said, however, that he had heard King Richard say that Gloucester would be put to death. All these lords naturally threw the guilt on to the ex-Governor of Calais, the exiled Norfolk, who had died at Venice. Their sentence was far milder than they could have expected, and the new King used his utmost influence to save them from the popular hatred. The three dukes were sentenced to lose their titles of Albemarle, Surrey, and Exeter, and became again Rutland, Kent, and Huntingdon. The new-made Marquis of Dorset and the Earl of Gloucester became again the Earl of Somerset and Lord Despenser. Lands and possessions acquired since 1397 by royal concession were taken away from them, a more serious loss than that of new-minted titles. They were released on sureties being given, and thus bound over to keep the peace.

The Commons murmured at this clemency, for which, indeed, Henry nearly paid dearly. They wished the Lords Appellant to be put to death. ' But,' says Holinshed, ' the King thought it best rather with courtesy to reconcile them than, by putting them to death, secure the hatred of their friends and allies, which were many and of no small power.'

Henry IV was, after all, brother-in-law to John Holland, Earl of Huntingdon, and first cousin to Rutland. He had also in 1397 acted more or less in co-operation with their party against Gloucester, Arundel, and Warwick, and had shared in the subsequent distribution of honours of Richard II, so that his position with regard to these lords was delicate. Also he was a true statesman, cautious, abiding his time, undiverted from his aims by passion, and striking at the right moment. The Earl of Huntingdon had been defeated in the great game by a brain superior to his own. He was like Hector to Achilles. He himself had given proof of vigour, daring, energy, and decision in the proceedings in 1397, but in later policy either he had shown want of judgment, or else he had been unable to control the childish impulses of his brother, King Richard. The restored Arundel, Archbishop of Canterbury, in an opening sermon to the Parliament which dethroned Richard, took for his text, ' Vir dominabitur vobis,' ' a man shall rule over you' (1 Reg. 9), and said, with truth, that the reign of Richard had been that of a child, whereas that of Henry would be that of a man. Young and rash counsellors would now, he said, be replaced by the wise and old.

CHAPTER VI

THE HOLLAND REVOLT

Much you had of land and rent,
Your length in clay's now competent ;
A long war disturbed your mind,
Here your perfect peace is signed.

Of what is't fools make such vain keeping ?
Sin' their conception, their birth weeping ;
Their life a general mist of error,
Their death a hideous storm of terror.
WEBSTER, Duchess of Malfi.

COULD the two Hollands, after Richard's deposition, have
been content to lead quiet lives on their hereditary estates
they would have been unmolested, and the young Earl of
Kent, at any rate, would soon have been taken into royal
favour, as was afterwards his younger brother, and might
have had a successful career in civil and military employment.
This kind of cool wisdom was not in them ; and not even
for a few weeks could they remain inactive and submissive
under their astute and clever relative. They had not the gift
of patience, and could not even await the inevitable reaction
which would have given them the ghost of a chance. Their
attempt was even more hopeless than that of Viscount Dundee, in 1689. They had just seen the whole realm abandon
Richard II and turn to Henry of Lancaster. They may,
indeed, have thought with some reason that, if they waited
longer, there would be no Richard to restore ; so that if they
were to strike at all, they must strike at once. For dramatic

131

purposes, it is well that they acted as they did, and put their fortune to the touch to win or lose it all.

The tale of their revolt is variously told by the chroniclers, French and English. The best account of it is probably that pieced together by Mr. Wylie in his laborious and erudite, yet amusing, ' History of England in the reign of Henry IV.' He is a great master of the records of the reign, and the present writer quotes him freely. It is vanity and waste of time to tell entirely anew in different words a story which has been well told already.

The plot began on Wednesday, December 17, 1899. The Earls of Huntingdon, Kent, Rutland, and Salisbury, the deposed Archbishop of Canterbury, Roger Walden, and the ex-Bishop of Carlisle, met in the house of William, Abbot of Westminster. This Abbot was supposed to be a supporter of Henry IV, but really hated him because he had heard him say, years ago when he was Earl of Hereford, that, in his opinion, religious men had too much property, and princes too little. Then there was a French physician, John Paul, whom Richard had left at Wallingford as one of the guardians of his child queen, and Sir Thomas Blount, a gentleman of Oxfordshire to whom Henry IV, only a month earlier, had given a grant of £20, charged on the revenues of the City of Hereford. A priest called Richard Maudelyn is also said to have been there. He was a retainer of Richard II, and resembled him curiously in face and figure.

The first idea of the conspirators was, according to the chroniclers, to invite the King to a tournament to be held at Oxford, and there capture him, but this project was abandoned. The King was at Windsor, and had himself sent out many letters of invitation for an entertainment, a jousting and ' mommying,' which was to be given there on January 6, the Feast of the Epiphany. The plan of the conspirators was this : armed men were to be introduced into the castle at

Windsor under the disguise of guards and drivers of carts full of tilt harness, as if in preparation for the jousting. The lords in the plot were to meet at Kingston on the evening of January 4, and ride thence in the night with their followers the short distance to Windsor. At a given signal, the men, previously entered in disguise, were to kill the guards and open the Castle gates. King Henry and his sons would then be captured. It was said that the conspirators intended to kill them forthwith, but perhaps they meant to hold them captive until Richard was restored. After this, the conspirators intended to announce that Richard was free and was with them, passing off Richard Maudelyn in that part until the real Richard could be recovered from his prison. The idea was altogether wild—the kind of plot a man might weave in his dream. They rashly imagined that Richard would be welcomed back by a sufficient body of supporters and that all the solemn legalities of the late Parliament could be undone. They did not, apparently, realise in the least how unpopular they were.

The conspirators drew out six bonds, in which they bound themselves to be true to each other and to restore Richard or die in the attempt. These were sealed and sworn, and each conspirator kept a copy. It proved impossible to keep a secret of this kind from December 17 until January 4. This was not surprising in view of the fact that the Earl of Huntingdon's wife was King Henry's sister, and that the Earl of Kent's mother was Archbishop Arundel's sister, and that the perfidious Earl of Rutland was in the plot,[1] and that his sister, Lady Constance, was wife of one of the conspirators.

[1] One story is that a Holland retainer told a lady of light character that some movement was on foot, and that she retailed the information to her next admirer, one of the King's attendants. If we are to *chercher la femme*, Constance, daughter of the Duke of York, sister of Rutland, and wife of Despenser, was more likely the traitress.

' There was evidently,' says Mr. Wylie, ' a general sense of some unknown danger impending, but nothing seems to have been known for certain until the appointed day, January 4. The King with his four sons and some few friends had been keeping Christmas in retirement at Windsor. He was out of health and needed rest. The Prince of Wales also and many of the royal household were ailing, and the usual suspicions of poisoning were abroad. Archbishop Arundel had been expected at Windsor, but Henry had sent him a message to keep out of the way at Reigate. A general uneasiness prevailed, and the King was heard to say that he wished that Richard, the focus of all intrigue, were dead. The Duke of York, the Earls of Northumberland, Westmorland, Arundel, and Warwick, with others, approached him with a petition that his wish might be carried into effect; but he refused with some show of indignation, though he added that if there should be any rising in the country, Richard should be the first to die.'

The other Lords were at Kingston on January 4, but Rutland was not there. A letter sent to him in haste required him without fail to observe his oath and join the rest at Colnbrook, whence the newly arranged attack on Windsor was to be carried out on the 6th. Rutland had made up his perfidious mind to break his oath and ruin his friends in order to save his own life and property. He took the letter and the bond, with the six seals attached, to his father the Duke of York at Windsor, who at once informed the King.[1] It was now late and dim in the Windsor streets on the afternoon of January 4. ' Horses were saddled,

---

[1] According to most of the chroniclers, the Duke of York saw the bond sticking out of his son's dress at dinner, seized and read it, was very angry, and said that he would at once inform the King, upon which Rutland anticipated his father by galloping off to Windsor and himself making a full confession. Mr Wylie does not, like earlier historians, accept this version, but if true, it would make the conduct of Rutland a shade or two less black.

The King with his sons and two attendants threw himself promptly into the adventure, daring all the chances of capture or ambuscade by the way.' He took the road to London, and arrived there in the dark at nine o'clock at night. Rumour had now spread far and wide, and on the way he met the Mayor of London, who told him the news, exaggerated by panic, that the rebels were in the field with 6000 men. 'Once in London, he threw himself on his people.' Letters were at once issued to the sheriffs of all counties to arrest those traitors—Thomas, Earl of Kent, John, Earl of Huntingdon, and the rest. Like letters were sent to the Governor of Calais, who was instructed to keep a close watch on French movements, for the father of Richard's queen might well be, in his own interests, and, perhaps was, in the plot. Orders were sent to the Channel Islands to look out for French ships, and to all the ports that no ships should be allowed to cross the sea. The Sheriffs of Leicester, Shropshire, Stafford, Derby, and Nottingham—counties where the rebels might be strong—were directed to call out their local forces. High pay was offered in London for military service for fifteen days, and, by the evening of Monday, January 5, more than 16,000 archers and bill-men had been enrolled. On Tuesday, the 6th, the King had 20,000 men under arms at Hounslow, and rode out to review them.

Meanwhile, Kent and Salisbury and their friends, finding, or suspecting, that their plot had been discovered, rode, after all, from Kingston to Windsor on the night of January 4, without waiting for Rutland, and the 6th. They reached Windsor in the early morning hours of the 5th too late. It was above twelve hours after Henry had left. They were at the head of 400 or 500 armed followers. They were admitted into the Castle, and searched it and the town for the King, and, says the chronicler, ' deden moche harme thereaboughts.'

They had missed their game, but still tried to raise the country. They sent messengers in all directions to say that Windsor Castle was in their hands, that Henry was a fugitive, and that Richard was free and was assembling an army. The young Earl of Kent rode on the 5th to Sonning on the Thames, where was residing Richard's queen, Isabella, a girl of thirteen. According to the chronicler, Kent entered the house wild and excited. He pulled the royal badges of King Henry's servants from the necks of the Queen's attendants and threw them on the ground, and said : ' Benedicite ! What makes Henry of Lancaster fly before me, he who used to boast so much of his courage ? Know all of you, that he has fled before me to the Tower of London with his sons and friends. I intend to go to Richard who was, and is, and will be, our true King. He has escaped from prison, and is now at Pontefract with 100,000 men.'

After that, the young Earl of Kent rode to join his friends at the rendezvous at Colnbrook where they had now increased their forces by a certain number of allies. The question was whether they should march on London ; a body of them had already gone in that direction as far as Brentford.

' At Colnbrook they were joined by the Earl of Rutland, whose dealings seem as yet to have been unsuspected. He told them that Henry was approaching with forces too large for them to cope with. A consultation ensued, and it was decided not to advance farther to the east, but to fall back to the west, where, with all Wales and Cheshire at their back, they could alone hope to make a stand.

' In all speed they drew off westward, but at Maidenhead Henry's advanced troops were upon them. The Earl of Kent made a successful stand at Maidenhead Bridge, and kept the assailants off till all the party and the baggage were in safety. The Earl of Salisbury, meanwhile, led off the bulk of the following through Henley and Oxford to Woodstock, where

the Earl of Kent soon joined them, having stolen off from
Maidenhead unperceived in the night. He travelled by
Wallingford and Abingdon, spreading still the rumour of
his sham success. The whole force, now much disheartened,
retired during the 7th hastily to Cirencester whither Sir
Thomas Blount, the ex-Bishop of Carlisle, and others of
their friends, had preceded them. Another body found their
way round to join them by St. Albans and Berkhampstead,
and the whole force encamped in some fields outside the
town of Cirencester.'

The French chronicler, De Wavrin, says that the rebel
lords themselves, with some followers, took lodgings at the
best hostel in Cirencester—no doubt in the *grande place* in
front of the great church which, though mostly rebuilt in the
fifteenth century, stands still where it then did. An archer of
King Henry's body-guard, on his way from Wales, happened
to put up at the same hostelry that night, and had a fire lit
in a room apart. The Earl of Kent came into the room and
asked the archer who he was. The archer recognised the
Earl, and replied : ' My lord, I come from Wales, whither I was
sent by the King.' At these words, the Earl took off the
badge the archer wore and threw it into the fire, saying :
' See what I do in contempt of Henry of Lancaster. You
traitor ! You came here to spy, but you shall be hanged.'

The archer got away and told the Bailiff of Cirencester
who the strangers were. The Bailiff collected forty archers
and came to the hostelry, and told Kent and the rest that they
must deem themselves under arrest, and not leave the inn till
the King was informed and gave orders. Then the fight began.
Mr. Wylie says : ' In the night the townspeople, headed by the
Bailiff, John Cosyn, surrounded the house in which the rebel
leaders were sleeping, barred up the entrances with beams and
timber, and, having closed all the approaches, began to assail
the inmates with showers of arrows, lances, and stones, the

women helping in the streets. A fierce attack was kept up from day-break through doors and windows, the disheartened troops outside the town having melted away, while the small band of leaders in the crowded building were left to defend themselves as best they might against the fury of the towns-folk. By nine o'clock on the morning of January 8 the mob had broken in, and the whole party surrendered under a promise that their lives should be spared until they should have an audience with the King. They were then lodged in the Abbey of the Austin Canons in the centre of the town, and news of the capture was despatched to Henry at Oxford.

'Already vast crowds had gathered into the town from all the country round, but in the afternoon, about three o'clock, when alarm and excitement were high, a fire broke out in some buildings in another part of the town. Supposing that this was the work of the conspirators, who might make their escape whilst the citizens were busied with the flames,[1] the mob rushed wildly to the Abbey, and demanded with threats of violence that the leading conspirators should be given up. Sir Thomas Berkeley, who had taken over the custody of the rebels and was making arrangements to conduct them to a place of greater safety, resisted for a time, but was over-borne, and on the night of January 8, the Earls of Kent and Salisbury were brought out and by torch-light ignominiously beheaded by the rustic plebeians in the streets.'

The monkish chronicler of St. Albans, Walsingham—that great hater of the Hollands and their friends—says ' the Lord thus paid them the penalty due to their faithlessness and unbelief.' He adds that ' both had been faithless to their King, who had just shown such favour to them; but the Earl of Salisbury, John Montacute—the friend of the Lollards,

---

[1] One contemporary account says that the fire was the work of one of their friends with that object, but the explanation in the text seems more probable.

the derider of images—died miserably, refusing the sacrament of confession, if the common account be true.' [1]

The party of Richard were all suspected of new ideas, and it was, on the other hand, the first Parliament of Henry IV, which passed, immediately after the Revolution, the first statute in England authorising the burning of heretics. It was Henry's reward to the Archbishop Arundel for his services. The enmity of the monastic orders to the Lollards was natural, because an essential part of Wycliff's open teaching had been that kings and lords had the right to deprive of its temporal possessions a Church which they deemed to be corrupt, and his lay follower, Lord Cobham, gave a practical point to the teaching by statistical calculations, showing how many feudal knight-soldiers the King could maintain for foreign war if he confiscated the monastic lands.

Another contemporary French chronicler gives this different portrait of the Earl of Salisbury. Mr. Wylie thus translates him in Saxon style.

' He was humble, sweet, and courteous in all his ways and had every man's voice for being loyal in all places and right prudent. Full largely he gave and timely gifts. He was brave and fierce as a lion. Ballads and songs and roundels and lays right beautiful he made. Though but a layman, still his deeds became so gracious that never, I think, of his country shall be a man in whom God put so much of good, and may his soul be set in Paradise among the saints for ever.'

Thus by a provincial mob were slain these two gallant young lords, loyal to their rightful King, Richard; disloyal

---

[1] Lord Salisbury was said to have taken down all the images of saints about his · house except one figure of St. Catherine which, because it was particularly revered by his retainers, he allowed to remain standing in his brewhouse. All his ballads, songs, roundels, and lays are unfortunately lost.

to the level-headed usurper. The official record judiciously stated that they were ' taken and beheaded by the King's loyal lieges without process of law.' One of the confederates, Lord Despenser, the ex-Earl of Gloucester, husband of Constance of York, escaped from Cirencester, but was captured and beheaded by a mob at Bristol on January 15, and his head was sent to London.

The bodies of the Earls of Kent and Salisbury were buried in the Abbey Church of Cirencester, and their heads were sent in a basket to King Henry—even as the head of Robert de Holland, Kent's great-grandfather, had been sent to Henry of Lancaster.

The King was at Oxford. The treacherous Rutland was now with him and had personally directed the despatch of troops, together with stores of shields and arrows, to Cirencester, Gloucester, and Monmouth, to be used against the associates to whom he had three weeks before sworn fealty. The King, at the Carmelite Monastery outside Oxford, received the heads of the Earls of Kent and Salisbury, and about thirty more heads of rebels killed at Cirencester. He sent these on to London to be fixed up there—some in sacks, and some slung on poles between men's shoulders. These ghastly trophies were borne through the London streets on January 16. The King himself re-entered London in triumph on the following day and was met by the Archbishop and a solemn procession of eighteen Bishops and thirty-two Abbots, who, with religious pomp, conducted him to St. Paul's, where the *Te Deum* was sung. The people of Cirencester were rewarded by the appointment of a Royal Commission to inquire into the usurpations and encroachments of the Abbot of the Monastery in that town. The worthy Bailiff, John Cosyn, not only had a tale to tell which must have lasted him till he died, but received an annuity of 100 marks for life. Four does from the Forest of Bradon

were to be presented to the townsfolk every year to com-
memorate their loyal services for ever.

Two days before Henry so gloriously entered London,
John Holland, Earl of Huntingdon, came to his violent
end. According to the English chronicler, Walsingham,
this Earl had neither taken part in the raid on Windsor,
nor accompanied the rest to Cirencester, but had remained
in London watching events until after the failure of the
attempt on Windsor.[1] Then he escaped in a small boat
down the Thames, but was driven by the weather to land.
He first went to Hadley Castle, the house of the Earl of
Oxford. 'Finding himself beset with spies, he stole out
of the Castle and hid himself in a mill in the marshes, waiting
for the weather to abate. He was accompanied by two
of his faithful followers—his esquire, Sir Thomas Shelley[2]
of Aylesbury, and his butler, Hugh Cade. For two days
and nights he lurked about disguised. Then, in desperation,
he tried the river again, but he was again driven ashore,
and took shelter in the night at the house of a friend, John
Prittlewell, at Barrow Hall, near Wakering in the flats near
Shoebury.

'But by this time, the hue and cry of the country was
on him. Acting on the King's proclamation, the men of
Essex surrounded the house. The Earl was captured while
sitting at a meal, and sent to Chelmsford. Here the mob
would have despatched him but for the intervention of
Joan de Bohun, Countess of Hereford, who sent him under

---

[1] A French chronicler says that Huntingdon had gone to Cirencester and had
escaped thence when the townspeople attacked the party. But, as Mr. Wylie
points out, it is not likely, if this were so, that he would have returned to the Thames
below London through the midst of his enemies ; he would rather have tried to
escape oversea from the Severn or Wales or Devonshire. Thus the English account
is more credible here.

[2] Sir Thomas Shelley was afterwards attainted. He was a brother of Sir
William Shelley, from whom descended all the Shelleys of Sussex.

a strong guard to her fortress of Pleshy, and reserved him for the sweetness of her private revenge.' [1]

John Holland had now, indeed, fallen into the hands of his deadliest foe. This Countess Joan was the widow of the last of the de Bohuns, Earls of Hereford. She had no sons, but two daughters—Mary and Eleanor. Mary had been the first wife of Henry IV, whence his ultimate choice of title as Duke of Hereford. Eleanor had been the wife of Thomas, Duke of Gloucester, and had brought to him the Castle of Pleshy and other de Bohun possessions. Eleanor, the Duchess, was no longer living in January 1400. The loss of her husband had been followed by that of her only son, Humphrey, who had died in captivity in Ireland. Eleanor, broken-hearted, had taken the veil at the Convent of Barking in Essex, where she may have met another nun —her maternal cousin, the Lady Bridget Holland of Kent. She died there on October 3, 1399, and was buried in St. Edmund's Chapel in Westminster Abbey. Thus Joan, Countess of Hereford, was not only mother of the late Duchess Eleanor, whose ducal husband the Earl of Huntingdon had been foremost in destroying, but her other son-in-law was Henry IV, against whose throne and life Huntingdon had just been conspiring. As though all this were not sufficient, Joan, Countess of Hereford, was born a Fitz-Alan. She was sister of Richard, tenth Earl of Arundel, whom Huntingdon had taken part in sentencing and had himself escorted to the scaffold in September 1397; and she was sister also of the Archbishop of Canterbury who had been condemned for treason, deposed, appointed to an obscure and impossible Scottish see, and driven into exile.

It is true that Joan's sister, Alice Fitz-Alan, had married Thomas Holland, second Earl of Kent, the brother of Huntingdon. That she held captive her sister's brother-in-law

---

[1] From Wylie's *Henry IV*. Pleshy is about seven miles from Chelmsford.

may only have added a more poignant flavour to Joan's revenge. Certainly John Holland had no chance of escape at all when he found himself once more at Pleshy Castle, and in the power of Joan, Countess of Hereford. The following account of his last hours is given by the French-Burgundian chronicler, Jean de Wavrin, Lord of Forestal, who wrote in his old age, between 1455 and 1471, a chronicle of English History. One never knows how far these chroniclers draw on their poetic imagination for details ; but De Wavrin was, in his youth, fighting on the English-Burgundian side in the wars in France and so had plenty of opportunity to learn from Englishmen about events within living memory. His early history of England is very mythical, but about events which happened in or near his own time internal evidence shows that he took great pains to get the best information he could. Men of the world like Froissart and De Wavrin are far better authorities than monastic chroniclers, to whom stories came distorted by ecclesiastical prejudice in the seclusion of monasteries. In any case, the story is well and dramatically told, and this is how De Wavrin tells it.[1]

‘ The Earl of Huntingdon being thus taken, the Countess wrote to the King, who was then in London, all that had happened, and that he would be pleased immediately to send the Earl of Arundel, his cousin, to see vengeance taken for his father, for her intention was to have the said Earl of Huntingdon hanged and drawn. King Henry rejoicing at the news, when he had read the letter, called to the young Earl of Arundel and said to him : “ Fair cousin, do you go and see your aunt yonder, and bring me all the prisoners she has, alive or dead.” ’ (A royal order dated January 10, 1400, to the Governor of the Tower of London to receive the Earl of Huntingdon as prisoner, is extant.) ‘ At which embassy

---

[1] From Edward Hardy's translation. London, 1891.

the Earl of Arundel much rejoiced, mounted his horse, and made such haste that he came to the town where his aunt the Countess was, who had collected around there more than 8000 peasants, all armed and supplied with weapons, and she caused the noble Earl of Huntingdon to be brought before them to be put to death; but there was certainly no one in all that company but what had pity on him, for he was a very fair prince, tall and straight, and well formed in all his limbs, who was there before them with his hands bound. At this very hour the Earl of Arundel arrived at the place and saluted his aunt, and seeing there present the Earl of Huntingdon, Duke of Exeter, he spoke thus to him: "My lord, what say you? Do you not repent that, by the advice of yourself and others, my father was put to death, and that you have so long held my land, and, besides, have wickedly governed my sister and myself till, by very poverty, I have been obliged to depart from the kingdom of England; and if it had not been for my cousin of Clarence, I should have died of want. And thou, villain, dost thou not remember how I have often taken off and cleansed thy shoes when thou hadst to taste before King Richard, and thou treatedst me as if I had been thy drudge. But now the hour has come when I will have vengeance on thee." And then he caused the Earl to be brought in front of the line of townsmen that they might kill him. The Earl of Huntingdon, seeing himself in this position and looking piteously at those who were going to kill him, he said to them: "My lords, have pity on me, for I have never done ill in anything to any of this country." And there was none of them who would have wished to do him any harm, or who felt not great pity for him, excepting the Earl of Arundel and the Countess of Hereford, who said to her men: "Cursed be ye all, false villains, who are not brave enough to put a man to death." There then drew near an esquire of the lady who offered himself to behead the said Earl of Huntingdon, and the Countess ordered him to do it forthwith, so the esquire, axe in hand, came forward, and, throwing himself on his knees before the Earl of Huntingdon, said : " My lord, pardon me your death, for my lady has commanded me to deliver you from this world." Then the Earl, who had his hands bound, fell on his knees and spoke thus to him who had asked pardon for his death. " Friend, art thou he who is to put me out of this world ? " " Yes, my lord," said the esquire, " by the command of my lady." And the Earl said to him, " Friend, why dost thou wish to take away the life God has given me ? I have done no harm to thee or thy lineage, and thou canst see very well that there are here seven or eight thousand people, of whom there is none who wisheth to harm my body excepting thee. Ah, my friend ! Why canst thou find it in thy heart and thy conscience to slay me ? " Then the Earl began to weep a little, saying : " Alas ! If I had gone to Rome, where our Holy Father the Pope sent for me to be his Marshal, I should not have been in this danger, but it is too late. I pray God to pardon my sins." When the esquire had heard the piteous words of the Earl of Huntingdon, such dread took possession of him that he began to tremble, and turned to the Countess, weeping, said to her : ' My lady, for God's mercy, pardon me ; for I will not put the Earl of Huntingdon to death for all the gold in the world." Then the lady in great anger said to him : " Thou shalt do what thou hast promised, or I will have thy own head cut off." Whereupon the esquire hearing the lady, was much dismayed, and returned to the Earl of Huntingdon, saying : " My lord, I pray of your mercy, pardon me your death." Then the Earl, throwing himself on his knees, spoke thus : " Alas ! is there no help for me but I must die ? I pray to God and the Virgin Mary and all the Saints in Paradise to have mercy on me." At which words the esquire swung up his axe and struck the

Earl such a blow with it that he fell to the earth badly
wounded on the breast and face, but directly the esquire
had withdrawn the axe the Earl sprang to his feet, saying :
" Man, why dost thou this ? For God's sake, deliver me
quickly." And then the esquire gave him eight blows with
the axe before he could strike home on the neck. Then said
the Earl again : " Alas ! why dost thou this ? " And then the
esquire drew a little knife with which he cut the throat of the
Earl of Huntingdon.' It was about sunset on that January
afternoon, says Walsingham, when the deed was done. John
Holland was about forty-eight or forty-nine years old when
his violent life came to this violent end.

Next came the triumph. The Earl of Arundel ' entered
London, his trumpets sounding and his minstrels before him,
and between the said Earl of Arundel and the minstrels
came the said prisoners and those who carried on a pole
the head of the Duke of Exeter, Earl of Huntingdon. The
Londoners showed great joy at this adventure, and cried
all along the roads and streets, " God save our noble King
Henry and the Prince, his son, and all the noble council." On
this very day there arrived in London the Earl of Rutland
who, in like manner, was having borne before him the head
of Lord Despenser, likewise set on a pole, his trumpeters
and minstrels before him, and a cart in which were twelve
prisoners bound hand and foot, who were all sent to the
Tower of London, and right behind came the said Earl of
Rutland with a great force of men-at-arms, and so he guarded
the prisoners to the Tower.'

There was nothing to be said in defence of that double-
dyed traitor Rutland, who entered London by the Oxford
Road, following the head of his sister's husband, but certainly
there was retributive justice in the procession which on the
same day came out of Essex by Mile End and Whitechapel,
whose hero was the youthful Earl of Arundel, and whose

glorious trophy the head of John Holland, Earl of Huntingdon Less than three years earlier, Holland, in the day of his power, ' riding a great horse,' had conducted the Earl of Arundel's father through London to the scaffold. Now Huntingdon's head was borne along the streets with joyful music sounding before,and the young Earl of Arundel riding behind. His body was buried in the collegiate church which had been founded at Pleshy by the Duke of Gloucester, and where that murdered Duke was himself buried. His head was fixed, with those of other leaders of the rising, over the Kentish end of London Bridge, to remain exposed ' as long as it should last and endure.' But, in little more than a month, on February 19, it was taken down, restored to the Earl's widow, and buried with the body at Pleshy.

The antiquary, John Weever, in his book on ' Funerall Monuments,' published in 1631, says that ' within the last few years the upper part of the collegiate church at Pleshy was taken down. This part of the church was beautified with divers rich funeral monuments, which were hammered to pieces, bestowed and divided according to the discretion of the inhabitants. Upon one of the parts of a dismembered monument, carelessly cast here and there in the body of the church, I found these words :

> ' Here lyeth John Holland, Erle [*sic*] of Exeter, Erle
> of Huntingdon and Chamberlayne of England,
> who dyed . . .'

Such fates attend rich monuments and the bones of famous men. The great Castle of Pleshy itself, where the Duke of Gloucester came out that summer morning into the court to meet Richard II and Huntingdon, and where, on a cold mid-winter evening, Huntingdon was slain in the presence of his fierce enemies, the Countess of Hereford and young Arundel, yet stood for some time, and was a favourite residence of Margaret of Anjou, queen of Henry VI. It had quite or almost vanished long years before John Weever came there.[1] But the Castle of the de Bohuns had been built within some far more ancient and far less perishable British earthworks, which still denote the spot. Pleshy is an unfrequented village, set amid homely Essex scenery, and lying two miles west from the high road from Chelmsford to Dunmow, and about seven miles from the nearest railway station, but the place is worth a visit. One can see very well where was the Castle keep, and where the entrance gate into the great court, and where was the middle of the court.

John Holland, Earl of Huntingdon, was a fine fighting man, bold and energetic, who, like his father and grandfather, rose by old and recognised methods—those of war and capture of woman ; and he died right well, keeping a crowd at bay, so noble was his mien, with none daring or willing enough to slay him, notwithstanding his attempt to overthrow the hero of the fickle populace. He had been an ardent sinner, but was not degenerate ; and for sins there is remedy, even in the hour of death, but for degeneration none. A good tree sometimes bears bad fruit, but a bad tree never bears good fruit. The Gospel, the Church, and Nature, teach that the distinction between, for example, the malefactor on the right cross and the malefactor on the left cross does not coincide with the distinction between what we call good

---

[1] Henry VIII gave the college buildings and the endowments to a gentleman of his chamber, named John Gates, who pulled down one part of the church for the material. There were in this church also some monuments of the Stafford family. There is nothing of the smallest historic interest in the church as now restored. All that remains of the masonry of the Castle is a one-arched brick bridge leading over the inner moat to the ancient mound on which the keep once stood, and some brick and flint foundations of the keep and of the gateway which once stood in a gap of the outer earthworks, and opened into the great court of the Castle, where a few cows now graze.

deeds and what we call evil. In the hour of death all
deeds vanish—good and bad alike; nothing remains but
the doer and that which he then essentially is. Yesterday
with its deeds, good and bad, is now as non-existent as a
day a thousand years ago. Many an example shows that
the words of the Calvinist hymn, 'As a man lives so shall
he die,' are not of strict necessity and always true. The
Catholic Church in absolving the sinner who dies truly
repentant does but follow in noble symbolism the unerring
guidance given by man's unsophisticated instinct.

John Holland was admired and liked by John Froissart,
who knew him well at different times of life, and terms him
a ' vaillant homme d'armes ' ; and by the other ' gentilhomme '
chronicler, John de Wavrin, who told with so much sympathy
the story of his last hours. Certainly it was a long way
from Sir John Holland, gloriously riding in summer at the
head of an English army under the sun of Spain, to the
Earl of Huntingdon hiding in winter among dismal muddy
Essex marshes, his last aspiring dream dissolved, and hopes
broken.

Evidently, no one much regretted the death of the man
who a few months before had held supreme power in England ;
but men, and women perhaps still more, were a little sorry
for the fate of Thomas Holland, the young Earl of Kent.
It was thought and said he had been misled by his unscrupulous uncle of Huntingdon working on his chivalrous feelings.
He was about twenty-four years old, and had shown gallant
qualities at Maidenhead Bridge and Cirencester. Froissart
tenderly says of him : ' Il estoit jeune et beau fils.' During
his brief career, the young Earl founded the Carthusian
monastery called Mountgrace, of which the spacious remains
still exist near Northallerton in Yorkshire, at the foot of a
steep rise leading to moors purple with heather in August.
The terms of foundation show that the young Earl of Kent

had piety towards his forbears and affection for kinsfolk and friends. The deed ordained that the priors and monks of the house should always in their orisons recommend to God the good estate of King Richard II, Queen Isabel, himself (the founder), and his wife Joan and their heirs; also the good estates of John Holland, Duke of Exeter, and John of Ingleby, and Ellen his wife, during their lives in this world, and also their souls after their departure hence; and the soul of Queen Anne, first wife to Richard II; likewise the souls of Edmund of Woodstock, sometime Earl of Kent, great-grandfather of the founder, Margaret his wife, Joan, Princess of Wales, Thomas de Holland, Earl of Kent, his grandfather, Thomas his father, and Alice his mother; and lastly the souls of Thomas de Ingleby and Catherine his wife, and Margaret de Aldenburgh, &c.

The headless body of Thomas, third Earl of Kent, was entombed at Cirencester Abbey until July 1412, when at the prayer of Lucia di Visconti, the widowed Countess of Edmund, fourth Earl, Henry IV permitted it to be removed to the new and still unfinished Abbey of Mountgrace.[1]

There stood his monument for more than a hundred years while Carthusian monks chanted solemn orisons, and then perished in the vast and wanton destruction which overwhelmed the monastic churches of England, and deprived us of countless memorials and sculptured effigies of our knightly ancestors and their beauteous and stately ladies. With what solemn indignation did that mighty Warwickshire antiquary, Sir William Dugdale, at the beginning of his book on the Baronage, denounce this history-destroying devastation! An old writer estimated that out of 45,000 churches, monastic and parish, which existed in England before the Reformation, only 10,000 were left, beside all the vast number of chapels and chantries destroyed.

---

[1] The Abbey was not completed until about 1440.

This number seems hardly credible, but those destroyed certainly included by far the greater number of cathedral-like churches containing the most interesting monuments.[1] At the Revolution there was a similar destruction of monastic churches and monuments in France. Most of the memorial brasses were stolen from the churches which survived in England. All this is more the pity because the art of portrait painting was in that age very immature, whereas carving of monumental effigies was in high perfection. What could be more lifelike than the image of the Black Prince at Canterbury or that of Richard II at Westminster? But of all the leading personages who figured in the interesting and dramatic reign of Richard, how many are known to us in this way? There are effigies of Richard II and Queen Anne at Westminster; of Henry Bolingbroke and Margaret Holland and her two husbands at Canterbury; of the poet John Gower in the Abbey Church of St. Mary in Southwark. Are there many others? The figure of John Gower is very lifelike, with the dignified gown worn by elder men after discarding the fantastical costume of the youth of that period, the forked and carefully cut beard, the hair falling below the ears and rolled up at the end. He supplies a good idea of how men of his time must have appeared.

The attempt of the Hollands and their friends to restore

[1] Within the walls of York, besides the cathedral—to take one instance—there were in the reign of Henry V, 41 parish churches, 17 chapels, 16 hospitals (in the old sense), and 8 monastic houses, and also the great monastic house just outside the Bar Gate. In the Tudor period, 18 of the parish churches and all the monasteries, hospitals, and chapels, were laid in the dust. Even the strong old Protestant writer Strype says of the man whom he calls 'the good Duke of Somerset' (the Protector): 'It must be reckoned among his failures, the havoc he made of sacred edifices. It was too barbarous, indeed, the defacing ancient monuments, and rooting out thereby the memory of men of note and quality in former times of which posterity is wont to be very tender (*Ecclest. Mem.* i. 12). Strype's feelings as historian and antiquarian almost get the best here of his admiration for the Protestant 'good duke.' But 'failures' indeed!

Richard caused the secret murder of the unhappy king in Pontefract Castle, a week or ten days after the rising. Archbishop Fitz-Alan of Arundel, rejoicing over the Cirencester affair, vindictively wrote on January 10, 1400, that the Earls of Kent and Salisbury had been beheaded by ' Sancta Rusticitas que omnia palam facit.' (' Saint Rusticity who does all things openly.') This rude openness of the Archbishop's new and singular saint was at any rate better than the secret murder of Richard, covered by the cold official falsehood, supported by the exhibition of his dead face to the London public, that the late king had died a natural death.

In those days of weak governments, full of apprehension because without standing army or police, a king deposed was a king murdered. It was an incident of change of government. ' Come, let us sit upon the ground and tell sad stories of the deaths of kings.' Even before he landed in England, Henry of Lancaster well knew that he would have to slay his cousin. Froissart relates a conversation at Paris between him and Archbishop Arundel, who urged upon him the venture. Henry did not immediately reply, but, leaning on a window that looked into the garden, mused awhile, and then, turning to the Archbishop, said that, if he complied, he would have to put Richard to death. ' For this,' he added, ' I shall be blamed by all men, and I would not willingly do so if any other means could be adopted.' The Archbishop replied, in full accord with later ' constitutional principles,' that Henry would act on the advice of counsellors, and so would avoid any personal responsibility.

Froissart, after relating the story of Richard's death, says : ' I was in the city of Bordeaux and sitting at the table, when King Richard was born, which was on a Wednesday, about ten of the clock. The same time there came there, where I was, Sir Richard Pountchardon, Marshal then of Aquitaine, and he said to me, "Froissart, write and put in memory that as now my Lady Princess is brought abed with a fair son on this Twelfth Day, that is, the day of the Three Kings, and he is son to a king's son, and shall be a king." This gentle knight said truth, for he was King of England twenty-two years; but when this knight said these words, he knew full little what should be his end.'

John Holland, Earl of Huntingdon, left three sons—Richard, John, and Edward—and a daughter, Constance. This daughter was married first to the Earl Marshal, beheaded at York for treason in 1405, son and heir to that Earl of Nottingham, for a time Duke of Norfolk, who had the quarrel with Bolingbroke, and secondly to Lord Gray de Ruthyn, who was ancestor of a new, long, and dull line of Earls of Kent. One of these later Earls of Kent, so descended from Constance Holland, sat on the commission which condemned Mary Queen of Scots, and he was present at her execution in the castle hall of Fotheringay. Mary held the Crucifix and said: 'As Thy arms, O God, were stretched out upon the Cross, so receive me into the arms of Thy mercy and forgive me my sins.' 'Madam,' said the Earl of Kent, 'you would better leave such popish trumperies and bear Him in your heart.' Mary replied: 'I cannot hold in my hand the representation of His sufferings, but I must at the same time bear Him in my heart.' An Earl of Kent of the nobler and earlier line would not so have insulted a dying queen and woman.

The Earl of Huntingdon's widow, Elizabeth, was, after all, sister of King Henry IV, and for this reason, although the estates were confiscated for his treason, manors were re-granted sufficient for the maintenance of his children, the King's nephews and niece, who were brought up at their late father's Hall of Dartington, near Totnes in Devonshire. Elizabeth mourned so little for the husband who had tried to overthrow her brother, that within two months after his death she married, without the consent of the King and to his displeasure, a certain gentleman called Sir John Cornwall, more noted for his great bodily strength than for any other qualities. He was afterwards made Lord Fanhope.

Waleran, Count of St. Pol and Luxemburg—he who had married Maud la Belle, sister of John Holland, Earl of Huntingdon—was pleased to add an epilogue of comedy to the tragedy of King Richard and the Hollands. It was the supreme glory of this Picard lord to have married the half-sister of the King of England, and he was exceeding wrath at the overthrow of his royal brother-in-law. His own great time had come to an end, and he could no longer enjoy visits to Eltham Palace and play the proud rôle of diplomatic agent between the kings of France and England. After meditating on these things for a year, the Count, in 1402, sent King Henry this insolent letter :

' Most high and puissant Prince Henry, Duke of Lancaster, I, Waleran of Luxembourg, Count of St. Pol, considering the love, affinity, and alliance which I had for the most noble and puissant Prince Richard, King of England, whose sister I have married, in the destruction of which noble King you are notoriously inculpated and very greatly dishonoured, and, moreover, the great shame I and my offspring descending from me may, or might, have in time to come, and also the indignation of God Almighty, and of all reasonable and honourable persons, if I do not hazard myself with all my power to avenge the destruction of him to whom I was thus allied ; wherefore by these present letters, I make known to you that in all ways that I can and that shall be possible to me, I will requite you henceforth, you and yours, and all the damage as well by myself as by my relations, all my men and subjects, that I can do, I will do to you, by sea and by land, always without the Kingdom of France, for the becoming reason of the thing above discoursed of, not in anywise for the matters which have taken place and are to take place between my most dread and sovereign Lord the King of France and the Kingdom of England. And this I certify you by the impression of my seal. Given in my castle of St. Pol on the eleventh day of February, year one thousand four hundred and two.'

The noble Count did not get a satisfactory answer to this letter, the composition of which must have given much trouble to him and his legal advisers.

' When King Henry,' says John de Wavrin, ' had received and caused to be read this letter, and had understood the contents of it, he thought a little, and then said to the messenger : '' My friend, return to your country, and say to your master the Count of St. Pol, that of his anger and threats, I take not much account, and say to him that my intention is so to meet his threats that he will have much to do to protect his person, his subjects, and his country.''

' Then the messenger, hearing the answer of the King, without replying, departed, and came to Dover, where he embarked in a boat and came to Calais and thence to Aire, where he found Count Waleran his master. When the Count had heard the messenger touching the answer of King Henry, he was much troubled in his heart, but passed it off as well as he could, and to keep his word he prepared himself to make war on the said King Henry and on all whom he might think wished him well. Also he caused to be made in his Castle of Bohaing, the effigy of the Earl of Rutland, son of the Duke of York, blazoned with his arms and a portable gibbet, which he caused to be taken secretly into one of his fortresses in the country of Boulogne, and soon afterwards the said Count ordered his people— namely, Robert de Reubetagnes, Aliane de Bectune, and other skilled men of war, who by his command placed the said gibbet and effigy by night close to the Gates of Calais, where the same gibbet was by them set up and the effigy of the said Earl of Rutland there hanging by the feet downwards.   After this was done, the two gentlemen returned to the place whence they had come.   When it came to pass in the morning that the people of Calais opened the gates they were much amazed to see this gibbet, and at once demolished it, and brought it into the town, and from this time were the English at Calais even more inclined to do damage to the Count of St. Pol, and his country and his subjects than they were before.'

The Burgundian chronicler thus solemnly relates this valorous feat of arms.

CHAPTER VII

EDMUND HOLLAND, FOURTH EARL OF KENT, AND HIS SISTERS

Twist ye, twine ye! even so,
Mingle shades of joy and woe,
Hope, and fear, and peace, and strife,
In the thread of human life.

WALTER SCOTT.

THOMAS HOLLAND, third Earl of Kent, slain by the Cirencester folk, left a young widow, the Countess Joan, but
no children. Henry IV gave means of support to Joan,
who lived till 1444. The earldom passed to the younger
brother, Edmund Holland, who was about sixteen in 1400,
when he became fourth Earl of Kent. Most of the Kent
and Huntingdon estates had been confiscated either before
or after the revolt, and both branches of the family depended
mainly on the King for support. Henry IV was placable
by temperament, and wished to win the great houses to
the support of his dubious, though parliamentary, title.
As soon as the young Earl of Kent came of age, he was
made high steward and received a command at sea. He
was made Knight of the Garter in 1403. Two years later
he first saw war in a naval expedition commanded by Thomas
of Lancaster, one of the King's sons, and himself, two youths
scarcely of age. He fought gallantly in an unsuccessful
attack on Sluys, and was twice hit so badly that the French
believed him killed.

Edmund was a youth distinguished and charming;

157

'inclytus et amabilis,' the chronicler calls him. Like his late uncle, John, Earl of Huntingdon, he won renown in the lists. In 1405, when he was about twenty-one, he was challenged to a match by a Scottish champion, Alexander Stewart, Earl of Mar, bastard son of the famous Earl of Buchan, the 'Wolf of Badenoch,' himself a son of King Robert II. The Earl of Mar came down from Scotland with a special safe conduct, and the fray was fought in Smithfield before London's beauty and fashion. The Earl of Kent defeated the Northerner, no doubt with vast applause, winning the double event—the combat on horse and the combat on foot.

Edmund, when still hardly more than a boy, was under the spell of the Lady Constance, sister to the second Duke of York, the whilom Earl of Rutland, who had betrayed Kent's dead brother. Constance was widow of the Lord Despenser who had taken part in the Holland revolt of 1400, and had been beheaded by the mob at Bristol. It was this fair and immoral lady who was concerned in the Yorkist plot of 1405, and smuggled the two Mortimer boys out of Windsor Castle, and afterwards, correctly no doubt, accused her own brother, the Duke of York, of treason, and tried to get one of her admirers to prove her allegation by ordeal of battle against him. A daughter named Eleanor was the fruit of the love affair between Edmund of Kent and Constance of York. This high-born passion-child married Lord Audley, of a family which continues to this day, and in 1431 she unsuccessfully tried in Court of Law to prove herself legitimate.

But now the young Earl of Kent had to discard this entanglement with the widow of a rebel lord whose estates had been confiscated, and make a rich marriage for the sake of his impoverished house. Holinshed says that, 'Edmund Holland, Earl of Kent, was in such favour with the King, that he not only advanced him to high office and great

honours, but also, to his great cost and charges, obtained for
him the Lady Lucia, daughter and one of the heirs of Lord
Bernabo of Milan.'

Bernabo was brother of Gian Galeazzo de Visconti, whose
daughter Violante, had, as his second wife, married Lionel,
Duke of Clarence, son of Edward III and uncle of Henry IV.
That marriage was celebrated at Milan in 1368 and was
the most glorious affair.   Violante was beautiful, and Lionel
far renowned as the handsomest of his good-looking race.
Violante had for her dowry 100,000 florins.   There was a
gorgeous banquet of thirty courses, the very leavings of
which, said the enraptured Italian chronicler, would have
fed 10,000 men.   Francesco Petrarcha, the poet laureate
of Italy, was there, and ' for the honour of his learning, was
seated among the highest nobility,' who were far more highly
honoured by his presence.   There were two hundred English
among the guests.   During one course were presented, as gifts
to the guests, ' seventy goodly horses, caparisoned with silk
and silver, and during others, silver vessels, falcons, hounds,
armour for horses, costly coats of mail, breastplates glistening
of massy steel, corslets and helmets adorned with rich crests,
apparel embroidered with costly jewels, soldiers' belts, and
lastly, certain gems of curious art set in gold, and purple
and cloth of gold for mens' apparel in great abundance.'

Unhappily, the Duke of Clarence was so exhausted by
Italian banqueting and love-making that he died in Piedmont
two months after his wedding, or he was poisoned by an
enemy, some said.   But such was the wealth and extrava-
gance of these Lombard Viscontis, into whose family the
young Earl of Kent was now to marry.   They could spare one
of their numerous daughters for an Earl of Kent to please
the King of England, but they were keen to make much
greater alliances.   One of their daughters had married into
the royal family of France, and a marriage had at one time

been talked of between Richard II and another daughter of Bernabo, and Michael de la Pole had been sent to Milan in 1379 to treat of it. These two Viscontis had amassed their great fortunes by taxing the people of the rich Lombard plain. Bernabo was a tyrant, and called the ' Scourge of Lombardy '; but all the same was a good patron of art and letters. He had twenty-nine children. When Henry IV, as Earl of Derby, was on his return from Jerusalem in 1898, he came to Milan, and Lucia Visconti, then fifteen years old, was so much smitten by this magnificent English stranger— he was then twenty-six—that six years later when they wanted her to marry a German Prince, Frederick of Thuringia, she cried, and would not let her maid put on her most showy frock, vowing that she would wait till her life's end to marry Henry of Derby, even if she had to die three days after she was wed.[1] Other proposals were made for her hand, but for one reason or another she did not marry till she was twenty-nine. The Earl of Kent was then about twenty-three, or six years younger than his Italian wife. Edmund Holland was contracted to the Lady Lucia at Milan in the summer of 1306, and was married to her in London on January 24, 1307, in the Church of St. Mary Overy, now called Southwark Cathedral, where the poet Gower, to whom Richard II was so kind, had been buried two years earlier.

The forsaken Lady Constance Despenser was sufficiently forgiving to attend this wedding. It was a grand social affair. The King himself gave away the bride—his former girl adorer—at the door of the church, and after the ceremony the guests all repaired to a grand banquet at the neighbouring palace of the Bishop of Winchester. According to Holinshed, Don Alfonso of Cainuola paid in the church to the Earl of Kent 100,000 ducats on behalf of Bernabo of

[1] *Eine Mailandisch-Thuringische Heirath's geschichte aus den Zeit König Wenzels.* Dresden, 1895.

Milan as a dowry. Perhaps, however, Don Alfonso only gave promissory and unhonoured notes, for in the following year the Earl of Kent was without means, and deep in debt. Edmund survived not his marriage long. In 1408 he was appointed 'Admiral for the North and West' in place of the Earl of Somerset, his brother-in-law, and soon afterwards was sent with a fleet to coerce Olivier de Blois, Count of Penthiévre, who owned the island of Breton off the coast of Brittany, was in rebellion against his suzerain, the Duke of Brittany, had been a kind of Channel pirate, and had refused to pay a sum due to the English Crown. The Earl of Kent, notwithstanding his supposed rich marriage, was in debt, and to raise £200 on this occasion from the moneylenders at Southampton, he had to pawn his spoons, forks, spice-plates, goblets and potellers, his silver gilt basins with the arms of Kent and Milan, his salt cellars inlaid with the lodged hart, his cups dotted with pearls, and 'balusters or pounced with ivy and the lids enamelled with falcons and mounted with fretlets of roses, apples eagles, green flowers and doves.'

The fleet sailed early in June 1408, and the island and castle were captured. But the young Earl of Kent was wounded to death. Riding recklessly near the walls without wearing his 'basinet' or iron cap, he was struck on the head by a shot from the castle, and died of the wound a few days later, September 5, 1408. His body was brought home and buried near that of his father at Brunne, or Bourne, Abbey in the fens of Lincolnshire. Edmund was the fourth of his family, since the Hollands had emerged from Lancashire, to meet a violent death. He died with no assets, without a will, and deep in debt. His widow Lucia received in 1412 an annuity of £333 6s. 8d. from manors in Lancashire, which confirms the supposition that most of her dowry had never been received or had been spent at

M

once in clearing off her husband's previous debts. She married again. The Elizabethan chronicler, Grafton, is responsible for the following statement. He does not put the matter as prettily as he should have done.

'This Lucye, after the death of her husbande, by whom she had none issue, was moved by the King to marry hys bastard brother the Erle of Dorset, a man very aged and evil-visaged, whose person neyther satisfied her phantasie nor whose face pleased her appetite. Wherfore she, preferring her owne minde more than the Kinge's desyre, delighting in him which should more satisfie her wanton desire than gayne her any profite, for verye love tooke to husbande Henry Mortimer, a goodly young esquire, and bewtifull bachelor. For which cause the King was not onely with her displeased, but also for marying without his license, he fined her at a great some of money, which fine King Henry V both released and pardoned and also made him knight and promoted him to great offices both in England and in Normandy.'

Lucia died on April 4, 1424, and was buried in the church of the Austen Friars in Bread Street, London. She seems to have been a pious soul, who lived an unhappy life, full of disappointments. By her will she bequeathed her body to be buried wheresoever it should please God. She left a thousand crowns to the Abbey of Brunne in Lincolnshire, where her husband lay buried, and a like sum to the Priory and Convent of the Holy Trinity, Aldwych Without, London, upon condition 'that they should provide a fitting priest to celebrate divine service daily to the end of the world, in every of these hereafter named religious houses, viz. St. Mary in Overy in Southwark, the Carthusian Minoresses, and Holy Trinity Without, Aldgate, and Abbey of Brunne, as also in the four houses of the Friars Mendicants in London, for the health of the souls of King Henry IV and King

Henry V. Likewise for the souls of Edmund, late Earl of Kent, her husband, as also for her own soul, and the souls of all the faithful deceased. And that in every one of those houses they should yearly celebrate the anniversary of him the said Edmund and her the said Lucia. Likewise that every brother and sister in each of those houses should every day say the psalm of *De Profundis* with the wonted orison for the dead, for the souls of him the said Edmund, and her the said Lucia, by name. Moreover that in each of those houses they should once every month in their Quire, say *Placebo* and *Dirige* by note for the souls of them, the said Edmund and Lucia by name, and once every year a Trental of St. Gregory for their said souls by name.'

Poor Lucia fondly imagined that these orisons would continue ' until the end of the world ' ! They lasted barely a hundred years. She also left a thousand crowns to the Provost and Canons of Our Lady de la Scala at Milan, not forgetful of the land of her girlhood, and another thousand crowns to the church where her father was buried.

Edmund and Lucia had been married only a year and a half, and they had no children. The Kent title therefore died out in the Holland line, though it was afterwards revived in favour of the Greys of Ruthyn, who long held it.[1]

Edmund's sisters and the young Earl of March, the son of one sister who had died, became co-heirs to his valueless possessions.

Thomas Holland, second Earl of Kent, besides his sons Thomas and Edmund, the third and fourth Earls, and two other sons who died young, had six daughters. One would have liked to see this family in their glorious youth in some

---

[1] The Greys of Ruthyn were connected with the Hollands by the marriage of Constance, daughter of John Holland, first Duke of Exeter. They remained Earls of Kent till the last of their male line, who became Duke of Kent in 1710 and died in 1740, and all the Kent titles died with him. The barony of Grey of Ruthyn continued through a female descent and still exists.

country estate. There is evidence to show that they were vigorous and beautiful. Some of the sisters became of importance in the descent of the royal line of England. Their names were :

1. Alianora.
2. Johanna, or Joan.
3. Margaret.
4. Eleanor.
5. Elizabeth.
6. Bridget.

Bridget became a nun, but the other five sisters married men of importance. The eldest, Alianora, married Roger Mortimer, Earl of March, who was son of Edmund Mortimer, Earl of March, and of Philippa, daughter of Lionel, Duke of Clarence, the third son of Edward III. Roger, Earl of March, was killed in the wars in Ireland in 1398. He was at the time formally recognised as heir presumptive to the Crown in default of children to Richard II, by virtue of his mother, Philippa, whose father was senior in order of birth to the Duke of Lancaster. If Richard II had died in, say, 1390, England would therefore have had a King Roger of the House of Mortimer, and a Queen Eleanor of the House of Holland. Henry IV would probably never have been King, and the Wars of the Roses might have been avoided.

This Roger, Earl of March, left four children, namely :
Anne, who was nine years old on her father's death.
Edmund, who was six.
Roger, who was then four.
Eleanor, who was younger.

By strict right or custom, as received in England, that right by which Edward III had claimed the crown of France, the boy Edmund should have become King on the deposition of Richard II. The right was put aside by Parliament in favour of Henry of Bolingbroke, and this passing over the

Mortimer claim was ostensibly the cause of the Wars of the Roses, the real cause being the Yorkist ambition.   The two Mortimer boys, as possible centres of conspiracy, were taken away from their mother by Henry IV and kept at Windsor Castle.   The attempt made in 1405 by that ambiguous lady, Constance Despenser, and her brother, the treacherous Duke of York (formerly Rutland and Albemarle) to smuggle them away to Wales was foiled.   The boys were recaptured in a wood near Cheltenham and placed in safer keeping.   Edmund was kept many years a prisoner in an Irish castle, and died there.   The two unfortunate youths were both dead before 1425, and left no children.   The claim then passed to their elder sister Anne.   She and her sister had been left with their mother, Alianora, born Holland, who, after her husband the Earl of March's death, married Lord Powys and died in 1405.

Anne Mortimer was married to Richard, Earl of Cambridge, younger brother of the existing Duke of York and son of Edmund Langley, not by Joan Holland, but by his first wife, the Spanish Princess.   This Earl of Cambridge was beheaded at Southampton in 1415 for his share in the Yorkist conspiracy against Henry V.   His elder brother, the Duke of York, died the same year at Agincourt without leaving sons.   Richard Plantagenet, the son of the Earl of Cambridge and Anne Mortimer, and so grandson of Alianora Holland, became Duke of York and was killed at the Battle of Wakefield in 1460.   He was father to Edward IV and Richard III and grandfather to Elizabeth of York, who married Henry VII and so reunited the Roses.   Thus, Alianora Holland was an ancestress of Henry VIII and his successors, Edward VI, Mary, and Elizabeth, and through the daughter of Henry VII, who married James of Scotland, was also an ancestress in the Stewart line.

Another daughter of Thomas Holland, second Earl of Kent, was Johanna, or Joan, a Beauty who married four times.

Her first husband, whom she married in 1393, was much older than herself, Edward III's son, the easy-going and ineffective Edmund of Langley, Duke of York, whose first wife had been Isabella of Castile. He was then about fifty and Joan not twenty. Froissart remarks that the Duke of Gloucester, who was jealous of his brother the Duke of Lancaster, 'cared nothing for his brother the Duke of York, a prince that loved his ease, and was without malice or guile, wishing only to live in quiet ; also he had a fair lady to wife, daughter of the Earl of Kent, who was all his pleasure, and with whom he spent most of his time that was not filled by hunting and other diversions.' Froissart, who had not been in England for twenty-seven years, arrived at Dover on July 16, 1394, a year after Joan's marriage, and met the Court two days later at Canterbury. All his old friends were dead, and he knew no one at first, but he rode in the train of the King by Ospringe and Leeds Castle, and thence, crossing again the chalk downs, to Eltham, conversing on the way about the events of the times with Sir William de Lisle and Sir Richard de Sturry. At Leeds Castle the Duke of York, to whom he had letters of introduction, presented him to the King, and a few days later at Eltham Froissart had an opportunity to present Richard his book on L'Amour handsomely written and illumined and ornately bound, studded and clasped.[1] No doubt he also addressed at Eltham his compliments to the young and beautiful Duchess of York and told her how well he remembered her grandfather, 'ce bon chevalier,' Sir Thomas Holland, and her grandmother, the Princess Joan of Kent. He stayed over three months at Court, moving about, at Eltham and Shene and Chertsey and Windsor, and must have seen a good deal of the

---

[1] A 'fair book, fair illumined and written, and covered with crimson velvet, with ten buttons of silver and gilt, and roses and gold in the midst, with two great clasps, gilt, richly wrought.'

Holland family.   The impression given by Froissart of the
first Duke of York, the most amiable of his race, tallies well
with that conveyed by the rhyming chronicler, Hardyng :

> That Edmund, hight ' of Langley,' of good chere
> Glad and merry, and of his own aye lyved
> Without wronge, as chronicles have breved ;
> When all the lords to council and to parleyment
> Went, he wolde to hunt, and also to hawkeying.
> All gentyll disporte, as to a lord appent,
> He used aye, and to the pore supportyng,
> Wherever he was, in any place bidyng,
> Without surprise or any extorcyon
> Of the porayle, or any oppressyon.

It is a picture of the eternal English country gentleman,
and it is a pleasing trait that when other lords went to quarrel
in Parliament, Edmund of Langley would go hunting.   He
is Shakespeare's ' good old York.'   In ' Richard II ' the
widowed Duchess of the murdered Gloucester sends a tragically poignant and discouraging invitation to him through his
brother, John of Gaunt :

> Commend me to thy brother, Edmund York.
> Lo ! this is all : nay, yet depart not so ;
> Though this be all, do not so quickly go ;
> I shall remember more.   Bid him—ah, what ?—
> With all good speed at Plashy visit me.
> Alack ! and what shall good old York there see
> But empty lodgings and unfurnish'd walls,
> Unpeopled offices, untrodden stones ?
> And what hear there for welcome but my groans ?
> Therefore commend me ; let him not come there,
> To seek out sorrow that dwells every where.

The Duke of York had to leave his hawks and hounds
and to die in 1402, having had no children by the beautiful
Joan Holland, who next married Sir William de Willoughby,
Lord D'Eresby.   He also died, and then she married Henry

Scrope, Earl of Masham, whose head was cut off at Southampton in 1415 together with that of the Earl of Cambridge, who was both her own stepson and the husband of her niece Anne Mortimer, for his share in the Yorkist conspiracy. Joan, after these adventures, aimed lower and, fourthly, married Henry Bromflete, a Yorkshire gentleman whose father had been chief butler to Richard II, and had then, with official adaptability to change of government, become Controller of the Household to Henry IV.   After this varied career, the Lady Joan died in 1434.

The second Earl of Kent's third daughter was the Lady Margaret Holland.   She is a lady of much importance in the genealogy of the Kings of England.   She married first, John Beaufort, Earl of Somerset, who was the eldest illegitimate-born son of John of Gaunt, Duke of Lancaster, and of Katherine Swynford.   The Duke's sons by this Katherine, namely (1) the said John Beaufort, Earl of Somerset, (2) Henry, who became the famous Cardinal Bishop of Winchester, and (3) Thomas, the Beaufort who fought at Agincourt and was created, for life, Duke of Exeter, were made legitimate by special Act under King Richard II. There was also a daughter, Joan, who married Ralph Nevill, first Earl of Westmorland.

In Parliament, on January 22, 1397, the King ' as sole Emperor of the realm of England ' (says the Tower Record), ' for the honour of his blood royal, willed that Sir John Beaufort, with his brothers and sister, should be legitimate, and created him to be Earl of Somerset.

' Whereupon, the said John was brought before the King in Parliament between two Earls, viz. of Huntingdon and Marshall (Nottingham) arrayed in a robe as in a vesture of honour, with a sword carried before him, the pummel thereof being gilded.   And the charter of his creation was openly read before the Lords and Commons, after which the King girded him with the sword aforesaid, took his homage and caused him to be set in his place in the Parliament between the Earls Marshall and Warr.'

John Beaufort, Earl of Somerset, took a leading and active part with his brother-in-law, Thomas Holland, third Earl of Kent, and with John Holland, Earl of Huntingdon, and their allies, in the overthrow of the Duke of Gloucester and his party in the summer of 1397. He was raised by Richard II at Michaelmas to the title of Marquess of Dorset, and was deprived of that title after the accession of his half-brother, Henry of Lancaster, becoming again Earl of Somerset. John Beaufort took no hand in the Holland revolt, and remained in royal favour in the new reign. He died on Palm Sunday, in the year 1410.

Margaret Holland of Kent bore to him the following children:

1. Henry Beaufort, who succeeded his father in 1410 as second Earl of Somerset, and died 1418, *s.p.*

2. John, who became Duke of Somerset, and died in 1444, without sons.

3. Edmund, who succeeded him as second Duke. He was leader of the Lancastrian party, and was slain at St. Albans in 1455.[1]

4. Joan, who married James I of Scotland.

5. Margaret, who married Courtenay, Earl of Devon.

These Beauforts died out in the legitimate male line, but John, the first Duke, left a daughter, Margaret Beaufort, who was thus granddaughter of Margaret Holland. This was the Lady Margaret famed for her goodness, religion, and understanding, who married Edmund Tudor, Earl of Richmond, and so became mother of Henry VII and ancestress of the royal house of Tudor. Child of the bright and tender re-dawn of Art and Letters, so soon, like the

---

[1] Edmund Beaufort's two sons were Henry Beaufort, third Duke, beheaded after Hexham fight in 1463, and Edmund, fourth Duke, murdered after Tewkesbury, 1471.

glorious morning of Shakespeare's sonnet, to be overcast by northern gloom, she endowed two chairs of divinity, and founded at Cambridge the fair colleges of Christ and St. John.   On her death, a beautiful funeral sermon—whence it appears that she was a very perfect lady—was preached by her chaplain, John Fisher, who in his saintly old age was martyred for being unable to admit that her grandson Harry was supreme head of the Church in England.   Lady Margaret had lived through the Wars of the Roses and had seen the woes of kings, and the crimes which they must, or do, commit in the name of State Policy.   Fisher says of her : ' She never yet was in that prosperity, but the greater it was the more always she dreaded the adversity.   For when the king, her son, was crowned in all that great triumph and glory, she wept marvellously : and likewise at the great triumph of the marriage of Prince Arthur, and at the last coronation wherein she had felt great joy, she let not to say that some adversity would follow ; so that either she was in sorrow by reason of the present adversities, or else when she was in prosperity she was in dread of the adversity for to come.' [1] Well might the Lady Margaret feel dark forebodings when she witnessed the marriage of Prince Arthur, laden with such disaster, and yet more at the coronation of her lusty young grandson Henry, who resembled not her, nor her son his excellent father Henry VII, but the bad York-Woodville breed.   She would have wept the more had she known for certain that he would slay her confessor, destroy venerable foundations which she loved, and break England away from the visible unity of the Catholic Church.

When she died, five days after this coronation, it was a symbol of the passing away of a more chivalrous and, as some would say, a nobler age.   Her admirable effigy,

[1] Henry VII's eldest son Arthur was born in 1486, was married to Katherine of Aragon as a boy, and died in 1502. The second, Henry, was born in 1491 and crowned June 24, 1509. Their grandmother, Lady Margaret, Countess of Richmond, was born 1443 and died on June 29, 1509.

with a delicately carved hart at her feet, lies in front of a vanished altar in the chapel built by her son at Westminster, and behind hers is the monument of her charming, ill-fated, descendant, Mary Stewart, Queen of Scots.

After the death, in 1410, of her first husband, John Beaufort, Earl of Somerset, the legitimated half-brother of Henry IV, Margaret Holland married Thomas, Duke of Clarence, whole brother of Henry V, and so half-nephew of her first husband. This royal duke had won fame in previous campaigns in France, but was killed in 1421 in the disaster which befell the English near Beaugé. In this same fight a son of Margaret by her first husband, John Beaufort, Earl of Somerset, and also her first cousin John Holland, second Earl of Huntingdon, were taken prisoners, so that the news must have given a shock to high English society, and especially to Margaret, Duchess of Clarence. The Duke of Clarence had desired to be buried like his father, King Henry IV, in Canterbury Cathedral. Margaret's first husband, the Earl of Somerset, was already there interred. The body of the slain Clarence was brought home from France. 'A new hearse was provided and a hundred torches were burned that night in various sacred places in the Cathedral.' The funeral cost £85, a great sum in those days. Margaret died, more than sixty years old, on December 31, 1440. She had made for her husbands and herself a fine monumental tomb, which still stands, not much injured, in St. Michael's Chapel at the south-east end of the nave. Her figure lies between those of her two husbands, who are both fully armed, whence the chapel is usually known as the 'Warriors' Chapel.' The face of Margaret, though she is shown as an elderly woman, indicates that in her youth she too was beautiful. On her head is a ducal coronet ; on her robes are depicted the arms of England within a bordure argent. Her personal device was represented in a window of the Cathedral—namely, a white hart couchant, gorged with a golden coronet and chain under a tree. It was the device of her grandmother, the Fair Maid of Kent.

Margaret Holland, Duchess of Clarence, five years before her death, heard of the tragedy which befell her daughter Joan, Queen of Scotland. The story of James I of Scotland and Joan Beaufort is well known but is worth repeating in a history of the Hollands. James, son and heir of Robert III, the first Stewart King of Scotland, was, for some political reason, sent at twelve years old in a ship to France. The ship was captured off Flamborough Head by an English rover, hailing from Cley, in Norfolk. The boy was taken to London. Henry IV said that he could learn French in England as well as in France, and kept him in strict custody. This happened early in 1406, and the same year James's father, King Robert, died and the boy became King of Scotland. Henry IV refused all demands by the Scots for the restitution of their boy King, and kept James close guarded, but gave him a far better education than he could have obtained in wild and barbarous Scotland. He learned all gentle accomplishments, law, and manners, and music, and to write poetry. While he was a prisoner at Windsor Castle in the Central Keep, or Round Tower, he sometimes saw from his window the lovely Joan Beaufort, daughter of the Earl of Somerset and Margaret Holland, walking or sitting with her maidens in the garden below, and became enamoured. The poet King thus describes his feelings in touching verse :

> And therewith kest I down mine eye again
> Where as I saw, walking under the Tower
> Full secretly new comen her to pleyne
> The fairest or the freshest yonge flower
> That ever I saw, methought, before that hour,
> For which sudden abate, anon astert
> The blude of all my body to my herte.

And though I stude abasit throw a lite,
No wonder was ; for why, my wittis all
Were so ourcome with plesance and delight,
Only throw latting of my eyën fall,
That suddenly my herte became her thrall,
For ever, of free will : for of menace
There was no token in her swëte face.

And in my head I drew right hastily
And eft sonës I leant it forth again
And saw her walk that very womanly
With no wight mo, but only women twain
Then gan I study in myself and sayn,
Ah Sweet, are ye a worldly creáture,
Or heavnly thing in likeness of nature ?

Or are ye god Cupid's own princess
And comen are to loose me out of band ?
Or are ye very Nature the goddess
That have depainted with your heavnly hand
This garden full of flouris as they stand ?
What sall I think !   Alas, what reverence
Sall I minister to your excellence.

Gif ye a goddess be, and that ye like
To do me pain I may it nocht astert :
Gif ye be worldly wight that doth me sike,
Why list God mak you so, my dearest herte
To do a silly prisoner this smart
That lufis you all, and wote of nocht but woe ?
And therefore mercy sweet ! sen it be so.

' Of menace there was no token in her swëte face.'   These
are the words of one who had seen menace in faces less
beauteous.   It was a love affair at the ' fair Castle of Windsor '
such as Joan Beaufort's great-aunt, Lady Maud Holland,
had there with a less strictly guarded captive, the young
Count of St. Pol, nearly fifty years earlier.

James was kept in captivity for eighteen years, until, in 1424, it suited the policy of Cardinal Beaufort, who was then virtually ruler of England, that the Scottish King should marry his niece and return to Scotland. James was then about thirty-one years old. The marriage of James and Joan was celebrated, like that of Edmund Holland and Lucia Visconti, in the church of St. Mary Overy, and again the banquet was in the palace of the Cardinal Bishop of Winchester. Joan's uncles and mother and other kinsfolk gave her great gifts, 'Plate, jewels, gold and silver, rich furniture, cloths of arras such as at that time had not been seen in Scotland, and, amongst other gorgeous ornaments, a set of hangings in which the labours of Hercules were most curiously wrought. And being thus furnished,' adds the chronicler, 'of all things fit for her estate, her two uncles, the Cardinal Beaufort and the Duke of Exeter, accompanied her and King James into his own kingdom of Scotland, where they were received of his subjects with all joy and gladness.' The joy and gladness lasted not long. James returned to his kingdom a cultivated gentleman with English ideas as to government and the protection of the people against powerful oppressors. It was almost as though a prince had gone with civilised notions and intentions to modern Albania. James I tried to introduce reform into Scotland, and had some degree of success. Drummond of Hawthornden said of him : 'Of the former Kings of Scotland it might be said the nation made the King, but this King made that people a nation.'

He was a man of action as well as a poet and a musician. He passed salutary laws and executed powerful robber chiefs, both in the Highlands and the Lowlands, but his reward was murder. At Christmas 1435, notwithstanding omens and sinister and mysterious warnings, he went to Perth to spend the feast at the monastery of the Black Friars. An aristocratic conspiracy had been formed to take his life. Its chief, Sir Robert Graham, a dark and determined character, aided by confederates in the court, made his way, with armed followers, on the night of February 20 into the royal chamber, where James was conversing with the Queen and her ladies before retiring to rest. He heard the fierce approach of the murderers, tore up some planks and hid himself in a recess below the floor, while a gallant girl, Katharine Douglas, tried to bar with her arm the door from which the bolts had been treacherously removed. The King was discovered, dragged out, and pierced with many swords, while the Queen clung to him, till, wounded herself, she was torn violently away. James was but forty-four years old. It was a far cry from the dreadful night scene in the gloomy Black Friars at Perth to the splendid marriage banquet in the palace of Cardinal Beaufort, or the tender love idyll in the fair royal gardens of Windsor.

James left a six-year-old child, who was crowned James II of Scotland, and for some years the boy king and his mother were in the hands of one or another of the ferocious feudal factions. It was then almost impossible for high-born women to live unprotected and alone in Scotland, and in 1439 Queen Joan married Sir James Stewart, known as ' The Black Rider,' and bore him three sons. She died on July 15, 1445, at Dunbar, and was buried by the side of King James I in the Carthusian Convent at Perth, which was destroyed at the Reformation.

Thus through her daughter, Joan, Queen of Scotland, Margaret Holland was an ancestress of the Stewart line as through her son, John Beaufort, Earl of Somerset, she was ancestress of the Tudor line. Since, by the marriage of James of Scotland to Margaret, daughter of Henry VII, these two lines were fused, Margaret Holland was by two streams issuing from her body an ancestress of our royal line. This line also having received a rivulet coming from Margaret's sister Alianora, through the York descent, and the marriage of Henry VII to Elizabeth of York, there was a good deal of not very remote Holland blood in, for instance, Mary Queen of Scots and her grandson, Charles I of England and Scotland. Possibly these unfortunate sovereigns derived from the Hollands their genius for adopting the unpopular and losing side.

Eleanor, fourth of the six daughters of the Earl of Kent, and the most fortunate, perhaps, of her family, married Thomas Montacute, Earl of Salisbury, son of that brave and cultivated third Earl of Salisbury who died in the first days of 1400 with her brother the third Earl of Kent, at Cirencester. The fourth Earl of Salisbury, says the historian Banks, ' was concerned in so many military exploits, that to give an account of them all would be to write the history of the reign of Henry V. Suffice it then to say that, as he lived, so he died, in the service of his country, being mortally wounded when commanding the English army at the siege of Orléans in 1428.' Salisbury was examining the defences of the town when he was wounded in the face by a stone shot from the walls, and died in a week. John de Wavrin, after narrating his death, says of this Earl, ' He was a good prince and was feared and loved by all his people, and he was also accounted in his time throughout France and England the most expert, clever and successful in arms of all the commanders who had been talked about during the last two hundred years ; besides this, there were in him all the virtues belonging to a good knight ; he was mild, humble and courteous, a great almsgiver and liberal with what belonged to him ; he was pitiful and merciful to the humble, but fierce as a lion or a tiger to the proud ; he well loved men who were valiant and of good courage, nor did he ever keep back the services of others, but gave

to each his due according to his worth.' In short, the
husband of Eleanor Holland was the very type of a noble
gentleman and great captain. He died eight days after he
was wounded, and was buried at Mehun on the Loire,
and his death marked the close of English success in
France.

Lord Salisbury left no son, and thus the earldom came
to an end of its tenure by the old Norman line of the Montacutes, or Montagus ; but Eleanor Holland gave him a daughter,
the Lady Alice Montacute, who was married to Sir Richard
Nevill, K.G., second son of Ralph Nevill, Earl of Westmorland. This Richard Nevill obtained the revival of the
Earldom of Salisbury. He was a Yorkist, and being taken
prisoner at the defeat at Wakefield, his head was cut off
and placed on a pole over a gate at York. His eldest son
was also slain in that Lancastrian victory. His second son
and successor, also named Richard, had married Anne
Beauchamp, heiress of the Beauchamps, Earls of Warwick,
and obtained for himself the title of Earl of Warwick, by
which name, and not that of Salisbury or Westmorland,
he is known in history as 'Warwick the Kingmaker.'
Thus this Nevill hero of the Wars of the Roses, a great
fighter, whom Shakespeare represents as a better judge of
a pretty girl, a horse, or hawk, than of political questions,
was a grandson of Eleanor Holland, and great grandson
of the second Earl of Kent. He was a second cousin once
removed to the Henry Holland, second Duke of Exeter,
against whom he fought in the civil war until Warwick
changed the colour of his rose from white to red, and then
they fought side by side in the disastrous battle of Barnet
Field.

The fifth daughter of the second Earl of Kent, named
Elizabeth, married another Nevill, a half-brother of the
Richard Nevill who married Alice de Montacute. This was

John Nevill, eldest son by his first marriage of the great northern lord of Raby and first Earl of Westmorland, Ralph Nevill. This Ralph Nevill married first Margaret, daughter of Hugh, Earl of Stafford, and secondly Joan Beaufort, daughter of John of Gaunt, Duke of Lancaster. By his first wife he had two sons and six daughters, and by his second nine sons and four daughters, twenty-one children in all. From this numerous brood descended the tribe of Nevills. The present lords of Abergavenny descend from Edward, his sixth son by Joan Beaufort.

One of Ralph Nevill's daughters by Joan Beaufort was Cecily, who married Richard, Duke of York, and became mother to Edward IV, Richard III, and to Anne, who married Henry Holland, third Duke of Exeter.

The John Nevill who married Elizabeth Holland, died, before his father, in 1422. Their son Ralph Nevill, second Earl of Westmorland, married a daughter of Henry Lord Percy, the famous 'Hotspur,' and his son John Lord Nevill, who also died before his father, married Anne, daughter of John Holland, second Duke of Exeter. Thus the two lines of the Hollands blended with two lines of the great clan of Nevill.

Lady Bridget, sixth and last daughter of the second Earl of Kent, became a nun in the ancient, wealthy, and famous Benedictine Convent of Barking in Essex, always the most fashionable house in England for great ladies. Some small remains of it, a church, a gateway, and a piece of wall, can still be seen by those who travel on electric tramcar in the obscure far east of London.

This then, is the close of the story—the little that can be recovered from darkness out of dim old chronicles—of those Hollands who became Earls of Kent, and for a fleeting moment held the Dukedom of Surrey. The ten children who once lived together, high-born, beautiful and vigorous, in the manors of the second Earl of Kent, experienced great fortune and misfortune.   Thomas had been killed by the rustic crowd at Cirencester, Edmund by the French in war, two other sons had died young ; Alianora's husband, the Earl of March, had been slain in Ireland ; Joan's third husband, Lord Scrope had been beheaded for high treason ; Eleanor's husband, the Earl of Salisbury, was wounded to death before the walls of Orléans ; Margaret's second husband, the Duke of Clarence, had been slain in battle in France ; and she lived to know of the murder of her royal son-in-law in Scotland, though not long enough to hear that her second son Edmund Beaufort, Duke of Somerset, was slain at St. Albans.   In those days the saying was true, ' Rara in nobilitate senectus.'

The Hollands of the younger branch derived from the marriage of Sir Thomas Holland with the Fair Maid of Kent, those who became Earls of Huntingdon and Dukes of Exeter, continued for a while longer in the male line, and the following two chapters relate their story, after which this leisurely chronicle must return to other and less distinguished descendants from the Hollands of Upholland in the County of Lancaster.

CHAPTER VIII

JOHN HOLLAND, SECOND DUKE OF EXETER

Fair stood the wind for France,
When we our sails advance,
Nor now to prove our chance
Longer will tarry ;
But, putting to the main,
At Caux the mouth of Seine,
With all his martial train,
Landed King Harry.

DRAYTON.

JOHN HOLLAND, first Earl of Huntingdon and Duke of
Exeter, had been deprived of both titles : of the dukedom
immediately after the deposition of Richard, and of the
earldom on his revolt and death.   By Elizabeth of Lancaster
he left a daughter, Constance, and three sons—Richard,
John, and Edward.   Richard and Edward both died unmarried.   Richard lived just long enough to come of age and
into possession of the great estates—some twenty manors
in Devonshire, Cornwall, and Somerset—which had apparently
been restored by the Crown ; but he died young, and the
estates passed to John when he came of age.   John was
born in 1394, and was six years old when his father tragically
died at Pleshy.   Something is known of his christening,
thanks to an inquisition made in the sixth year of Henry V.[1]

Thomas Codling testified that the ' Abbot of Tavistock, in

---

[1] These inquisitions were made when a minor, entitled to a manor held directly
from the Crown, came of age. he had to prove his age, as the Crown was entitled
to profits during a minority.   As to these particular inquisitions, see *Cal. Inquis.
post mortem*, vol. IV. p. 24.

the County of Devon, being one of the godfathers, immediately after the baptism gave him a cup of gold, with a circle about it, framed after the fashion of a lily, and ten pounds of gold therein; and to the nurse, twenty shillings. Also that the Prior of Plympton, who was the other godfather, gave him twenty pounds in gold, and forty shillings to the nurse. And Joan, the wife of Sir John Pomeraie, carried him to the chancel to be christened—the same Sir John Pomeraie, her husband, and Sir John Dynham, knight, conducting her by the arms. Likewise, that twenty-four men did proceed before them with twenty-four torches; which torches, as soon as he was baptized by that name, were kindled.' Evidently it was a provincial baptism intended to be worthy of the baby nephew of the reigning king. He was, indeed, in every way a high-born babe. On the side of his mother, Elizabeth of Lancaster, the small John Holland was great-grandson of King Edward III, and also descended in two separate lines, through John of Gaunt and his wife, Blanche, from King Henry III. By another line, through his paternal grandmother, the Fair Maid of Kent, he descended from King Edward I.

The reason why the baptism was in Devonshire was that John Holland was born at Dartington Hall, close to Totnes. This was a manor which had fallen in to the Crown through the failure of heirs of the Lords Audley, its previous holders, and had been granted by King Richard, with many other manors in the western shires, to John Holland, Earl of Huntingdon, the ill-fated father of the present John. That Earl intended to make Dartington his chief seat, and built, or rebuilt, the house. Some of his work still remains, in a ruined condition, adjacent to the more modern buildings. Dartington Hall stands high above the beautiful banks of the Dart river. It consisted formerly of two large quadrangular courts, divided by a great hall, kitchen, and other

buildings.   John Holland's great hall, with the kitchen
and entrance porch, is still standing, but the roof was taken
off in the nineteenth century.   It measures seventy feet
in length by forty-five in width, with side walls rising thirty
feet to the spring of the roof, and the pitch of the roof was
fifty feet from the ground.   The windows are large and
pointed, and the outside is embattled and buttressed.   On
the walls are still visible spandrel angels, carved in the fourteenth century, bearing effaced coats of arms, and in the roof
of the portal of the hall is carved a rose and a hart couchant
—the device of the Fair Maid of Kent.   In the eighteenth
century there was still painted glass in the windows, and in
one the picture of the Duchess of Exeter, praying for the
soul of her son.   After the extinction of the Hollands, in
the reign of Edward IV, Dartington Hall, after intervening ownerships, passed, in the reign of Elizabeth, into
the hands of the Champernownes, who built a long low house
at right angles to the Hall ; and they still cling to the place
—which has now, however, a decayed and deserted appearance.[1]   Sir John Pomeraie, or Pomeroy, who took part in
the christening with Joan, his wife, was a neighbour of
Norman descent living at Berry Pomeroy, a stately castle, of
which the ruins are to be seen at the summit of a high cliff
three miles south of Totnes.   The Sir William Pomeroy of
the year 1549 led the insurgent Catholic gentry and peasantry
of Devonshire against the Protestant Reform Government,
and the Pomeroy estates were then confiscated for that
treason.

John Holland and his elder brother, Richard, and his
younger brother, Edward, and their sister, Constance, were
bred as children at Dartington, and sported by the banks
of the Dart, and rode their ponies about the lovely Devon

---

[1] The present Champernownes, however, assumed the name, inheriting the
place through a female descent.   The last in the male line died in 1774.

country. John soon received royal favours, notwithstanding his father's treason of 1400. After all, the boy was the nephew of Henry IV, and the first cousin of Henry V. The latter young hero succeeded to the throne on March 20, 1413, when John was nineteen, and made him on the coronation occasion a knight of the new Order of the Bath. John took the symbolic bath, with fifty other novices of the Order, on April 8. All night they watched their arms in the chapel of the Tower, and next morning rode as escort to the King through the City by way of Cheapside to Westminster Abbey for the Coronation.

In 1415, John Holland was made Knight of the Garter; and in 1417, his elder brother having died, the Earldom of Huntingdon was restored to him by Act of Parliament. The lost Dukedom of Exeter was now with the Beauforts. Thomas Beaufort, brother-in-law of Margaret Holland, had been created Duke of Exeter for life only, on November 18, 1410, and he did not die till December 30, 1426. It was this Duke who distinguished himself at the Battle of Agincourt, and is celebrated in Shakespeare's heroic verse.

With the accession of Henry V, glorious times had come for loyal kinsmen of the House of Lancaster. Henry IV had come into power partly upon the tide of opposition to the peace with France policy espoused by Richard II and his Holland brethren, and had said to his first council: 'Now we will have peace with the Flemings and war with every one else.' But his throne had been too insecure, and threatened by too many internal conspiracies, to allow him to gratify the dominant English passion for invasion of France. Probably he desired it little himself; he had had very friendly relations with the House of France; and he seems to have cherished a vague idea of crusading against the Turkish infidels. With the accession of Henry V —young, handsome, and popular, with his laurels to win—the lovers of war were again in the ascendant, and the Orleanist-Burgundian feud beyond the sea gave an opportunity for a re-assertion of the English claims.

Lord Bacon, in his ' Discourse of the Government of England,' observes that ' Scotland was a country yet incompetent for the King's appetite. France was the fairer mark and better game, and though too big for the English gripe, yet the Eagle stooped and spread himself so well as within six years he fastened on the sword and sceptre and a daughter of France, and might have seized the Crown, &c.' In Bacon's time it was still unnecessary to put forward great moral reasons for war.

In 1414 the King held a Parliament at Leicester, and the question of foreign policy was discussed. The Archbishop of Canterbury advocated the invasion of France to subdue that kingdom to the British Crown. It is alleged by a chronicler that he did this in order to divert attention from a Bill for the confiscation of some monastic lands. He was opposed by the Nevill, Earl of Westmorland, warden of the Marches, who argued that Scotland should first be conquered, quoting the saying : ' He who France would win, must with Scotland first begin.' John Holland, or perhaps his eldest brother, not yet dead, seems to have replied, and the assembly voted for war with France by acclamation, shouting : ' War, war, France, France.'

On June 16, 1415—almost exactly four hundred years before the day of Waterloo—young Holland was riding with his royal cousin through the City of London after a service at St. Paul's Cathedral, and down the road to Southampton. Near Winchester, in the Bishop's Hall at Wolvesey Castle, the King received the French Embassy, which had come in hot haste via Dover to negotiate, and had followed the Court from London along the south-western road. ' The King,' says the chronicler, ' leant against a table, bareheaded and clad from head to foot in cloth of gold, with a chair placed beside the throne, which was splendidly draped with gold trappings. At his right hand stood his three brothers, together with the Duke of York, Sir John Holland, and others; and on his left, the Chancellor, Bishop Beaufort, together with Bishops Courtenay and Langley, who introduced the envoys, all of whom knelt as they entered.' Henry received the envoys again on the next day, and gave them a banquet. Negotiations continued until July 6, and then broke down. The Frenchmen offered much, but were not able to accede to the immense English demand for the best half of France—all Aquitaine, Normandy, Anjou, Touraine, Poitou, and Maine.

· At Southampton, the King discovered a new Yorkist plot against his throne and life. The leading conspirators were Richard, Earl of Cambridge, brother to the Duke of York and cousin to the King, Lord Scrope of Masham, and Sir Thomas Grey of Heton. An inquest of twelve jurors of the county found that the Earl of Cambridge and Sir Thomas Grey had conspired to proclaim the Earl of March as King, and to call in a Scottish army, and that Lord Scrope was guilty of treason also. Grey was forthwith beheaded, but Cambridge and Scrope claimed trial by their peers, and a commission was appointed on which John Holland sat, and these lords were also found guilty and beheaded. Thus it was John Holland's duty to assist in condemning to death the Earl of Cambridge, who was the stepson of his first cousin, Joan Holland, and Lord Scrope, who was the same Joan's present husband. The Duke of York, no doubt, was behind this conspiracy, but nothing could be proved against him. The man who, as Earl of Rutland, had been an appellant against Gloucester, Arundel, and Warwick, who had shared in the honour and plunder derived from that stroke of state, who had been

loved by Richard and had forsaken him on his fall, had then
joined in the conspiracy of the Hollands, and had betrayed
them to Henry IV, who had conspired against the King in
the Mortimer plot, and had been denounced by his own
sister and given her the lie, was really capable of anything.
He escaped, for the time being, from punishment of his
sins and treacheries, and went on to Agincourt, where he
was one of the very few Englishmen of rank who fell. He
was knocked down by a stroke from the battle-axe of the
gallant Duke d'Alencon, who had cut his way to the Royal
standard and to Henry V himself. The Duke of York was
not wounded by the blow, but, being fat, was smothered
inside his armour in the press : ' smouldered to death,' says
the chronicler, ' by much hete and thronggidd.' He well
deserved this end for his base betrayal of the Hollands.

After these executions, Henry V crossed the Channel
with about 30,000 men and besieged Harfleur, which surrendered on September 22 ; then marched for Calais with
9000 men, and on his way won the Battle of Agincourt.
Holland took a leading part in the siege of Harfleur, but it
does not appear whether he was with that division of the
army which won that glorious victory.

In the autumn of this year the young Earl of Huntingdon
was made a Knight of the Garter, filling, curiously enough,
the vacancy caused by the death of Thomas, Earl of Arundel
—the same who, as a vindictive boy, had presided over the
execution of Huntingdon's father, fifteen years earlier,
and had made that triumphant entry into London preceded
by the head of his foe. The following year, 1416, there was
a banquet of the Order at Windsor—famous because it was
honoured by the presence of Sigismund, the Holy Roman
Emperor, who was installed as a knight. The Emperor
landed at Dover on May 1, and on the 2nd was escorted
by 800 men of his own Imperial cavalry and many great

English lords, of whom Huntingdon was one, to Canterbury, and thence by short stages in four days along the Roman road to London, there to meet the victor of Agincourt.

In the same summer of 1416, John Holland had a commission at sea with the Duke of Bedford, Henry's brother, and they relieved Harfleur, which was being besieged by the French. In 1417, the Earl of Huntingdon, as Holland had now formally become, was sent by the King to clear the Channel of hostile ships before the second expedition made the passage.

'The King,' says the chronicler, 'before he crossed over himself, sent the Earl of Huntingdon to search and scour the seas. The lusty Earl, called John Holland (son to the Earl of Huntingdon, otherwise Duke of Exeter, beheaded in the time of Henry IV, and cousin to the King), with a great many ships, searched the sea from the one coast to the other, and in conclusion encountered with nine of those great carracks of Genoa, the which the Lord Jacques the Bastard had retained to serve the French King, and set on them sharply.'

After a running fight for most of a summer's day, three of the carracks and the Lord Jacques himself were captured, three were bulged in and left as wrecks, and three got away. Huntingdon then returned to Southampton, where he found the King, who thanked him greatly. In 1418, Huntingdon commanded one side of the English investing army at the long siege of Rouen. The city was reduced by famine to surrender on January 16, 1419. Later in that year, in May, he was with Henry during the negotiations with the French near Meulan, on the Seine. In July he took part in the capture of Pontoise. Then he was Governor of Gournai, in Normandy, and ravaged the country thereabouts, 'with fire and sword.' In 1420 he besieged Clermont unsuccessfully and ravaged those regions also. In the same year he was in a battle near Mons, in which the French were severely defeated. The agreement was now made with the French King by which Henry V was to marry his daughter Catharine, and be the next heir to the Kingdom of France, the Dauphin being set aside. In December 1420, Henry entered Paris in state with the King of France. The two kings rode in from Corbeuil side by side. They were immediately followed by Henry's brothers, the Dukes of Clarence and Bedford. In the next group rode John Holland, Earl of Huntingdon, first cousin of the King of England. Then came a long retinue of English and French lords. Philip, Duke of Burgundy, Henry's powerful ally, and the richest Prince in Europe, rode at the head of a splendid procession of his own. They were met at the gate by representative citizens of Paris, and passed through streets bright with tapestry and rich with cloths of divers colours. Then met them a procession of clergy, and conducted the two kings to Notre Dame, where they made their orisons before the High Altar. Wine flowed night and day in the streets, and the people, freed, as they vainly thought, from the horrors and privations of war, shouted for joy. Are not all these things related in the chronicles of Jean de Wavrin, seigneur of Forestel, of Enguerrand de Monstrelet, and others ?

The Dauphin and his party continued to resist the transfer of the succession to the Crown of France. In 1421 the Earl of Huntingdon was in the Angevin country with a force commanded by the Duke of Clarence, his own maternal first cousin, and the husband of his first cousin, Margaret Holland, and brother of Henry V. On March 22, the English —a fashionable and aristocratic company of warriors—were chasing a mixed force of French led by the Seigneur de la Fayette, and 5000 Scottish allies led by the Earl of Buchan. The English leaders and horsemen, pressing too rapidly upon their retreating foes, left their indispensable bowmen behind, and got into marshy ground by a river. Then the enemy, seeing their advantage in numbers and position, and the absence of the dreaded archers, suddenly turned and assailed them. Twelve hundred English were killed, among them the Duke of Clarence; and 300 were taken prisoners, among them the Earl of Huntingdon and his cousin, the Earl of Somerset. It was a rich haul for the French and Scots. It was, financially, unlucky for them that Clarence was killed, not taken. He was killed as he was trying to remount his horse after a fall, with a spear, by John Swinton, a Scot, and he had round 'his helmet a circlet of precious stones,' which the Scot took, and sold to John Steward at Derby for 1000 angels. Huntingdon ransomed himself, but the price which he had to pay impaired his fortune, and, at a later date, he applied for a grant from the Crown on this account.

Henry V died at Vincennes on August 31, 1422, and Henry VI, at nine months old, became King of England and France under the recent treaty. The Duke of Bedford, his uncle, was made Regent or 'Protector' by Parliament, with a council to assist him. The Dauphin, Charles, on the other side, was proclaimed King of France at Poitiers, and so the war went on, with, at first, new successes for the English.

The Earl of Huntingdon, after his costly release, continued to flourish during the Regency. In 1430 he was retained to serve the Crown, with three knights, seventy-six men-at-arms, and 240 archers; crossed from Dover to Calais, and was sent with a force, by the Duke of Bedford commanding in France, to assist the Burgundians at the siege of Compiègne. It was during this siege, before Huntingdon's arrival, that the wondrous maid, Joan of Arc, was captured during a sortie from the gates.

The Earls of Huntingdon and Arundel commanded the English reinforcements—about 2000 in number. In October, 4000 French advanced in order to revictual the town. The Burgundian-English besiegers marched three miles to meet them, and there was some fighting in the forest, towards the old castle of Pierrefonds. The French found a way into the town with provisions, and they made a successful sortie upon the siege works of their enemy. The English and Burgundians quarrelled, and Huntingdon and Arundel marched away declaring that the pay to the English promised by the Burgundians was in long arrear. Consequently the Burgundians, in face of the increased French, had to retire also, and so much in haste that they left their valuable siege artillery behind. In the following year, 1431, the Earl of Huntingdon was doubtless present when the nine-year-old boy, Henry VI, was crowned King of France by Cardinal Beaufort in Notre Dame in Paris. The affair was not a success, and the Parisians grumbled much that the festivities were so meagre and badly arranged.

The failure of the long siege of Compiègne was, after Orléans and Rheims, the most important sign of the turn of the tide against the English-Burgundian allies in France. The Burgundians grew weary of endless war, and the English had a series of small disasters and loss of places. In 1435 the Earl of Huntingdon was one of the English Ambassadors sent to the Court of Philip, Duke of Burgundy, at Arras, to assist at the negotiations for peace which were then taking place between the Burgundians and the French. In order to maintain his dignity and to impress the foreigners, Huntingdon obtained licence from the Crown to carry with him gold, silver, plate, and jewels, twenty-four pieces of woollen cloth, and other things to the value of £6000. The other members of the Embassy were Cardinal Beaufort,

Bishop of Winchester, the Archbishop of York,[1] the Bishop of St. Davids, the Earl of Suffolk, William Lyndewoode, Lord Privy Seal, and four others. Their instructions were to offer the French all France south of the Loire, except Gascony and Guyenne, and, if they would not accept this, to offer next that the French should retain all that they actually possessed, and nothing more.

This congress, held at Arras from July to September 1485, was a very great affair. It had been initiated by the Pope and the Council then sitting at Bale, who were anxious, as the Church authorities had been throughout these long wars, to terminate the miseries and impoverishment of France, and to re-unite Christian Princes against the ever-advancing Turks who threatened Constantinople both from the south and the north. The Papal Legation arrived towards the end of July at Arras, attended by fifty horse. The great Duke Philip rode into his good town of Arras at the head of a glittering cavalcade of 800 horse. The Duchess and her son arrived another day, well attended by valiant knights and lovely Burgundian ladies. The English Embassy brought 500 horse. On July 31, arrived the French Ambassadors with 900 horse. There were also diplomatic agents from the Emperor of the West, and from Sicily, Spain, Portugal, Denmark, Poland, and the Italian Republics. It was the first great European peace conference.

Jean la Fére, the Burgundian chronicler, was there—enjoying himself very much.

'On this day,' he says, 'there entered into the said town of Arras, the Bishop of Liége, accompanied by noble knights, squires, gentlemen, and others, richly apparelled, to the number of 246 horse [all white horses, says another

---

[1] This Archbishop was John Kemp, of the Kemps of Olantigh in Kent. He was afterwards Archbishop of Canterbury.

account], and went to the hotel of the Duke. On the same day the English Embassy entered the town of Arras, for which cause the Duke mounted on horseback to go and meet them very nobly accompanied by his servants, counts, barons, knights, and squires. Likewise there assembled all the Cardinals, and all the Archbishops and Bishops, who were in the said town, and went to meet the said Embassy. In which Embassy were the Cardinal of Winchester, the Count of Suffolk, the Count of Huntingdon, and several others who came from the Kingdom of England.[1] All the said company accompanied them as far as the Church of Notre Dame in the City, where the said Cardinals and Lords of England were lodged. And there great honours and reverences were made, and then they separated. The Cardinal of Winchester and the Count of Huntingdon were nobly accompanied by noble barons, knights, and squires, very richly and notably apparelled and mounted, to the number of 500 horse or thereabouts.'

The Duke of Burgundy, three or four days later, gave a dinner at his hotel—' a very noble dinner,' says Jean la Fére—' to which were invited the noble lords of England, the ambassadors. At the high table sat, in this order, the Archbishop of York, the Cardinal of Winchester, the Duke, the Duke of Guelders, the Bishop of Liége, the Duke of Vuillon, the Count of Suffolk, the Count of Huntingdon ; and then at the other tables, according to their rank, the noble barons, knights, and squires,' and among them, Jean le Fére, making his notes. ' How they were served,' he adds,

---

[1] Jean la Fére may have mistaken the Archbishop of York for the Cardinal-Bishop of Winchester, since it seems that the latter did not arrive till later, towards the end of August   According to Enguerrand de Monstrelet, the Earl of Huntingdon did not come at first, but with the Cardinal. It was difficult to be accurate in those things when there were no morning newspapers or printed lists at banquets. See Barante, *Ducs de Bourgogne*, vol 1 p 560, and Sir James Ramsay, *Lancaster and York*.

'need not be asked, for the Duke, while he lived, was a treasure of honour.'

From July to September, 480 years ago, the ancient town of Arras overflowed with rich attire, beauty, gallantry, love-making, and diplomacy. The proceedings were enlivened by jousts and dancing. The congress met for business on August 31, in the hall of the Abbey of St. Waast, the Cardinal of Santa Croce presiding in the name of the Pope. The French offered that if the English would renounce their claim to the French throne, and give up Paris and other possessions, they should be allowed to keep Aquitaine. Afterwards they offered to cede also the dioceses of Avranches, Bayeux, and Evreux in Normandy, if the English would also release without ransom their princely captive, Charles, the poetic Duke of Orléans. The crisis came in the last week of August and the first of September, after the arrival of Cardinal Beaufort, who was seen one day arguing so hotly with the Duke of Burgundy that perspiration streamed down his face. The final offer of the English was that each side should retain the possessions which they actually held. This the French refused, and the English Embassy left Arras on September 6. Negotiations, however, went on between the French and Burgundians, and led to a formal treaty of peace between them, disastrous to the English, who were not able to hold their possessions in France without allies. On April 10 in the following year (1436) they were badly defeated at St. Denis, and, three days later, lost Paris under the combined effect of an assault from without the city and a popular rising from within. The Parisians were delighted to be rid of them. According to a French chronicler, the people said : ' Ah ! one could see the English were not in France to stay. They have never been seen to sow a field of wheat, or build a house ; they destroyed their lodgings without ever thinking of repairing them. No one but their Regent, the Duke of Bedford, cared for making buildings and giving work to the poor. He was worth more than them, and would have wished for peace, but the natural character of these English is always to make war with their neighbours ; also they all come to a bad end ; and, thank God, more than 70,000 of them have already died in France.' Enguerrand de Monstrelet, writing of the final campaign of Charles VII, says : ' It was evident that Heaven was against the English, and they were deserving of it ; for it is true that they have always encroached on their neighbours, as well in the Kingdom of France, as in Scotland, Ireland, Wales, and elsewhere. Many violences have been most unjustly done by them.' Within fifteen years from the treaty at Arras, the English had lost every place they had ever held in France, except Calais. Cardinal Beaufort would have done far better to close with the offer of Aquitaine and a handsome slice of Normandy.[1] But a curse was now upon the English.

In 1436 Huntingdon was joined in a commission with the Earl of Northumberland to guard the ' east and west borders ' towards Scotland. He was also made Lord High Admiral of England and Lieutenant of Aquitaine. In 1438 he was retained to serve the King in Guyenne for six years, with sixteen knights, 280 men-at-arms, and 2000 archers. The English in Guyenne were much harassed by soldiers of fortune, who collected ' companies ' and were in pay of the French King or lived on the country. One day Lord Huntingdon found himself in presence of such a force captained by Rodrigue de Villandrando, son of a poor escudero, or squire, near Valladolid, who had become a famous partisan

---

[1] This Cardinal was a very mundane prelate, and the terrible chief responsibility for the burning of Joan of Arc, now Beata, rests on him. He might well, as he did, order to be written on his tomb in Winchester Cathedral : ' Tribularer si nescierem misericordias tuas ' (' I should be troubled did I not know Thy mercies ').

leader. Huntingdon wished to see him—curious to know what kind of man it was who had raised himself from a low estate to power and glory—and invited him to an interview at a place between the two armies on the banks of a stream called the Leyre. The Spaniard rode up to the spot.

'I wished to see you in person,' said Huntingdon, 'since the fates have brought us together here. Will it please you to eat a few mouthfuls of bread and drink a cup or two of wine with me? And after that, the battle will fare as it please God and my lord St. George.'

But the Captain Rodrigue replied: 'If that is all you wish, it is certain that I will not do so, for, should fortune make us encounter in this fight, I should lose a great part of the anger I ought to have in fighting. I should strike my sword less fiercely against thine, remembering that I had eaten bread with thee.'

Lord Huntingdon, according to the Spanish chronicler, was so much struck by these words and by the look of the speaker, that, because of them, and also because his force held the worse position, he decided not to fight on that occasion, although superior in numbers, saying, according to the Spanish chronicler: 'One had best not fight with a Spanish head at the time of its fury.' ('Non es de pelear con cabeza espanola en tiempo de su yra.') This invitation to a drink before battle seems to have been a practice of the sportsman-like English. Even the great Duke of Bedford sent a herald with a like invitation to the Franco-Scottish commander, Douglas, before the Battle of Verneuil. But the serious Spaniard regarded fighting as more of a business and less of a game than did the English.[1]

In 1441 Huntingdon presented a petition to the King

---

[1] This account is taken from the Spanish chronicler Hernando del Pulgar, quoted in the *Rodrigue* of M. Quicherat. The Spanish account says that the Englishman was Talbot, but M. Quicherat shows by dates that this was an error and that it must have been Huntingdon.

stating that the lands which King Richard had granted to his father to maintain his dignity as Earl were then worth 2000 marks a year, but now only 500, which shows that these estates, or some of them, had long ago been restored after confiscation. Also that he had been put to heavy expense for his ransom when taken prisoner in France in 1421 on the King's service. He was accordingly given 500 marks a year, charged on the port revenues of London, Bristol, and Hull. In the same year he was made one of a Royal Commission, whose reference was to inquire ' of all manner of treason and sorceries which might be hurtful to the King's person.'

The Earl of Huntingdon was, in politics, opposed to his half-uncle, the haughty Cardinal Beaufort. Humphrey, Duke of Gloucester, addressed in 1440 a protest to the King in which, amongst other complaints against the Cardinal, he alleged that the Cardinal and the Archbishop of York ' have had and have the governance of your Highness, which none of your true liegemen ought to usurp, nor take upon them, and have also estranged from your Highness, me your sole uncle, my cousin of York, my cousin of Huntingdon, and many other lords of your kin, to have knowledge of any great matter that might touch your high estate.' [1]

On January 6, 1443, John Holland, Earl of Huntingdon, attained what was, probably, the main object of his ambition. He was created Duke of Exeter, and so recovered the title which his father had borne from 1397 to 1399. The warrant gave him the privilege that he and his heirs male should ' have place and seat in all parliaments and councils ' next after the Duke of York and his heirs male. In 1446, the Duke of Exeter was made Lord High Admiral for life, and

---

[1] Lord Bacon calls this Cardinal Beaufort ' so great a man both for birth, parts of nature, riches, spirit, and place as none before him had ever had the like; for he was both Cardinal, Legate, and Chancellor of England.'

in 1447, Constable of the Tower of London, which was the last of the numerous high appointments in his very successful career.

The Duke of Exeter was thrice married, in each case to a widow. His first wife was Anne, widow of the Edmund Mortimer, Earl of March, who had died young without children, the son of Roger, Earl of March, and his wife, Alianora Holland. Anne was the daughter of Edmund, Earl of Stafford, the younger brother of that Ralph Stafford, whom John Holland, first Earl of Huntingdon had killed in a fit of passion at Beverley. Thus the second John Holland married the niece of his father's victim. By her he had a son named Henry Holland, who became third Duke of Exeter, in whose unhappy fate, as in that of the third Earl of Kent, who also married a Stafford, the superstitious might have seen a curse in this alliance between Staffords and Hollands.[1]

Anne's mother was a daughter of Thomas Plantagenet, Duke of Gloucester; so that Anne was a cousin of Henry V She died in 1432. Shortly afterwards, Huntingdon married Beatrice, widow of Thomas, Earl of Arundel—that same Earl whom the first John Holland had held in custody as a boy, and who had presided at his execution. Beatrice was an illegitimate, or perhaps legitimated, daughter of John I, King of Portugal, by Donna Agnese Perez. By her, Exeter had a daughter called Anne, who married first, John, Lord Nevill, eldest son of the first Earl of Westmorland, who died before his father, and secondly Sir John Nevill, the uncle of her first husband. Sir John was slain

---

[1] The Staffords were an unlucky race. They took first the Lancastrian and then the Yorkist side. They became at this time Dukes of Buckingham, an ill-fated title whether borne by them or afterwards by the Villiers. The first Duke of Buckingham was put to death by Richard III, and the second Duke by Henry VIII. The Staffords came to an obscure and melancholy end in the seventeenth century, having been great people since the Norman conquest.

at Towton battle in 1461, leaving, by Anne Holland, a son, Ralph, who became third Earl of Westmorland. From him descended the Nevill Earls of Westmorland down to Earl Charles, who took part in the Catholic rising against Queen Elizabeth in 1570, was attainted and lost his earldom. He died in France, in exile, in 1584, leaving only daughters.

Beatrice, Countess of Huntingdon, died at Bordeaux on October 23, 1439, and was buried by her first husband at Arundel. Huntingdon then married, lastly, Anne, widow of Sir John Fitz Lewis, and, before that, widow of Sir Richard Hankford. She was daughter of John Montacute, third Earl of Salisbury, who married Eleanor Holland of the Kent line, and was slain at Orléans. The Duke of Exeter left no children by his third wife, and had only the two legitimate children, Henry and Anne, already mentioned. But he had two bastard sons, William and Thomas, to each of whom he left an annuity of £40 by his will.

The Duke of Exeter died on August 5, 1447, at the age of fifty-three. He was the most long lived, the most successful, and the most prudent of his fortunate-unfortunate line. The chronicler, Thomas of Elmham, calls him ' circumspectae probitatis miles nobilissimus, militaris industriae multiplici fulgore coruscans, leonini pectoris magnanimitate praeful-gidus.' The style is flamboyant, like that of the co-temporary architecture, but it expresses the fact that this Holland was a cool-headed, trustworthy, and brave soldier, who deserved his rewards. He was happy in the era of his active career lying between the storms of the reign of Richard II and the Wars of the Roses, and, coinciding with energy turned to foreign war, and with the duration of English Empire in France.

By his will, dated July 16, 1447, he directed his body to be buried in a chapel of the Church of St. Catharine, beside the Tower of London, at the north end of the High Altar, in a tomb there ordained for him and Anne, his first wife, as also for his sister Constance, and Anne, his other wife, then living. He bequeathed to the High Altar of the said church a cup of byril garnished with gold, hearts, and precious stones, to use for the Sacrament; also a chalice of gold, with the whole furniture of his chapel. And he appointed that another chalice, two candlesticks of silver, with two pair of vestments, a Mass-book, a pax-bred, and a pair of cruets of silver should be delivered to that little chapel, where he so intended to be buried with his wife and sister, for the priests that should celebrate divine service therein, and pray for their souls. To the priest and clerks, and other of the House of St. Catharine, for their great labour and observance on the day of his obit, and the day of his burying, he bequeathed forty marks, ordaining that four honest and cunning priests should be provided, yearly and perpetually, to pray for his soul in the said chapel, and for the soul of Anne, his wife, the soul of his sister Constance, and the soul of Anne, his present wife, when she should pass out of this world, and for the souls of all his progenitors. To his daughter, Anne, he bequeathed his white bed with popinjays, &c.—the same solemn white bed, perhaps, which John of Gaunt in his will bequeathed to his daughter Elizabeth, Duchess of Exeter.

The Duke of Exeter's third wife, Anne Montacute, lived until the year 1457. In her will, made April 20 that year, may be discerned a touch of the coming change of religion in England, towards which Lord Salisbury, her father, had inclined. She bequeathed her body to be buried in the same chapel, ' expressly forbidding her executors from making any great feast, or having a solemn hearse or any costly lights, or largess of liveries, according to the glory or vain pomp of the world, at her funeral ; but only to the worship of. God after the discretion of Mr. John Pynchebeke, doctor of divinity, and one of her executors.' She bequeathed six and eightpence to the master of St. Catharine if he were present at the Dirige and Mass on the day of her burial, and made some small bequests to the priests, sisters, and bedesmen of that college. Her executors were ' to find an honest priest to say Mass, to pray for her soul, her lord's soul, and all Christian souls in the said chapel for seven years after her decease, for doing which he should have yearly twelve marks; and to say daily, Placebo, Dirige, and Mass, when so disposed.'

The history of this Church of St. Catharine's by the Tower is curious. The Hospital and Church of St. Catharine was founded by Mathilda, the queen of King Stephen. It was to be the collegiate home of certain religious brethren and sisters, who were to celebrate divine offices and pray for souls, and the patronage and control was always to be in the hands of the reigning Queen of England. Philippa, queen of Edward III, was a great benefactress, and added to the endowments. Owing to this royal patronage, the Hospital escaped the storm of the Reformation. It was, indeed, at first suppressed, but placed upon a new charter by Queen Elizabeth. The Duke of Exeter's byril cup and golden chalice vanished in those days of plunder. The church was untouched by the Fire of London in 1666. In 1825 it was necessary to remove the Church and Hospital buildings in order to make the London docks. New buildings and a new chapel were erected facing Regent's Park, near Gloucester Gate, and the tomb of John Holland, Duke of Exeter, was with great care and with much cost removed and set up against the north-eastern corner of this chapel. It is a strikingly fine monument, in the Late Pointed style, highly decorated with carvings of angels and strange beasts, and with coloured devices. Recumbent on the monument are the figures of the Duke of Exeter, and two noble-looking ladies, all in perfect preservation, and evidently most

faithful representations from life. The figure of the Duke lies on the outside of the table, and those of the two ladies on his left hand. All these figures wear coronets. Three leaden coffins were removed with the monument from St. Catharine's by the Tower.

It is to be hoped that his skull was replaced in the coffin before it was removed. A contemporary journalistic account says : ' We were yesterday led to examine a tomb in the very ancient church of St. Catharine, which workmen are now pulling to pieces for the purpose of forming a new dock. It was the tomb of John, Duke of Exeter, who was, we believe, cousin to Henry V. His skull is now in the possession of the surveyor. The cranium is small and retiring, which those who profess to be learned in such matters say is evidence of royalty and legitimacy, as well as of valour. The teeth are remarkably perfect.' [1] So may a great Duke's skull some day be handed round among workmen, and come into possession of a surveyor.

The Duke of Exeter's will contemplated that he, his sister, and his first and third wives, should be buried under the same monument, his second wife having already been buried by her first husband at Arundel. But his sister was buried elsewhere, the Lady Constance Holland, who married first the Earl Marshal, commonly called second Duke of Norfolk, who was beheaded at York with Archbishop Scrope, in 1405, for conspiring against Henry IV, and afterwards she married Lord Grey of Ruthin. The two dames represented on the tomb are the Duke's first wife, Anne Stafford, and his third wife, Lady Anne Montacute.

[1] The figure of the Duke on the tomb does not show a small and retiring cranium at all, but a fine straight forehead. Possibly the skull in question belonged to one of his wives.

CHAPTER IX

Richard Plantagenet of York :

> Let him that is a true-born gentleman,
> And stands upon the honour of his birth,
> If he suppose that I have pleaded truth,
> From off this brier pluck a white rose with me.

Somerset :

> Let him that is no coward, nor no flatterer,
> But dare maintain the party of the truth,
> Pluck a red rose from off this thorn with me.
>> SHAKESPEARE, *Henry VI*, Pt. 1. Act II.

HENRY HOLLAND was born in the Tower of London on June 27, 1430. We know something of his baptism from the evidence taken by the Inquisition made when he came of age. His aunt, the Lady Constance, widow of the Earl Marshal, Duke of Norfolk, carried him in her arms from the Tower to 'Cold Harbour,' and thence in a barge to St. Stephen's, Westminster, where he was christened. This house, called ' Cold Harbour,' is shown in a picture of London viewed from the south side, made in 1616, and is there underwritten 'Cole Harbour.' A large and lofty house it was, of several stories, with gables and small irregular windows, standing on the bank of the river, near All Hallows Lane, just east of the existing Cannon Street railway bridge. Stow, in his history of London, written at the end of the seventeenth century spells it ' Coal Harbour,' and

gives its history in much detail. In the reign of Edward II
the house, then spelled ' Cold Harbrough,' belonged to
Sir John Abel, and after passing through other hands was,
in 1397, the town house of John Holland, Earl of Huntingdon. It was ' the fair and stately house behind All Hallows
Church in Thames Street,' where Richard II and his friends
dined with John Holland before the eventful ride to Pleshy.
Cold Harbour continued to be the town house of the Hollands of Huntingdon and Exeter, until this branch of the
race ended in the Wars of the Roses. At one time, in the
sixteenth century, it belonged to the Bishops of Durham,
but the Crown deprived Bishop Tunstal of it in 1553, and
gave it to the Earl of Shrewsbury. In the following century
the then Earl of Shrewsbury—the house having fallen into
decay and the situation being no longer in fashion—' took
it down, and in the place thereof built a great number of
small tenements, now let out ' (says Stow) ' for great
rents to people of all sorts.' The site is now covered with
warehouses, and, although there are plenty of barges,
none of them ever convey princely babes to fashionable
baptisms.

Little is known of Henry Holland's further life until
the Wars of the Roses began. He was married to Anne,
daughter of the Duke of York, and sister to the Princes
who afterwards became Edward IV and Richard III. A
poet of the day, in a long account of that family, wrote:

> To the Duke of Excestre Anne married is,
> In her tender youth.

He could not, like his ancestors for three generations, win
early distinction in the wars in France, for by the time he
was twenty-one, the English had been driven out of France.
Their last hold on Normandy was lost in 1450, and they
were expelled from their most ancient possession, Bordeaux,

in 1453. Now they held not an acre oversea beyond Calais and its environs. Such was the end of their hundred years' effort to annex France, and of all the misery thereby caused. They now turned fierce swords against each other.

In 1449, although but nineteen, the Duke of Exeter had, like his father before him, become Lord High Admiral. In this capacity he aided the Opposition Lords, Warwick and Salisbury, against the dominant Earl of Suffolk, a favourite of the beautiful and vigorous young Queen, Margaret of Anjou. When Suffolk was trying to escape to France, Exeter placed some ships of war at the disposition of the confederate lords. Suffolk was caught at sea and rudely beheaded by sailors of a barque called the 'Nicholas of the Tower,' off Dover. A few years later, Exeter appeared as a strong Lancastrian, and remained on that side till his death, although his wife was a lady of the House of York.

Now began the Wars of the Roses, which ruined so many great families, and, among them, the House of Holland. In 1453 when the Duke of Exeter—who was then, barring the York claim, heir-presumptive to the Crown—was in his twenty-fourth year, Queen Margaret bore on October 13, seven years after her marriage, a son, who was named Edward. The rumour spread that he was not really Henry's son, and his birth brought to a head the dormant question of the superior claim of the York family to the throne. The Lancastrians were led by the Duke of Somerset, the son of Margaret Holland, and grandson of John of Gaunt by the Katherine Swynford amour. At the close of 1453 the quarrel came to a crisis; Somerset was sent to the Tower, and soon afterwards King Henry having fallen into an imbecile condition, Parliament declared Richard, Duke of York, Protector of the Kingdom. In 1454 Ralph Lord Cromwell 'demanded in full Parliament the surety of the peace of the Duke of York against Henry Duke of Exeter, the which was granted.' The Lancastrian nobles gathered round the Queen and in a few months she recovered power.   Early in 1454 the Duke of Exeter was in the north, acting on her behalf.   John Studeley wrote to the Pastons in Norfolk on January 19, 1454 : ' Item, the Duke of Exeter, in his own person, hath been at Tuxforth and Doncaster in the north country, and there the Lord Egremont met him, and the two been sworn together, and the Duke is come home again.'   Somerset was set free, but the Duke of York, popular in the south, raised his standard and, on April 22, 1454, the Red Rose and the White fought in the streets and suburbs of St. Albans.   The Duke of Somerset was slain and his followers defeated.   Exeter is not named as having been in this action.   On July 24 the Privy Council charged the Duke of York to keep the Duke of Exeter in custody in Pomfret Castle.   In 1456 there was reaction, and the Duke of York had to resign the Protectorship.   In January 1458, a conference between the high opposing nobles was held in London, and they arrived from the provinces attended by great armed retinues.   The new Duke of Somerset and the Duke of Exeter, with 800 followers lodged outside Temple Bar and in Holborn.   On March 27 there was what the chronicler Fabian calls ' a dissimulated Loveday.'   The King and Queen wearing crowns and royal robes attended by all the prelates and peers, walked in solemn state to St. Paul's Cathedral.   The great lords were arranged in antagonistic couples.   The Duke of Somerset and his foe the Earl of Salisbury headed the procession, and next came Henry Holland, Duke of Exeter, and his cousin and enemy, Richard Nevill, Earl of Warwick.   Behind the King, who walked alone, came the Duke of York holding Queen Margaret by the hand, which must have been a great trial to her.   A poet of the time, foolishly happy, wrote in the unromantic and prosaic style of south-English folk-bards of all times :

> Our sovereign lord, God, keep alway !
> And the Queen and Archbishop of Canterbury,
> And other that have laboured to make this loveday,
> O God ! Preserve them, we pray heartily,
> And London for them full diligently ;
> Rejoice England ! In concord and unity.

This loveless love lasted not long. Almost the same day there was an affray in the London streets between Warwick's men and the King's. The Duke of Exeter had already been alienated because his hereditary command of the fleet had been taken away as part of the arrangement and given to the Earl of Warwick. Botomer, in his letter of February 1, 1458, to the Pastons, says : ' The Duke of Exeter hath taken great displeasure that my Lord Warwick occupieth his office, and taketh the charge of the keeping of the sea from him.' The Duke was inadequately appeased by the grant of £1000 from the exchequer, and henceforward was a most unswerving foe to the Yorkists, married though he was to Anne, daughter of Richard Duke of York.

Exeter's deposition from command at sea was partly a concession to popular feeling, for in the preceding year, 1457, he had failed to protect the Channel Coast from French raids, under the able Pierre de Brézé, Seneschal of Normandy, who had sacked Sandwich in Kent and burned Fowey in Cornwall.

Civil dissensions came to a new crisis in 1459. Queen Margaret's friends raised a force in loyal Cheshire and Lancashire. The Duke of Exeter, Lord Beaumont, and others took the field, according to the well-informed and trustworthy contemporary writer, Jean de Wavrin, at the head of

15,000 or 16,000 men, all horse. On the other side, the Earl of Salisbury and his son Richard, Earl of Warwick, raised a more democratic force. Warwick was especially successful in recruiting because he knew how to address the commoners in familiar and persuasive language. Their little army consisted of about 6000 or 7000 men, among whom there were only twenty-five knights, and no mounted men-at-arms. It was a plebeian force of archers. The two Earls came across the aristocratic army led by Exeter and Beaumont, at Blore Heath, on the borders of Derbyshire and Lancashire, on April 29, 1459. Their men took up a good position, entrenched and staked themselves in, and awaited attack. The Duke of Exeter charged with his division of horse, and was met by so vigorous an arrow fire that between five and six hundred of his men were killed or wounded. He withdrew out of range, charged again, and lost another hundred men. Lord Beaumont then dismounted his division—about four thousand in number—and advanced against the Yorkist position on foot, and fought for half an hour, but had the worst of it. One of his knights, who led five hundred men, was so much disgusted that Exeter's horse did not charge a third time, as he had expected, that he began to fight on the side of the Warwickers. In the end, the Lancastrians had lost Lord Audley, killed, and Lord Dudley, captured, and over two thousand men, and the Yorkists less than a hundred, and the latter retained possession of the field. It was the old story of the wars in France—the superiority of English bowmen over mounted chivalry.

The Duke of York with Salisbury and Warwick, then raised the rebel standard at Worcester. A royal army, with the King, advanced against them and pursued them to Ludlow, where the Yorkist force dissolved. In November 1459, the King held a Parliament at Coventry, to which the

Duke of Exeter was summoned as leading peer, and an Act of Attainder was passed against the Duke of York and his chief allies.

In January 1460 the Duke of Exeter was at York. In the French Records there is this curiously spelt document. ' The yere of Our Lord, MCCCCLX, the XX day of Janvier at the City of York, in the presence of the most excellente Princess Margaret, Queen of England and of Ffrance and Lady of Ireland, by the lords whose names were underwritten hit was graunted and promysed that they shal labour by alle moyennes resonable witoute inconvenience to the moost high and migghty Prince Henry VI, King of England and of France and Lord of Ireland, thaire souverain lord that suche articles as were commoved at the College of Lyncluden in the royaulme of Scotland, the Vth day of the saide moneth, the yere above said, that it may please his grace they may take gude and effectual conclusion. Signé, Excester, Somerset, W. Byschof of Carlyls, Northumberland, Westmorcland, Devonshire, John Coventry, Byschof Nevyll, H. Fitzhugh, Roos, Thomas Seymour, H. Dacre.'

After the Yorkist dispersal at Ludlow, the Duke of York went to Ireland, and the Earl of Warwick to France, where he held possession of Calais against the Duke of Somerset, who lay outside the walls and tried in vain to recover the town. Warwick had some ships, including a large one which he obtained by descent on Sandwich Haven, and in the spring of 1460 sailed with his little fleet to Ireland to visit the Duke of York and concert a campaign. It was agreed that the Duke should land in the north, and the Earl in Kent. Warwick then returned towards Calais.

The Duke of Exeter—who had been on business at York at the end of January—now again High Admiral, sailed west from Sandwich in Kent, with four great ' carracks '—one of which, called the *Grace Dieu*, was his Admiral ship—and ten smaller 'caravel' vessels. He swore a vow that Warwick, his enterprising cousin, should never get back to Calais. Off the Devon coast he came in sight of Warwick's numerically inferior squadron, and wished to engage. The wind was blowing from the south or south-west, and Warwick got to windward of Exeter. The Earl called together his captains and asked them if they would fight, and they replied joyously that they would like nothing better. Exeter got a different response from his captains. They refused to fight, turned about their ships, whether by his order or not, and ran with the wind into Dartmouth. Warwick did not pursue, but passed on up Channel to Calais, for he had only just enough provisions left to last that distance.

The chronicler, Grafton, says ' the captains of the Duke of Exeter's fleet murmured against him, and the mariners dispraised and disdained him, glad to hear of the Earl of Warwick's good success, by which occasion he neither would nor durst meddle once with the Earl's navy.' This, no doubt, is true. Warwick had done well at sea against the French as High Admiral, and had captured the hearts of the sailors; nor could Exeter compete with him either in wealth and power of largess, or in ingratiating manners. Warwick was a good, bluff orator, and threw his money about generously, and was the popular hero along the shores of Kent and Essex and the Thames, and in all the jolly southern and midland taverns.

The War of the Roses was essentially fought between the north and west on one side, and the south-east and midlands on the other; a line of division of feeling which seems to rest on something racial, for it reappears at the Reformation, in the Civil War of the seventeenth century, and, more or less, in modern general elections.[1] ' The Kentishmen,' says a good old chronicler, ' desired the Earl of Warwick's

---

[1] Sir Thomas Malory, a Lancastrian, says that they of London, Kent, Sussex, Surrey, Essex, Suffolk and Norfolk 'held the most part ' with the wicked Mordred, against King Arthur.

return and longed for his coming.' They had not long to
wait. Warwick landed, together with Edward, Earl of
March, at Sandwich on June 20, 1460, and was met by the
nobles and gentry of Kent and Archbishop Bourchier,
whom he had already seduced at Calais, and then went on
to London by Canterbury and Rochester. Thousands joined
from the towns, and gentlemen and yeomen poured in from
every side road to swell his army. Triumphantly he entered
London on July 2, cordially received by the City authorities,
and was reinforced by thousands of Londoners and Essex men.
He left the Tower blockaded, and marched up the North Road
—scene of most of the fighting in this war—to Northampton, where the Lancastrians with King Henry had assembled
some 50,000 men. Exeter, according to one account, was
with them. After some parleying, there was a great battle.
Warwick, with the Earl of March, assisted by the treachery
of Lord Grey de Ruthin, who deserted to the Yorkists at
the last moment, utterly defeated the Lancastrians. ' Ten
thousand tall Englishmen,' says the old Tudor chronicler,
Hall, ' were slain or drowned in attempting to pass the river,
and King Henry himself, left all lonely and disconsolate,
was taken prisoner.[1] Queen Margaret fled into Wales, and
there soon the Duke of Exeter came to join her.

Now the Duke of York, returning from Ireland, entered
London and claimed the throne by virtue of his descent
from Lionel, Duke of Clarence, through that Duke's daughter

---

[1] Jean de Wavrin, who was living at the time in Northern France, and had the
best sources of information, says that 12,000 Lancastrians were killed at Northampton. Why, then, should Professor Oman of Oxford, living in the twentieth
century, say, without giving his authority, that only 300 were killed here ? (See
Political History of England, vol. iv. p. 393) As to incidents in the Wars of
the Roses, the present writer has mainly followed Wavrin, who was at this time
completing his life and his chronicle. Internal evidence shows that he took
great pains to be accurate by getting information from Englishmen who had
been engaged in the affairs described, as also did his contemporary, de Comines.

Philippa, and the Mortimers.[1] This descent was superior to that of Henry VI, if descent through two female links were admitted ; nor could any Englishmen deny this female principle upon which the English kings still claimed the throne of France. The House of Lords had to choose between the Parliamentary title of Lancaster and the legitimist claim of York. They compromised by agreeing that Henry VI should nominally retain the crown for life, but that on his death it should devolve not upon Edward, his son, but upon Richard Plantagenet, Duke of York. The proud and powerful lords of the Red Rose—the Northumberlands, Dacres, Nevills, and Cliffords—were of another opinion ; and Queen Margaret and Henry Beaufort, Duke of Somerset, who had his father's death to avenge, were soon at the head of a new feudal army. They might have said in the words of Walter Scott's cavalier lay :

Go tell the bold traitors in London's proud town
That the spears of the North have encircled the Crown.

Henry Holland, Duke of Exeter, was with them—now thirty years old and a good warrior by land, whatever his failures by sea. He fought in the battle of Wakefield on December 30, 1460, where the Duke of York's southern army was gloriously defeated, himself slain, and his young son, Rutland, taken and killed by the fierce Lord Clifford. Exeter must have seen with mingled feelings the head of the Duke, father of his own young wife, scornfully adorned with a paper crown and spiked on a pole over a gate of York.

This was the hour of Margaret's triumphant revenge. Lord Bacon observes in his ' Historical Discourse ' that ' wha

---

[1] The reader remembers, of course, the great fact that Lionel, Duke of Clarence, was third son of Edward III, John Duke of Lancaster fourth son, and Edmund, Duke of York fifth son, and that the second son, William of Hatfield, died without issue.

the French could not effect by arms in their own field, they did upon English ground by a Feminine Spirit, which they sent over to England to be their Queen, and, in one civil war, shedding more English blood by the English sword than they could formerly do by all the men of France, were revenged upon England to the full at the Englishmen's own charge.'

Ill fortune has strangely attended English Kings who married French Princesses. Henry V died young, within three years from marriage ; Edward II, Richard II, Henry VI, and Charles I were dethroned and murdered.

The Duke of Exeter, ever loyal to the fierce Feminine Spirit, received a grant of the late Duke of York's Castle of Fotheringay, where his own wife, Anne, had been born in 1439. And now the victorious Margaret, with Somerset, Exeter, Northumberland, Clifford, and the rest, marched southward, and the northerners sacked every town on the road after they had crossed the Trent. On February 16, 1461, they defeated Warwick's army, which lay across the road at St. Albans, and threatened London. The opportunity was lost owing to the attitude of the Londoners, and to the hesitation of gentle and religious Henry. He had been brought out of the Tower to battle by the Yorkists, had been recaptured on the field by his wife, had been shocked at the treatment of St. Albans by the northern troops, and liked not the idea of a sack of London. Relieving forces arrived, and the Lancastrians returned to Yorkshire with their King and their plunder. Edward, now Duke of York, only twenty-one years old—a vigorous fighting man, extremely good-looking, affable, and immensely popular among the southern English—at the request of a deputation of select peers and prelates and London citizens, enthroned himself at Westminster on March 4, as Edward IV. Parliament was not consulted by these Legitimists. Meanwhile, the Red Rose chiefs collected a great host round the warrior

Queen and King Henry at York, and the White Rose King left London on March 12 and went north to fight them. When the armies met, the Lancastrians had about 60,000 men, and the Yorkists between 40,000 and 50,000, but the numerical inferiority of the southerners was compensated by better training and archery. They were more disciplined and were led by veteran officers who had learned war in France.

The first action was fought by Edward's vanguard on Saturday March 28, against a Lancastrian out-post, for the possession of the North Road Bridge, or Ferrybridge, across the river Aire. The Yorkists forced the passage by six o'clock that evening, and here the fierce and zealous Lord Clifford was killed by an arrow through his throat, together with some 3000 men on the two sides. Edward's army crossed the river all through that night, and ranged themselves in order of battle on the other side.

The main body of the northern host marched from York, when news came of Edward's approach, and took up a position eight miles south of that city and two miles north of the Aire River, along a ridge between the villages of Towton and Saxton. The great battle began about nine o'clock on the morning of Palm Sunday. The northerners advanced with banners flying, and loud shouts of ' King Henry.' Exeter and Somerset commanded on the right, and the Earl of Northumberland led the centre, where floated the royal standard ; the Earls of Dacre and Devon commanded on the left. The south wind blew a shower of snow-sleet in the faces of the Lancastrians and disconcerted the aim of their archers, while the shooting of the better-trained southern bowmen was all the more effective. The Lancastrian arrows fell short and stuck in the ground, impeding the advance of their men-at-arms. But a rush of 14,000 men, half of them Welsh, in Exeter's division, broke

Lord Fauconberg's horse and drove them in flight for miles. On the left, Dacre and Devon pressed hard on Warwick, who was himself wounded. But in the centre, young King Edward prevailed, after a long and fierce fight, over the main Lancastrian host.

'Here,' says the Burgundian writer, 'was the battle furious and the slaying great and pitiable, for the father spared not son, nor son the father.' At noon the Duke of Norfolk arrived with a fresh Yorkist contingent, and assailed the Lancastrians on their left flank. At the end of six hours of hacking and hewing, the Lancastrian centre and left, about three o'clock, were rolled up and driven into a little river (the Cock) to their right rear, and here was murderous killing and drowning. The stream ran, they say, so red with blood, that even the water of Wharfe River, into which it flowed two miles away, was discoloured. No fiercer, bloodier battle has ever been fought on English soil than that on this cold Palm Sunday, celebrated, as an old chronicler says, 'with lances instead of palms.' The Dukes of Exeter and Somerset escaped, probably because they led the 'victor vanward wing,' but Northumberland, Dacre, and Devon, and all the flower of the Red Rose nobles and gentlemen, and a vast multitude of their followers, perished this fatal day.

> ' Witness Aire's unhappy water,
> Where the ruthless Clifford fell,
> And where Wharfe ran red with slaughter
> On the day of Towton's field,
> Gathering in its guilty flood
> The carnage and the ill-spilt blood
> That forty thousand lives could yield.
> Cressy was to this but sport,
> Poitiers but a pageant vain,
> And the work of Agincourt
> Only like a tournament.' [1]

[1] Robert Southey.

This horrible disaster was, the Burgundian chronicler thinks, just retribution for the treason by which Henry IV, sixty-two years earlier, had deprived Richard II of the throne, and caused him to be murdered ; for, he remarks, ' Chose mal acquise ne peult avoir longue duree.'

William Paston, writing from London on April 4 to his brother, John Paston in Norfolk, says that ' a letter of credence,' sent by King Edward ' under his sign manual ' to his mother, the Duchess of York, had arrived at eleven o'clock that day, Easter Eve, and ' was seen and read by me, William Paston.' The letter was probably despatched from York on the Wednesday or Thursday, after the heralds had had time to count the dead and to identify their chiefs. It announced that the King had ' won the field,' and had upon the day after the battle ' been received into York with great solemnity and processions,' and that ' King Henry, the Queen, the Prince, the Duke of Somerset, Duke of Exeter, and Lord Roos be fled into Scotland and they be chased and followed.' This official despatch gave the names of the leading chiefs slain on both sides, and added that 28,000 other of the opponents had been slain, as ' numbered by the heralds.' [1] The number of the rank and file slain on the

---

[1] See Fenn's *Paston Letters*, vol. 1. p. 216. Croyland says that those who buried the dead said that, taking both sides, 33,000 fell. Wavrin, the well-informed contemporary, says that the Lancastrians had 60,000 men and that, on both sides, 36,000 were killed. Hearn's fragment says 33,000 ; Fabian, 30,000 ; Hall, for the two days' fighting, 36,776. The chronicler Stow (1631) says ' the whole number slain was accounted by some to be 33,000, but by others some 35,091 ; The precision of that last ' one ' is pleasing. The official figure for the Lancastrian dead, given in Edward's despatch, is probably about correct. But since there is this first-rate evidence that 28,000 Lancastrians were killed, why does Professor Oman say in the *Political History of England*, vol. iv. p 406, that there were only ' 15,000, or 20,000,' of them in the battle ? Has modern Oxford some inspired source of information better than that of the heralds who actually counted the dead ? There are good reasons for thinking that in the fifteenth century the population of many parts of rural England was much greater than it is now. Except at harvest time there would have been no great difficulty in raising two armies of 60,000 and 40,000 or 50,000 respectively for a four or five weeks' campaign.

Yorkist side is not stated in this despatch, but, according to other accounts, amounted to something like seven or eight thousand.

The Duke of Exeter, after his flight from Towton Field to Scotland, tried, with his usual ill success, to head a resistance in Wales. Henry Wyndesore, writing from London on October 14, 1461, to John Paston at Norwich, tells him as an item of public news that ' all the castles and holds, both in South Wales and North Wales, are given and yielded up into the King's hand ; and the Duke of Exeter and the Earl of Pembroke are fled and taken the mountains, and divers lords with great puissance are after them. And the most part of gentlemen and men of worship are come in to the King.' It is not known what happened to the hunted fugitives among the autumnal Welsh mountains.

Parliament now passed an Act to confirm Edward's right to the Crown, and Acts of Attainder against the Queen, the Dukes of Somerset and Exeter, the Earls of Northumberland, Devonshire, Wiltshire, and Pembroke, the Lords Beaumont, De Roos, Rougemont, Dacre, Nevill, and Hungerford, and a hundred and fifty knights, esquires, and priests. Their estates were confiscated and divided among the chiefs of the victorious faction. A number of slain Lancastrian lords were included in the Act, in order that the ' corruption of blood ' effected thereby might bar any future claim by their heirs against the new grantees.

The Dukes of Exeter and Somerset, however, seem to have succeeded in making, for the time, some kind of arrangement with the victorious Government, doing homage in exchange for part of their estates—at any rate, this was certainly the case with Somerset. But when undaunted Queen Margaret made her new attempt from France in the autumn of 1462, the Duke of Exeter joined her. Margaret was supplied by Louis XI of France with three ships and 800 Frenchmen under Pierre de Brézé, all landed in Northumberland, near Bamborough, on October 21. The Castles of Bamborough, Dunstanborough, and Alnwick, had already fallen into the hands of the northern Lancastrian lords. King Edward IV, an excellent soldier, marched north, and by January 6, 1463, had captured all three castles. Later in the year, Alnwick and Bamborough again fell into the hands of the Scot-aided Lancastrians. They besieged also Norham Castle, but Warwick and his brother, Lord Montague, relieved it. Margaret fled to Scotland, and eventually, in March 1464, went by sea to Sluys, thence to Bruges, where she lodged with the Carmelite nuns, and then to Barre in Lorraine. During these hunted wanderings, she and her son had fearsome adventures in the wilds of Northumberland, related by chroniclers, her abode in the generous robbers' cave, and so forth. She gave some account of them to the Duchess of Bourbon at St. Pol in the presence of Georges Chastellain, the herald of the Golden Fleece. Henry Holland, Duke of Exeter, was with the Queen in these wanderings, or part of them, and went with her to Sluys. After fighting so ardently and long against his usurping brother-in-law, the last representative of the once great House of Holland was now a completely ruined man. From 1463 to 1470, like other Lancastrian lords who had not changed the colour of their rose, he lived destitute in foreign lands. The Burgundian chronicler, de Wavrin, says that at one time he was an exile in Ireland, but he was after this, at any rate, in Flanders.

At first, some of the exiled Lancastrians received a slight assistance from the Duke of Burgundy. The glorious Duke Philip of Burgundy had married the Infanta of Portugal, whose mother was Philippa, daughter of John of Gaunt, Duke of Lancaster, and sister of Elizabeth, who married

John Holland, first Duke of Exeter. The heart of the Duchess was English, and she had before his first marriage with a French princess, wished her son Charles to marry into the House of England. At one time she had wished him to marry Anne of York, who became Duchess of Exeter.

Duke Philip was proud of his Lancastrian connection, and still more so was his son, the Count of Charolais, who had this blood in his veins. De Commines says that Charles of Charolais cordially hated the Yorkists after they had dethroned his nearest English relatives. But the Dukes of Burgundy, for trade and political reasons, as lords of the weaving Flemish cities supplied with English wool, were bound to keep on good terms with the *de facto* Government of England, and in 1467 Charles, who had lost his first wife, Isabelle de Bourbon, and succeeded in that year to the dukedom, entered into a contract of marriage with Margaret of York, sister of Edward IV, and sister, also, of Anne of York, the faithless wife of the exiled and ruined Duke of Exeter. Charles said, in 1467, to the Constable of St. Pol, who came to him on behalf of the King of France : ' Is it not true that my relationship and affections were for the House of Lancaster and for King Henry against the House of York and King Edward ? If now I wish to marry Madame Margaret, is it not necessity which has inspired me with this design ? '

This marriage, so fatal to the Lancastrians, was the more necessary because that deadly and subtle enemy of Burgundy, Louis XI, was soliciting the hand of Margaret of York for one of his sons. After this marriage, Charles of Burgundy, though hating the Yorkists as well as ever, had to be careful not visibly to favour the Lancastrian exiles or countenance their conspiracies. John Paston, the younger, was at Bruges on July 8, 1468, and wrote to his mother describing the marriage there of the Duke and Margaret of York.[1] He says : 'The Duke of Somerset and his bands departed well beseen out of Bruges on the day before that my lady the Duchess came thither, and they say that he is [going] to Queen Margaret that was, and shall no more come here again, nor be holpen by the Duke.' This Somerset was Edmund Beaufort, the fourth Duke, son of Edmund who fell at St. Albans, and brother and successor of the third Duke, Henry Beaufort, who was beheaded after Hexham fight in 1464. He was himself destined to be beheaded after Tewkesbury. No doubt Exeter was one of those who rode out of Bruges with him, probably on a sorry horse.

Philippe de Commines, at that time a servant of the Duke, observes in his memoirs that in the Wars of the Roses, ' three score or four score persons of the blood royal were cruelly slain. Those that survived were fugitives, and lived in the Duke of Burgundy's court ; all of them young gentlemen whose fathers had been slain in England, whom the Duke of Burgundy had generously maintained before this marriage as his relations of the House of Lancaster. Some of them were reduced to such extremity of want and poverty, before the Duke of Burgundy received them, that no common beggar could have been poorer. I saw one of them, who was Duke of Exeter, but he concealed his name, following the Duke of Burgundy's train, bare-foot and bare-legged, begging his bread from door to door. This person was the next ' [in succession, he means, to the crown after Prince Edward of Wales] ' of the House of Lancaster ; he had married King Edward's sister, and, being afterwards known, had a small pension allowed him for his subsistence. There were also some of the family of the

---

[1] A description of these marriage festivities is given in immense detail by Olivier de la Marche.

Somersets, and several others, all of them slain since in the wars.'

De Commines adds, with much justice : ' The fathers and relations of these persons had plundered and destroyed the greater part of France, and possessed it for many years, and afterwards they turned their swords upon themselves, and killed one another ; those who were remaining in England, and their children, have died, as you see ; and yet there are those who affirm that God does not punish men as He did in the days of the children of Israel, but suffers the wickedness both of princes and people to remain unpunished.'

Certainly, if this be so, the Hollands had no right to complain of retributive justice ; they had taken their full share in the ravaging of France. Yet one can feel for the victims of even just retribution, when the sins of the fathers are visited upon the children ; and it is rather a touching picture, this authentic vision of the chief of the once haughty House of Holland, begging bare-foot for his bread, too proud to reveal his name. The contrast was the more poignant in that, in these last years of Duke Philip le Bon, the Court of Burgundy was by far the most wealthy and splendid and luxurious in Christendom, and that the Duke of Exeter was second cousin to the Count de Charolais, Duke Philip's son and heir,[1] who succeeded in 1467. It seems strange that Henry Holland, who had landed in Flanders with Queen Margaret in 1463, should have been allowed by the richest and most magnificent and bountiful of dukes to fall into such complete distress and oblivion, and when rediscovered should only have received a small pension. But unsuccessful relatives had best not put their trust in Princes.

[1] Brantome says : ' Je crois qu'il ne fût jamais quatre plus grand ducs, les uns après les autres, comme furent ces quatre ducs de Bourgogne.'

For weary years the Duke of Exeter lived in Flemish cities, consuming his heart in poverty and despair, and then for a brief space, Fortune turned her wheel. In 1470 his ' king-making ' and vain-glorious cousin, Richard Nevill, Earl of Warwick, who thought himself treated with vile ingratitude by Edward IV, and was especially indignant because that popular King preferred to take counsel of ' low born men ' rather than of great lords, quarrelled with his Yorkist allies and, after various manœuvrings, retired to France. He was well received by Louis XI, who, since the Burgundian-Yorkist marriage alliance, had been hoping to obtain through a Lancastrian restoration a Government in England more favourable to himself. By the advice of that astute monarch, Warwick gave his daughter, Anne Nevill, in marriage to Edward, son of Henry VI, the exiled Prince of Wales. Another of Warwick's daughters had already been married to George Duke of Clarence, younger brother of Edward IV, a prince of feeble character, who on this occasion followed for awhile his father-in-law against his royal brother. Warwick now was ready to attempt a restoration of the House of Lancaster. Calais was again in his possession, and de Commines saw its old fishy and narrow streets full of men wearing the Nevill badge of the bear and ragged staff. Warwick borrowed ships from Louis XI, landed with a small force at Dartmouth on September 13, 1470, and at first was completely successful. Edward IV, gallant and energetic in war, was indolent and improvident in peace. ' King Edward,' says Philippe de Commines, who knew him well, ' was a very young prince, and one of the handsomest men of his age at the time he had overcome all his difficulties ; so he gave himself up wholly to pleasures and took no delight in anything but ladies, dancing, and festivities, and the chase, and in this voluptuous course of life, if I mistake not, he spent almost sixteen years till the quarrel happened between him and the Earl of Warwick.'[1] Warwick's raid took Edward by surprise. He had suddenly to quit his hunting and love-making, and escape from the east coast to Holland. Warwick entered London, and the imbecile Henry was brought out of the Tower of London and proclaimed King once more. At the beginning of this brief Restoration, the Duke of Exeter was engaged on a diplomatic mission. De Commines says:

'That very day on which the Duke of Burgundy received the news of King Edward being in Holland, I was come from Calais and found him (the Duke) at Boulogne, having heard nothing of that nor of King Edward's defeat. The first news the Duke of Burgundy heard was that he was killed, and he was not at all concerned about it, for his affection was greater for the House of Lancaster than for that of York, and there were at that very time in his court the Dukes of Exeter and Somerset, and several others of King Henry's party, so that he thought by their means to be easily reconciled to that family, but he dreaded greatly the Earl of Warwick. Besides, he knew not after what manner to carry himself to King Edward, whose sister he had married, and, moreover, they were brethren of the same Orders, for the King wore the Golden Fleece and the Duke the Garter.'

It was an awkward situation for the Duke of Burgundy. For trade and other reasons, it was essential to be on good terms with the English Government, and for the moment it was not clear which dynasty would

---

[1] 'After his final success over Warwick,' says de Commines, Edward IV 'fell again to his pleasures, and indulged himself in them more recklessly than ever. From this time he feared nobody, but grew very fat,' &c. After the treaty of Pecquigny in 1475, Edward lived happily on 50,000 gold crowns paid to him by Louis XI, annually, at the cost of the unhappy French tax-payer, as an insurance against new English invasions.

prevail. It was all the more important to make no error, because the Duke was being hard pressed in war by the French.

King Edward arrived at the Duke's court at St. Pol in January 1471, and urged him to grant assistance for the recapture of England. On the other hand, says de Commines, ' the Dukes of Exeter and Somerset violently opposed it, and used all their artifices to keep him firm to King Henry's interest. The Duke was in suspense, and knew not which side to favour ; he was fearful of disobliging either, because he was engaged in a desperate war at home ; but at length he struck in with the Duke of Somerset and the rest of their party, upon certain promises which they made him, against the Earl of Warwick, their ancient enemy.[1] King Edward was present at the place and was much dissatisfied to see how unsucessfully his affairs bent ; yet he was given all the fair words imaginable, and told that all was dissimulation to keep off a war against two kingdoms at once ; for if the Duke were once ruined, he would not be in a position to assist him afterwards, if he were even so inclined to do so. However, finding King Edward bent upon return to England, and being unwilling, for many reasons, absolutely to displease him, the Duke pretended publicly that he would give him no assistance, and issued a proclamation forbidding any of his subjects to accompany him, but privately he sent him 50,000 florins, and furnished him with three or four great ships, which he ordered to be equipped for him at Terveene in Holland, which is a free port where all persons are received ; besides which, he hired secretly fourteen Esterling [2] ships for him, which were well armed and were engaged to transport him into England, and serve him

---

[1] ' Their ancient enemy,' but present ally They had to promise to throw over Warwick, or keep him down, after success.

[2] The German shipowners were known as Esterlings.

fifteen days afterwards, all which supply was very great considering those times.'

After this artful arrangement, the Duke expressed to de Commines the opinion that ' the affairs of England could not go amiss for him, since he was sure of friends on both sides.' He had shown on this occasion a caution and cunning which were worthy of his enemy Louis XI, and did not justify his nickname of ' Le Témeraire.' It had, indeed, been a very curious position. The Duke of Burgundy was the husband of Margaret, one sister of Edward IV, and the Duke of Exeter was husband of Anne, another sister. Edward was thus soliciting aid from one brother-in-law, and was violently opposed by the other.

The Duke of Exeter, always unsuccessful, returned to England in time to take part in the crowning disaster of Barnet. King Edward left Bruges with his brother Richard of Gloucester, Lord Rivers, Lord Hastings, and others, and about 1200 men, and on March 2 embarked at Flushing. He was held up by adverse winds for a few days, but on March 12 touched at Cromer in Norfolk. He found Norfolk full of enemies, and sailed on to Ravenspur at the mouth of the Humber, where, like Bolingbroke in 1399, he landed. He marched straight to York, where he arrived on March 16, and had a mixed reception. Some were for him and more against him. In order to keep quiet these last, he gave out that he had returned only in order to claim his hereditary duchy of York. Then he marched south by Tadcaster and Wakefield, passing old battle-fields, to Doncaster and Nottingham. The Duke of Exeter and Lord Oxford had raised a force of 4000 men in the Eastern Counties, and lay across the road at Newark. They retired, however, on Edward's approach, and so did the Earl of Warwick from Leicester. Warwick threw his force into Coventry, a fortified town, and refused battle to Edward who arrived before the walls on

March 30.   Edward passed on to Warwick town, and met at Daventry his brother Clarence, with 4000 men, who made submission to him.

Clarence—' false, fleeting, perjured Clarence '—had, says the French chronicler, found himself uncomfortable amongst his new Lancastrian friends.   During Edward's absence abroad an active intrigue to undermine his faith to his father-in-law, Warwick, had been kept on foot by his mother (Cecily Nevill), and by his sisters, the Duchess of Burgundy, and Anne, Duchess of Exeter—the last faithless in every sense to her husband.   Edward in Flanders, through the Duchess of Burgundy and the other two ladies in England, had played upon the fears and feelings of his weak brother.

After this scene of submission, or reconciliation, Edward attended Mass—it was Palm Sunday—in the Church of St. Anne at Daventry.   Here happened a good omen.   A sacred image of St. Anne was fixed to one of the pillars in a shrine covered by folding doors fastened, except when the image was exhibited for devotion, by iron clamps.   When Edward drew near, the doors flew open of themselves and disclosed the gracious saint.   It was important to have miraculous signs in a time when many powerful people were only anxious to know beforehand which would be the winning side, so as to join it betimes.

Edward challenged Warwick once more beneath the walls of Coventry, and then marched south.   He rode with his army into London on the Thursday before Easter Sunday, April 11, 1471, and was well received by the middle-class citizens.   According to de Commines, this was due partly to the great debts which he owed to the merchants who could only hope to get paid through his restoration, and partly to the ladies of quality and citizens' wives, who loved his good looks and gallantries, and were on his side to a woman, and forced their husbands and brothers and cousins to be so also. The sympathies of the poorer class were probably more with Warwick.

On entering London, Edward first went to St. Paul's Cathedral, and then to Westminster Abbey, where 'he made his prayers devoutly to God, to his glorious mother, to St. Peter, and to St. Edward.' Then he paid a visit to his wife, the Queen, who was already in London. On the Saturday, he marched with his army out of London and drove Warwick's advance parties in on their main body, who were now a mile and a half north of the village of Barnet, near where the road to St. Albans branches from the north road to Hatfield. Edward then passed through Barnet, and, under cover of darkness, established his force on the far side, close to the enemy's line.[1] Both armies had the new implements of cannon, but Warwick had many more than Edward. He had them fired at intervals all night, but they did no damage owing to a mistake as to Edward's position.[2]

Next morning, that of Easter Sunday, April 14, Edward rode through his army just before daybreak encouraging his men. Edward, who, like Warwick, posed as a jovial democrat, once told Philippe de Commines that when he saw that a battle was won, he used to mount his horse and shout to his men to spare the common people and kill the gentlemen. He did not do so on this occasion, because he was angry with the common people for the hearty good reception which they had given to Warwick on his last landing. Warwick had always been mightily popular, partly by reason of his lavish expenditure on eating and

[1] Edward's sister, Margaret, Duchess of Burgundy, in a letter to her mother-in-law, written a week later, says that Edward began the battle with his face to the village, and ended it with his back to the other side But she wrote on not very good oral information and, according to Wavrin, it was as in the text.

[2] Warkworth's chronicle says ' Near Barnet, on Holy Saturday, eche of them loosede gonnes at other all the nyght. And fought on Easter day in the mornynge unto X of clokke the forenone ' A pretty way in which to spend the Feast of Easter !

drinking. 'When he came to London,' says Stow, 'he held such an house that six oxen were eaten at a breakfast, and every tavern was free of his meat; for he who had any acquaintance in that house, he should have as much boiled and roast as he might carry on a long dagger.' When Edward and Warwick quarrelled it was a rift in the popular party.

This was the last fight in which the Holland banner was seen in battle. Exeter commanded the Lancastrian right wing, mainly consisting of his East Anglian levies ; Oxford led on the left wing, and Warwick in the centre. Before the battle the lords and gentlemen of both sides dismounted, sent to the rear their horses, according to English custom, and fought on foot. A thick mist hung over the field that morning, raised, it was said, by the incantations of Friar Bungay, a skilful magician. Between 5 and 6 A.M., Edward advanced through the fog, displaying banners and sounding trumpets, his archers shooting as they went forward. The fighting was fierce, and on their right the Lancastrians had the best of it at first, and some of the fugitive Yorkists never stopped till they came to London, spreading news of a defeat. But Warwick's right, after this success, 'fell to ryfling,' and did not turn to the aid of their centre and left. It is said that Exeter's men, in the course of the confused fight, shot at the Earl of Oxford's, mistaking in the mist their badge of a star for the badge of a sun worn by Edward's men, and that Oxford's men suspecting treachery left the field. Edward, valiant and bold, was fighting in person in the midst of the battle, and killed many with his own royal hand. His brothers, Clarence and Richard of Gloucester, also fought bravely, and so did Lord Rivers, Lord Hastings, and others of the Edwardian set. On the other side, Lord Montagu, Warwick's brother, did great feats, until at last he was killed. Warwick saw or heard of his brother's fall, was dejected and unmanned, and in the end was himself slain. Exeter fought 'manfully,' but was sore wounded in the middle of the fight. The battle lasted some four hours, and then the Lancastrians were driven off the ground. It was one more success for better discipline and training against numbers. Edward had no more than 9000 men against about 30,000 : 'Comme il fut sceu de vray non plus n'en avoit,' says de Wavrin. This looks as though the Londoners had not joined Edward largely.

King Edward returned to refresh himself at Barnet, and then marched in triumph to London. He entered St. Paul's as vespers were being sung, and offered up his own banner and that of Warwick as a thank-offering. Meanwhile, his brother-in-law, Henry Holland, last Duke of Exeter, lay sore wounded amid the slain. Wavrin says : 'Aussi fut abattu le duc d'Excestre, tenant le part de Warewick, moult fort navré et tenu pour mort avec les occis qui en grant nombre estoient non cognoissant que ce feust il.'

Presently plunderers despoiled the slain, and stripped him naked. But about four o'clock in the afternoon of that blood-stained Easter Sunday, there came to the field an old retainer of his, named Ruthland, who lived in or near Barnet. He searched for his lord's body and when he found it, saw that he was not dead, and took him to his own house where his wounds were attended to by a surgeon, and, on a later day, conveyed him into sanctuary at Westminster Abbey.

Edward IV, meanwhile, in a proclamation dated April 27, 1471, proclaimed the leading Lancastrians to be 'open and notorious traitors and rebels and enemies.' The list names Queen Margaret and Edward her son, and 'Henry, late Duke of Exeter, Edmund Beaufort calling himself duke of Somerset,' the Earls of Oxford and Devonshire, Viscount Beaumont, seven knights, two squires, three Clerks, and one Friar.

A mist hangs over the subsequent fate of Henry Holland,

Duke of Exeter. According to the chronicler Fabian, who was followed by most subsequent historians, his body was found a few months later floating in the sea between Calais and Dover and none knew how it came there. Sir James Ramsay, in his learned book ' Lancaster and York,' vol. ii. p. 370, has, however, shown that Exeter was in the Tower of London after his sanctuary and was living until June 1475.[1] Sir James adds that the Duke ' apparently was set at liberty to join the expedition ' (to France, in 1475), ' though his name does not appear on the Muster Rolls, and on the expedition he died, drowned at sea on the way to Calais, the last male of his aspiring House, and the only life lost in the campaign.'

This last statement rests on the authority of Richard Grafton, the Tudor continuator of Hardyng's Chronicle, who says that in this expedition to France ' none was slain saving only the Duke of Exeter, the which man was in sanctuary before, and, commanded to follow the King, was put to death by drowning, and cast over a ship by Sir Thomas St. Leger, which afterwards married his wife, contrary to the promise made.' The ' afterwards ' is in any case incorrect, as St. Leger married the Duchess long before 1475.

Sir James Ramsay, following the line indicated by Grafton, adds in a footnote : ' If there was any foul play in the matter, suspicion ought to rest not on Edward, but on his sister Anne, the Duchess of Exeter, and her second husband Sir Thomas St. Leger.' The argument is as follows : Anne, Duchess of Exeter, was born in 1439, and she obtained a divorce from the Duke on November 12, 1467, and then married Sir Thomas St. Leger. The Duke of Exeter's estates were confiscated in 1461, after Towton, when his wife was twenty-

---

[1] On June 21, 1471, a bill of 6s. 8d. was paid to William Sayer, purveyor to the Tower of London for food for ' Henry, called Duke of Exeter,' for seven days, from May 26, and again 6s. 8d. for the week beginning May 31.—Rymer, vol. xi. p. 713.

two years old, and after that he was in exile. As she was the sister of King Edward IV, the Holland estates in Devonshire and other south-western counties and elsewhere were re-granted to her to hold as a woman sole. An Act of Parlia-ment, passed in 1464, enabled that ' such gifts and grants as the King shall make to Anne, his sister, wife to Henry, Duke of Exeter, shall be to all intents good in law to the only use of the said Anne, and that she plead and be impleaded by the name of Anne, Duchess of Exeter.' (Tower Records) In August 1467, there was a settlement or re-settlement of the Exeter estates. King Edward granted to Anne, his sister, sundry castles, manors, &c., in Wales, Cornwall, Devon, Somerset, and Wilts, and other counties, to herself for life, with remainder to her daughter by the Duke of Exeter, the Lady Anne Holland, in general tail, and then, in default of that daughter living and having issue, to the Duchess Anne in general tail. On November 12, 1467, the Duchess obtained a divorce from the Duke and then married Sir Thomas St. Leger, by whom she had a daughter also named Anne. ' But,' says Sir James Ramsay, ' we find it alleged that the re-settlement of 1467 was obtained at the instance of Sir Thomas St. Leger to enable his daughter to succeed Anne Holland and her issue. If this was so, Anne St. Leger must have been born before her mother's divorce from the Duke. The Duke's liberation would be very inconvenient to the St. Legers.'

According to one old historian, Lady Anne Holland, while she was still a child, was contracted about 1465 to Thomas Woodville, a brother of Edward IV's queen, and this was one of the grievances of the Earl of Warwick, who had marked down this high-born heiress for a kinsman of his own. This match did not come off, and some time after 1467, Anne Holland died unmarried, and her mother, the Duchess of Exeter, died in 1476. The way now stood open for the advancement of Anne St Leger. An Act of Parliament in 1482 recites the facts, and states that Anne St. Leger was now intended to be married to Thomas, son of the Marquess of Dorset, and the King by authority of the Act confirmed to Anne the estates comprised in the settlement of 1467.[1]

One can well understand that, in those unscrupulous days, when things so stood, Anne Holland, hapless girl, should have died in favour of Anne St. Leger; all the more since she was also in the Lancastrian line of succession to the throne. The Duke of Exeter's misfortune in having a wife of the faithless and wicked House of York bore natural fruits. But Grafton's words, ' contrary to the promise made,' indicate that, according to tradition, on which he was writing, St. Leger's murder of Exeter, if he were the murderer, was instigated by higher authorities. Edward IV, or his courtiers, or perhaps the unscrupulous Duke of Gloucester, can hardly be acquitted of Exeter's death, because they had as much interest in it as the St. Legers, or even more. There is no good proof that Exeter was in the expedition of 1475, and it rather is probable that he was removed from the Tower to that convenient prison at Calais and drowned in the sea, or otherwise murdered and thrown into the sea. In some violent way, in any case, the last man of legitimate birth of this branch of the Hollands came to his end at the age of forty-five. It is singular that the first Holland Duke of Exeter should have lost his life in trying to dethrone his royal brother-in-law of the House of Lancaster, and that the third Duke should have lost his in the result of an attempt to dethrone his royal brother-in-law of the House of York.

Henry Holland, Duke of Exeter, is rather a dim figure in history, and his continuous failures make one feel that his was

[1] Anne St. Leger was eventually married to Sir George Manners, Lord de Ros, and from whom descend the present Lords de Ros and Dukes of Rutland.

not a formidable personality. He was like the Jacobite
lords of a later time—a loyal and brave adherent of a doomed
and unpopular cause. There is something pale and dreamlike
about the whole record of this Holland, especially about his
last years. He does not stand out in bold relief like his
grandfather. Perhaps it is for want of an historian like
Froissart. There were certainly excellent dynastic reasons
and motives of high policy for his disappearance from the
scene. After that Edward, Prince of Wales, had been killed
by his Yorkist cousins, in 1471, at the battle of Tewkesbury,
Henry Holland, Duke of Exeter, stood first in succession to
the Crown on the Lancastrian side. His claim was superior
to that which Henry Tudor, Earl of Richmond, successfully
asserted against Richard III on Bosworth Field. Holland
descended from Elizabeth, daughter of John, Duke of Lancaster, by a marriage previous to that which the Duke contracted with Katherine Swynford, whence came the Beauforts,
and from them, through Margaret of Richmond, Henry VII.
Also the first Beauforts were born of a doubly illegitimate
union, though they were afterwards legitimated. The Duke of
Exeter, if he had lain concealed and had not gone, or been
taken to, Westminster Abbey, might easily have escaped, as
he did after Towton Field, and again after the campaign in
Northumberland. He might have lived beyond the sea
until 1485, when he would have been fifty-five years old,
the year when the wicked House of York, having almost
devoured itself like a sinful clan in a Greek tragedy, fell
amidst the applause of a weary and indignant nation. Had
this been his fortune, to him, and not to Henry Tudor,
would most naturally have fallen the duty of asserting
in arms the Lancaster claim. In that event there might
have been, for better or worse, a Royal House of Holland
instead of a House of Tudor. This very claim made almost
certain his murder, for it was deadly to possess a claim

even more remote than that of Henry Holland. Henry VII himself told de Commines that ever since he had been five years old till Bosworth Field, he had been either hiding or in exile.

The three allied Houses of Lancaster, Beaufort, and Holland fell together in the storm of the Roses. The existing Dukes of Beaufort descend from an illegitimate son of Henry Beaufort, Duke of Somerset, who was beheaded after Hexham fight. Thus the modern Beauforts have for one of their ancestresses that important lady, Margaret Holland, daughter of the second Earl of Kent, who was also an ancestress of the Tudors and Stewarts.

A Lancashire historian,[1] reflecting on the poor body found floating off Dover, remarks that ' such was the melancholy end of this branch of the great feudal House of Holland, the most powerful of subjects and the most unfortunate of men.' The Hollands, indeed, ran a brilliant and disastrous course, but they never really were a ' great feudal house,' in the sense, at least, of the Fitz-Alans, Percys, Nevills, Staffords, Mortimers, Beauchamps, Montacutes, Mowbrays, or Bohuns. They were the descendants of Thurstan de Holland, who, only two hundred years before the Battle of Barnet, was a Lancashire squire of no high descent or great possessions, and throughout their history they were probably in the view of great Norman-descended lords merely Saxon-derived adventurers, or soldiers of fortune, who had married much above themselves, and whose importance was adventitious rather than intrinsic.'[2]

Beltz, in his stately and admirable ' Memorials of the Order of the Garter,' expresses mild surprise that seven Hollands in three generations should have been Knights

---

[1] J. Croston, in his *History of Samlesbury Hall*, once a Holland property.

[2] The Saxon name of Thurstan—rather common in old Lancashire—as well as their original social standing, makes it almost certain that the Hollands were of English and not of Norman descent

of that noble Society, for, says he very coldly, they ' derived no particular lustre from ancestry,' and came of ' a gentle but inconsiderable stock.' But, then, Mr. Beltz's ideals as to the origin of species were very lofty. The seven Hollands, K.G's, with their numbers in the list, were :

Sir Thomas Holland, 1st Earl of Kent, 14th Knight.
Sir Otho Holland, 23rd Knight.
Sir Thomas Holland, 2nd Earl of Kent, 59th Knight.
Sir John Holland, 1st Earl of Huntingdon and Duke
    of Exeter, 69th Knight.
Thomas Holland, 3rd Earl of Kent and Duke of Surrey,
    89th Knight.
Edmund Holland, 4th Earl of Kent, 107th Knight.
John Holland, 2nd Earl of Huntingdon and Duke of
    Exeter, 126th Knight.

The third Duke of Exeter never was a K.G., owing to his usual ill-luck. Probably there was no vacancy, and then the Civil War intervened.

The following tables may be useful illustrations of the alliances of the Hollands in this distinguished period of their history. Names not useful for the purpose are omitted.

THE HOLLANDS AND THE HOUSES OF PLANTAGENET AND LANCASTER

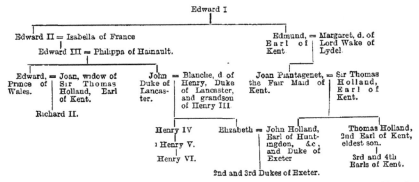

1 Margaret Holland, d. of 2nd Earl of Kent, married (*s.p.*) Duke of Clarence, brother of Henry V, as her 2nd husband.

THE HOLLANDS AND THE HOUSES OF MORTIMER AND YORK

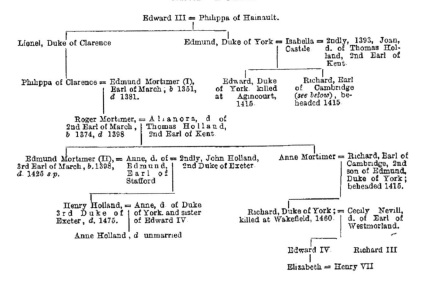

THE HOLLANDS AND THE HOUSE OF BEAUFORT

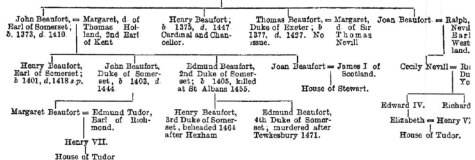

John of Gaunt, Duke of Lancaster = (3rd wife) Katharine Swynford; b. 1350, d. 1396.

John Beaufort, = Margaret, d. of   Henry Beaufort;   Thomas Beaufort, = Margaret,   Joan Beaufort = Ralph,
Earl of Somerset;   Thomas Hol-   b. 1375, d. 1447   Duke of Exeter; b   d. of Sir   Nevil
b. 1373, d. 1410.   land, 2nd Earl   Cardinal and Chan-   1377, d. 1427. No   Thomas   Earl
     of Kent.   cellor.   issue.   Nevil   West
           land.

Henry Beaufort,   John Beaufort,   Edmund Beaufort,   Joan Beaufort = James I of   Cecily Nevill = Ri
Earl of Somerset;   Duke of Somer-   2nd Duke of Somer-   Scotland.   Du
b. 1401, d.1418 s.p.   set, b. 1403, d.   set; b. 1405, killed   Yo
     1444.   at St Albans 1455.   House of Stewart.

Margaret Beaufort = Edmund Tudor,   Henry Beaufort,   Edmund Beaufort,   Edward IV.   Richard
     Earl of Rich-   3rd Duke of Somer-   4th Duke of Somer-
     mond.   set, beheaded 1464   set; murdered after   Elizabeth = Henry VI
           after Hexham   Tewkesbury 1471.
   Henry VII.   House of Tudor.

   House of Tudor

THE HOLLANDS AND THE HOUSE OF NEVILL

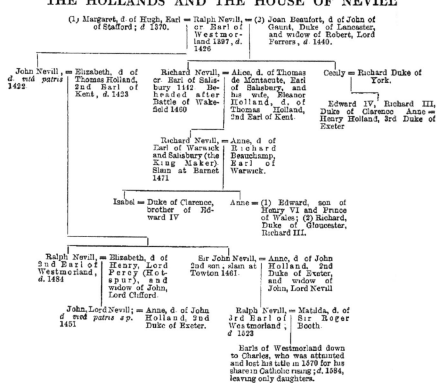

(1) Margaret, d. of Hugh, Earl = Ralph Nevill, = (2) Joan Beaufort, d of John of
of Stafford; d 1370.   cr Earl of   Gaunt, Duke of Lancaster,
                   Westmor-   and widow of Robert, Lord
                   land 1397, d.   Ferrers, d 1440.
                   1426

John Nevill, = Elizabeth, d of   Richard Nevill, = Alice, d. of Thomas   Cecily = Richard Duke of
d. vitâ patris   Thomas Holland,   cr Earl of Salis-   de Montacute, Earl   York.
1422.   2nd Earl of   bury 1442. Be-   of Salisbury, and
     Kent, d. 1423   headed after   his wife, Eleanor   Edward IV, Richard III,
           Battle of Wake-   Holland, d. of   Duke of Clarence Anne =
           field 1460   Thomas Holland,   Henry Holland, 3rd Duke of
                   2nd Earl of Kent.   Exeter

                   Richard Nevill, = Anne, d of
                   Earl of Warwick   Richard
                   and Salisbury (the   Beauchamp,
                   King Maker).   Earl of
                   Slain at Barnet   Warwick.
                   1471

       Isabel = Duke of Clarence,   Anne = (1) Edward, son of
              brother of Ed-   Henry VI and Prince
              ward IV   of Wales; (2) Richard,
                          Duke of Gloucester,
                          Richard III.

Ralph Nevill, = Elizabeth, d of   Sir John Nevill, = Anne, d of John
2nd Earl of   Henry, Lord   2nd son, slain at   Holland, 2nd
Westmorland,   Percy (Hot-   Towton 1461.   Duke of Exeter,
d. 1484   spur), and   and widow of
      widow of John,   John, Lord Nevill
      Lord Clifford.

   John, Lord Nevill, = Anne, d. of John   Ralph Nevill, = Matilda, d. of
   d vitâ patris s p.   Holland, 2nd   3rd Earl of   Sir Roger
   1451   Duke of Exeter.   Westmorland;   Booth.
                         d 1523

                     Earls of Westmorland down
                     to Charles, who was attainted
                     and lost his title in 1570 for his
                     share in Catholic rising; d. 1584,
                     leaving only daughters.

CHAPTER X

The solemn rites, the awful forms,
Founder amid fanatic storms ;
The priests are from their altars thrust,
The temples levelled with the dust.

WORDSWORTH.

WHILE the Hollands who went south led perilous and stormy
lives, and were at last killed out, other branches from the
old Upholland stem remained in Lancashire, and were
mainly distinguished by the tenacity with which they
adhered through centuries to various patrimonial estates.
The earliest of these branches was that of the Hollands of
Sutton.

The first Robert de Holland, owner of Upholland, who
lived in the reign of Henry III, and married Cecily, daughter
of Alan de Columbers, had by her three sons. From one
of these, Adam, came the Hollands of Euxton ; from another,
Richard, descended the Hollands of Sutton ; and from the
eldest of the three, Thurstan, came the Barons Holland,
the Earls of Kent and Huntingdon, and the Hollands of
Denton, Clifton, &c.

Richard de Holland married some lady not known,
and had for a son Robert de Holland, who married Agnes
de Molyneux. This Robert acquired from John de Sutton,
in the reign of Edward I, the manor and estate of Sutton
in south-west Lancashire, which remained in his posterity
until the reign of Queen Anne, and part of it still longer.

237

HOLLANDS OF SUTTON

Richard de Holland = d. of ——
(younger son of
Robert de Holland
of Upholland).

Robert de Holland, = Agnes de Molyneux.
living 1331.

William Holland, = Godith, d of ——
d. before 1356.

John Holland, = Ellen, d. of ——
living in 1390.

John Holland, = d of ——
d. 1402.

Richard Holland, = Elizabeth Eltonhead.
2 years old in 1402.

Henry Holland, = Jane Ecclestone.   Hugh   Four
living in 1476.   Holland.   daughters.

Richard Holland, =   and a daughter.
temp Henry VIII.

William Holland, = Catharine   Two other sons,   Four
living 1567.   Leigh.   Richard and Ralph.   daughters.

Alexander Holland, = Ann, d. of John   Three other sons,   Nine
d. 1588.   Bold of North   Henry, Thomas,   daughters.
                     Meals.   and Peter.

Richard Holland, = Anne ——   Henry Holland, S.J.
b. 1575, alive 1611

William Holland = Margaret Mileson   Thomas Holland, S.J.;
                                       executed 1642.

Richard Holland, = Anne   Alexander   Henry   Three
d. 1649.   Ewen.   Holland, S J. Holland. daughters.

Edward Holland, =   Richard   Anne.
b. 1640, d. 1717.

Thomas Holland   Richard Holland, S J
(alive 1717)

The pedigree of the Hollands of Sutton in the table herewith is based upon the part pedigrees given in Flower's heraldic visitation of Lancashire in 1567 and Dugdale's visitation in 1664, and upon records earlier than either quoted in the Chetham Society Papers and the 'Victorian History of Lancashire' and other books.[1] Nothing is known of their history until the sixteenth century, though they certainly handed down the manor with unbroken regularity. In that century and the next they do modestly appear on the page of history.

While the Hollands of Denton, as will be seen, were after the Elizabethan settlement strong Protestants, and even Puritans, their distant kinsmen, those of Sutton, adhered staunchly to Rome. There was, however, one striking exception : Roger Holland, burnt at Smithfield in 1558, appears to have been of this family. An account of him is given in Foxe's 'Acts and Monuments,'[2] commonly called the Book of Martyrs. This Roger came up from Lancashire, and, as was then common enough with younger sons of lesser, but good families, became a London apprentice, with one Master Kempton, at the Black Boy in Watling Street, a merchant tailor. He served his apprenticeship, says Foxe,

---

[1] A note in the Chetham Society publication of Lancashire Inquisitions says : 'The Holands of Clifton entered at the Visitation of 1567, as did also the Holands of Sutton whom the Heralds seem to have treated as an offshoot from Clifton, but this is manifestly erroneous, as Robert de Holand, son of Richard (younger brother of Thurstan, the grandfather of Sir Robert who was raised to the peerage), acquired in the reign of Edward I from John de Sutton, that estate which was inherited by his posterity.'

[2] There is no direct evidence that Roger Holland belonged to the Hollands of Sutton Hall, but there is a Lancashire tradition to this effect. The record of his trial shows that he belonged to a well-connected and obstinately Catholic family in Lancashire, and the fact that one of his kinsmen present at the trial was Mr. Ecclestone, makes it seem almost certain that Roger belonged to the Sutton family, since we know that Henry Holland, owner of Sutton, who was living in 1476, married Jane Ecclestone. Roger Holland may have been his nephew through his younger brother, Hugh. The learned and careful authors of the *Victorian History of Lancashire* accept the relationship.

'with much trouble to his master in breaking him from his licentious ways which he had before been trained and brought up in, giving himself to riot, dancing, fencing, gaming, banqueting and wanton company, and besides all this, being a stubborn and obstinate papist.'[1] One day he lost at dice £30 belonging to his master, and was about to fly to Flanders or France, says Foxe,' but first disclosed his disaster to ' a servant in the house, an ancient and discreet maid, whose name was Elizabeth, which professed the gospel, with a life agreeing to the same, and at all times rebuked the wilful and obstinate papistry, as also the licentious living of the said Roger.' Elizabeth luckily happened to have in hand £30 of her own, the fruit of a recent legacy. This she gave to Roger Holland on condition that he would reform his life, forswear wild company, never gamble again, attend every day the lecture in All Hallows and, on Sunday, the sermon in St. Paul's (it was in the reign of Edward VI), cast away ' all books of papistry and vain ballads,' get a Testament and prayer-book, read the Scripture and pray. Roger obeyed these conditions and, in half a year, became ' an earnest professor of the truth, and detested all papistry and evil company.' He went down to Lancashire and tried in vain to persuade his father and kinsmen to abandon the ways of their benighted ancestors. His father, however, gave him £50, and on his return to London he repaid Elizabeth her £30, and said to her : ' Elizabeth, here is thy money I borrowed of thee, and for the friendship, goodwill and counsel I have received at thy hands, to recompense thee I am not able otherwise than to make thee my wife.'

So in the first year of Queen Mary's reign, Roger Holland

---

[1] As ever, the revellers supported the Conservative cause, and sour Puritans or Radicals complained of this   An official report of 1562 at the beginning of Eliza- beth's reign, says that ' a great part of the shires of Stafford and Derby are gener- ally illy inclined towards religion and forbear coming to church and participating of the Sacrament, using also very broad speeches in alehouses and elsewhere.'

married the 'ancient and discreet maid.' They had a baby, who was baptized in their own house by Master Rose, and not in church by a priest.

In 1558, the last year of Mary's reign, Roger Holland was brought up, on the charge of heresy, before Bishop Chedsey, and others. Dr. Chedsey, 'with many fair and crafty persuasions,' tried to 'attune him unto their Babylonical Church,' but Roger stoutly held his own, using strong terms of abuse against that Church. Afterwards, he was examined before Bishop Bonner, who was evidently anxious to save his life if possible, within the law: the more so, because Roger belonged to a higher class family. The Bishop said that he had conceived, from private talk with him, that Roger was a man of good sense, though somewhat over-hasty, and added : 'See, Roger, I have a good opinion of you that you will not, like these lewd fellows, cast yourself headlong from the Church of your parents, and your friends here, that are very good Catholics, as is reported to me.' These friends in the Court were Lord Strange, ancestor of the Earl of Derby, Sir Thomas Jarrett, Mr. Ecclestone, a cousin of the Sutton Hollands, and 'divers others of worship, both of Cheshire and Lancashire, that were Roger Holland's kinsmen and friends.' Bishop Bonner spoke so kindly that these gentlemen gave him ' thanks for his good will and pains that he had taken on his [Roger's] and their behalf.' But Roger could not be moved, and in reply to the test question, which at last the Bishop reluctantly put, said : ' As for the Mass, transubstantiation, and the worshipping of the Sacrament, they are mere impiety and horrible idolatry.'

He was then condemned to be burned in Smithfield, with two others, under the old statute *de haeretico comburendo.* At the last, 'embracing the stake,' Roger said, according to the Foxe narration : ' Lord, I most humbly thank Thy Majesty that Thou hast called me from the state of death

R

unto the light of Thy heavenly word, and now into the fellowship of Thy saints, that I may sing and say " Holy, holy, holy, Lord God of Hosts." Lord, into thy hands I commit my spirit. Lord, bless these Thy people, and save them from idolatry.' 'And so he ended his life, looking up into Heaven, praying and praising God, with the rest of his fellow saints.'

So Roger Holland died, valiantly, like an honest Englishman, refusing to save his life by going back upon himself and saying that he accepted a doctrine which he did not in fact accept. If he had escaped burning for a few months, he would have escaped it for ever. His burning, and that of two others who suffered at the same time, was the last that ever took place in Smithfield, for Queen Mary died on November 17 in this same year. Had she only died in the spring instead of the autumn, Roger Holland, so far from being burned, would have seen his views as to the Mass substantially adopted by the Elizabethan Government, and embodied in milder words in the restored Articles of the Church of England.[1] He would have beheld—perhaps not with complete satisfaction—a renovated prelacy, and, after a time, as a prosperous merchant tailor and alderman, might have seen Catholic priests hung, drawn, and quartered for celebrating what were, in his opinion, idolatrous rites.

The other Hollands of Sutton did not follow this example. They continued to be Catholics, and suffered accordingly in person and estate. Alexander Holland, who then owned Sutton Hall, was noted as a ' suspected person ' in 1584. A year earlier, in 1583, Robert Holland, said to belong to this family, and very likely a brother of Alexander, had been convicted at the Manchester Quarter Sessions of the statutory crime of twelve months' non-attendance at his parish

---

[1] Articles 28–31. Many modern Anglicans, it is true, now accept the full Catholic doctrine on this subject. Under the Test Act everyone for 150 years who took a seat in either House of Parliament, including the bishops, denied expressly the doctrine of ' Transubstantiation.'

church, was fined £240 (£20 for each month), and committed, together with ' a great number of Lancashire gentlemen and ladies,' to the prison for recusants at Salford.

He was unlucky in living in the Manchester district, where there was a majority of Puritan magistrates. In the same year, according to an official report, no convictions of recusants could be obtained at the Quarter Sessions held at Lancaster, Preston, and Wigan, though there were many charges brought, ' and there were many notorious recusants in every of the said divisions.' Probably in these three divisions most of the squires who met at sessions were themselves more or less concealed Catholics, and others had been left, by repeated changes, in a state of religious indifference, and were certainly not disposed to worry, and fine, and send to prison, neighbours whom they met out hunting.

The apathy of the magistrates was not the only difficulty which the Government had to encounter in Lancashire. As late as 1602 the Bishop of London wrote to the Secretary Cecil. ' Also they in Lancashire and in those parts stand not in fear by reason of the great multitude there is of them. Likewise I have heard it reported publicly among them that they of that county have beaten divers pursuivants extremely and made them vow and swear that they would never meddle with any recusants more, and one pursuivant in particular was forced to eat his writ.' This last feat was done by a Lancashire Catholic gentleman, called Geoffrey Poole, who captured a pursuivant bearing a writ for his own arrest, and said : ' Look here, fellow ! I give thee thy choice, either eat up this writ presently, or else eat my sword, for one of the two thou shalt do before we depart hence.'

In 1591 the Government took vigorous steps to remedy want of zeal among the Lancashire magistrates. A commission was issued for the apprehension of seminary priests and Jesuits and for ' reducing recusants to conformity,' and on one night fifty Lancashire Catholic gentlemen were seized and committed to prison on the vague charge of harbouring priests and not attending church. On October 22, an order from the Lords of the Council was issued to ' oure verie, loving friends,' Sir John Byron, High Sheriff of Lancaster, Sir Edward Fytton, Richard Asheton, Richard Brereton, and Richard Holland of Denton, directing that sessions of the peace should be holden before November 22 following, at which every justice of the peace should be required to take the oath of supremacy, and ordering the removal from the commission of the peace of every justice not repairing to church, or whose wife, or son and heir, if he lived in the county, should refuse to go, or not usually go, to church. Thus the magistracy was tuned to the right key.

From Salford prison Robert Holland was taken to London, and imprisoned in the Marshalsea. A report made in 1586, by Nicolas Berden, Walsingham's prison spy, is extant, in which the prisoners in the Marshalsea are classified in several groups with such notes as ' mete to be hung,' or ' should be sent to Wisbech.' Robert Holland and several other lay gentlemen are bracketed with a note : ' These nether welthy nor wyse, but all very arrant.'

After much suffering, Robert Holland died, like so many others, in that insanitary prison, in June 1586, aged forty-eight, and is therefore named in the catalogue of ' confessors of the faith.'

Edmund Campion, S.J., whose brief English mission lay chiefly in Lancashire, wrote in a letter, dated October 1581 :

' The heat of the persecution now raging against the Catholics, throughout the whole realm, is now fiery—such as has never been heard of since the conversion of England. Gentle and simple, men and women, are being everywhere haled to prison ; even children are being put in irons. They are despoiled of their goods, shut out of the light of day,

and publicly held up to the contempt of the people in pro-
clamations, sermons, and conferences, as traitors and rebels.'
And further he writes : ' They [the Government] have filled
all the old prisons with Catholics, and now make new, and
in fine, plainly affirm that it were better so to make a few
traitors away than that so many souls should be lost. Of
their martyrs they brag no more, for it is come to pass
that, for a few apostates and coblers of theirs burnt, we have
bishops, lords, knights, and the old nobility, patterns of
learning, piety, and prudence, the flower of the youth, noble
matrons, and of the inferior sort innumerable, either martyred
at once, or by consuming punishment dying daily. At the
very writing hereof, the persecution rages most cruelly. The
house where I am is sad ; no other talk but of death,
flight, spoil of their friends ; nevertheless, they proceed
with courage.'

This style may appear to some moderns to have too
aristocratic a flavour, because of its reference to coblers.
However, and this is one defence of families like the Hollands
of Sutton for not obeying the laws, there can be no doubt
that the English Reformation, viewed over its whole course,
was, like most revolutions, the work of an energetic and
capable and keenly interested minority, operating, through
the medium of an undecided public opinion, against an
established system which was, indeed, corrupted by many
abuses, and weakened by long prosperity, security, monopoly,
and wealth.

The first break with Rome was the work of Henry VIII
and one or two advisers. Parliament and the Southern Convocation, though not at first the Northern, passed whatever
their formidable monarch required, and the heads of a few
leading opponents—like Bishop Fisher and Sir Thomas More—
were taken off ; and three saintly Carthusian Priors, and
afterwards some great abbots, were hung, to strike intimida-

tion. In Edward VI's reign the Service and Prayer-book, which gave so lasting and strong a stamp to the Church of England, was drafted by a Royal Commission of selected bishops and divines—virtually by Cranmer ; it was formally at most submitted to Convocation, and was made law by Act of Parliament. Bishop Burnet, in his right Protestant and right honest history of the English Reformation, says that, in Edward's reign, the two Archbishops, Cranmer and Holgate, adopted this course because ' the greater part of the bishops being biassed by base ends, &c., did oppose them, and they were thereby forced to order matters so that they were prepared by some selected bishops and divines, and afterwards enacted by King and Parliament.'

Even poor and remote Lancashire squires, like the Hollands of Sutton, could hardly be expected to revere Tudor parliaments. In twenty-five years, from 1534 to 1559, Parliament had passed the measures by which Henry VIII broke England off from Rome : the later reactionary Six Articles of Doctrine by the same monarch ; the Act of Edward VI establishing a book of common prayer in direct opposition to those Articles ; the repeal under Mary in 1554 of Henry's Acts against Rome and complete restoration of Catholicism, and, finally, the Elizabethan legislation renewing the breach with Rome, and re-settling religion on the Edwardian lines, very slightly modified.

The English separation from the visible, organic, and international society which centres at Rome, whatever may seem to different minds its merits and results, was, in fact— both under Henry VIII and under Elizabeth—the achievement not of the Church, nor of the nation, but of a strong, hard, and determined Government, pursuing a fixed policy by cruel methods, and supported by a section of mostly new nobles and large squires eager for monastic lands, under Henry, and solidly founded upon them under Elizabeth, by a very powerful and energetic section of the urban and commercial middle class, and by a number of real, but bitter and narrow-minded, Puritan religionists.

The separation of England from the main body of the Catholic Church in communion with the Apostolic See of Rome was, no doubt, as it happened, part of the providential design in history, and this thought should soften animosities and temper recriminations. But nothing is less true, as a matter of history, than to say that the Church of England deliberately broke itself off, if by 'Church' is meant the majority of clergy and laity. In Henry's reign the mass of the clergy and laity were taken by surprise, as indolent conservatives always are. The long previous decline of religious fervour had left them without much zeal or understanding, and there was general agreement in Europe that many practical reforms were needed, such as were afterwards advised by the Council of Trent, and more or less carried out by the Popes. Clergy and laity, intimidated and unable to marshal their ideas, reluctantly acquiesced at first in the bewilderingly rapid series of actions by the Government. 'Upon the first expulsion of the Pope's authority,' says a Protestant writer of two generations later, 'and King Henry's undertaking of the supremacy, the priests, both regular and secular, did openly in their pulpits so far extol the Pope's jurisdictio and authority, that they preferred his laws before the King's. Whereupon the King sent his mandatory letters to certain of his nobility, and others in especial office, thinking thereby to restrain their seditions, false doctrines, and exorbitancy.' [1]

After the reigns of Edward VI and Mary it had become clear that the real issue at stake was union with or separation from the main body of the Catholic Church, and oppo-

[1] Weever, *A Discourse on Funeral Monuments*, p. 86.

sition to separation from the Apostolic See took definite
shape. The final breach at the beginning of Elizabeth's
reign was opposed by vote in the House of Lords by every
bishop except Kitchin of Llandaff, who alone of them was
consequently not deprived of his see.[1] It is admitted by
most Protestant historians that the separation thus carried
against the bishops' vote was more or less distasteful to
the majority of the clergy, probably to the great majority.
Some of these, especially in the higher ranks, also refused
to take the oath, and were deprived. The vast majority of
the clergy did conform; but for a time, till the generation
died out, many of them were but external conformists, and
adhered at heart to the old religion. These were usually
called by Catholics of the time ' schismatics ' as distinct
from the Puritan ' heretics.'

Elizabeth and her advisers were, perhaps, compelled
by the circumstances, at home and abroad, in which they found
themselves to make their compromise between the conflicting
religious opinions of the commercial and territorial classes.
But the separation from Rome, and still more, the radical
change in doctrine and ritual, the overthrow of the old
Catholic doctrine and cult of the altar, was disliked by the
conservative county families, and by most of the yeomen
and farmers, more especially in the region of the Red Rose
party, the north and west of England. There is plenty of
evidence as to this, apart from the armed risings in the north
and west. The following passage, for one instance, is quoted by
Bishop Milner from a writer in Elizabeth's reign, one Rishton.
Speaking of the state of parties at the beginning of that reign,
Rishton says : ' Item, praeter plurimos ex optimatibus praeci-
puis, pars major inferioris nobilitatis erat plane Catholica.

---

[1] The bishops were deprived for refusing to take the oath of supremacy, which
the Act thus carried against their vote imposed upon all the clergy. Many of the
bishops had, of course, been appointed in Mary's reign.

Plebeii quoque qui agriculturam per totum regnum exercebant novitatem istam imprimis detestabant.' That is: 'Except many of the chief aristocrats, the larger part of the lesser nobility was fully Catholic. The lower class also, who were engaged in agriculture throughout the kingdom, at first detested this novelty.' And the population was then quite four-fifths agricultural. It was what one would expect, because men of the squire, farmer, and yeoman kind, always are conservative and attached to the ways of their forefathers.

Bishop Burnet fully admits in his history that the changes were disliked by a majority of the clergy and laity, but he argues that minorities are usually right, and majorities wrong, in their views. The earlier voluminous Protestant writer, Strype, makes the same admission in many passages, well supported by original documents. The Reformation was closely connected with the commercial development of England. A Catholic writer in Elizabeth's reign, quoted by Froude in his ' English Seamen of the Sixteenth Century,' said, no doubt with exaggeration, that ' the only party that would fight to the death for the Queen, the only real friends she had, were the Puritans—the Puritans of London, the Puritans of the sea-towns.'

In course of years the old clergy died out, and were gradually replaced by men of the new opinions—at first a most queer parsonhood. Meanwhile the error made by Pius V in issuing his Bull of excommunication and deposition against Elizabeth, the patriotic and anti-Spanish motive, so closely linked with the English Reformation (an immensely powerful and in itself meritorious motive), the monopoly of education and of the public pulpits, the invisibility of the old form of worship, which could only be carried on in hunted secrecy and under severest penalties involving not only the life of the priest, but also—though this

was rarely carried out—the lives of those who ' harboured '
him, and the discomforts, disabilities, and, above all, the
heavy and steady special taxation inflicted upon ' popish
recusants,' drove into conformity or indifference most of the
recalcitrants, and thus in England, as in other European
lands, the will of Government prevailed. Once more were
fulfilled the words of the prophet concerning the rulers of this
world : ' Diviserunt sibi vestimenta mea et super vestem meam
miserunt sortes.' ' *Cujus regio ejus religio,*' was, then, the
maxim adopted, and more or less rigorously enforced, throughout Christendom, both in Catholic and Protestant states.
The Duke of Alva was enforcing it in the Netherlands far
more cruelly than Elizabeth in England. Out of these
elements, still confused in the sixteenth century, arose the
Reformed Church of England, which, in the seventeenth, bore
a fair and definite aspect, had already fully evolved its
characteristic theory, and had by this time gained the support
of the majority of the natural Conservative party, though
not that of the Radicals, in religion.

Devout and learned men, educated later than the Elizabethan separation—such as the ' judicious ' Hooker, Jeremy
Taylor, Isaac Barrow, George Herbert, Bishop Bull, Bishop
Pearson, Sir Thomas Browne, and many others, who were
Catholics by native inclination and temperament—now
adorned and strengthened the Protestant and Reformed
Church of England, and, with the practical genius of their
countrymen, made the best out of what had happened. They
were the founders of the High Church party. If Henry VIII
and his successors had not broken off England from communion with Rome, who can doubt that men of this character, attached to established and traditional institutions,
would, like Bossuet, have been firm, though temperate,
adherents to the Roman See? But now Conservative
affections, under opposition to the developing religious

radicalism of the Puritans, and especially under the stimulus of the Civil War, gathered round the new form. Thought being, as Shakespeare remarks, the ' slave of life,' adapted itself to the new ways of its master, and found justification of what he had already done. In its inception, however, and in itself, the actual **Tudor** breach with the International Catholic Church, and with the old mould of religion, was, it must be repeated, undeniably in the nature of revolutionary action carried out by Government, supported by a strong and energetic Radical minority, in opposition to Conservative traditions and feelings. Anglican Churchmen in modern England seem inclined, on the whole, mildly to regret that the action of Henry VIII, Edward VI, Elizabeth, and their advisers, went quite so far as it did ; and certainly modern Conservatives, at any rate, ought to sympathise with the numerous plain, honest, and stubborn country families who held to the ways of all their forefathers and declined to change their religious allegiance to the central and apostolic See of Rome, their doctrines and customs, at the command of a violently reforming and by no means high principled secular Government. These mostly obscure families stood splendidly for religious freedom and for Conservative principle. They only had to attend sometimes the parish church, receive Communion there, and take an oath or two, and all English life was open to them, but they refused the immense temptation They disobeyed statutory law, but they were not bound in the Court of Conscience to accept the blended results of the action of Henry VIII and Thomas Cromwell, Cranmer, Somerset, Elizabeth, and the worldly-wise Cecils. *Principibus placuisse viris non ultima laus est.*

This has been rather a digression, but it was necessary to make some defence of the recalcitrant Hollands of Sutton, who, like many old Conservative families, obedient to the traditions and customs of all their fathers and forefathers, but disobedient to the new laws of their country, adhered to the Church of Rome long after Elizabeth had been gloriously buried at Westminster, and doomed themselves to gradual extinction or complete obscurity.

Richard Holland of Sutton, who was twenty-five years old in 1600, and Anne his wife, were in 1597 and 1603 heavily fined as recusants—persons, that is, who would not attend the parish church. Anne, as a widow, appears on the Recusant Roll in 1634. A younger son of theirs, Thomas Holland, became a Jesuit priest and a Catholic martyr.[1] 'His parents,' says de Marsys, in his French narrative, 'had always been remarkable for their piety, their constancy, and their faith.' Thomas Holland was born at Sutton Hall in 1600. He was put to death in the company of two ordinary malefactors—robbers—at Tyburn, on December 12, 1642, at the beginning of the Civil War, when the usurping power, dominant in London, recommenced these cruel punishments of men for being Catholic priests in England, for they had been suspended during the happy period in which Charles I ruled without the assistance of Parliament.

There are full accounts of this tragedy by co-temporary writers. One is the 'Certamen Triplex,' written in Latin by Father Ambrose Corbie, and published at Antwerp in 1645, of which an English translation was published in 1858. It gives the story of Thomas Holland and of two other priests of the Society of Jesus who suffered about the same time. An account is also given by de Marsys, in his 'De la Mort Glorieuse,' &c., also published in 1645. On these are based the accounts given by Bishop Challoner in his 'Memoirs of Missionary Priests,' published in 1742, and by Foley, S.J.,

---

[1] The name of this Thomas is not given in Dugdale's pedigree of the Sutton Hollands, printed in the Visitation of 1664. Possibly it was not given by the family, for prudential reasons. But he is stated in contemporary accounts to have been the son of Richard and Anne Holland of Sutton in Lancashire, and a nephew of Henry Holland, S J , and this was no doubt the fact

in his 'Records of the English Province of the Society of Jesus.'

When still very young, Thomas Holland went to St. Omer, where he spent six years in the English College of the Society of Jesus, which had been founded there in 1593. He was much esteemed there, and was elected Prefect of the Sodality of the Blessed Virgin. In August 1621, he was sent to the English College of the Society at Valladolid to study philosophy. While he was there the Prince of Wales, afterwards Charles I, came to Madrid with a view to marrying the Infanta Maria. Thomas Holland was chosen, for his power of speech, to address the Prince on behalf of the young Catholic Englishmen who were then studying in Spain. He made a Latin oration, of which the Prince, in replying, admired the style and approved the sentiments.

After three years in Spain, Thomas Holland returned to Flanders, was admitted into the Society, and entered the novitiate of the English Province at Watten in 1620. He then studied theology at the College of Liège—' the House of Divinity of the English Province '—and was ordained priest. After an interval at Ghent, he was appointed Prefect of Morals and Confessor to the scholars at St. Omer's. He was remarkably successful as a teacher of the Divine life. His 'industry in promoting spiritual conversation was observed by many, not only abroad, but afterwards in England, who remarked that he was absolutely made up of spiritual things, and called him a walking library of pious books. He was long remembered by the youth of the seminary with particular affection.' Some stories about his life at St. Omer were given by Thomas Cary, S.J., one of his pupils, and then of Liège College, in a letter which he wrote on February 4, 1643, soon after Holland's martyrdom. He says, among other things, that ' he seemed to be all inflamed, and his eyes would almost sparkle, as he was speaking of Almighty God ; and, in chiding those who were immodest, would with such zeal and fervour reiterate " *Dominus Deus videt nos*," as did clearly manifest what a lively sense and feeling he had of His Divine Majesty.   And although he would speak sometimes in chiding with that voice and gesture which would make a man believe he was on fire, yet we did see clearly that he was not angry, but spake only out of zeal, for as soon as he had ended his speech, he was as present to himself, and as meek and quiet as if he had not been in the least moved. . . . He was an exceeding good ghostly Father, and so beloved of his penitents that four or five years after his departure from the seminary his name was famous for so singular a talent, and divers of his penitents did protest never to have found the like, or received that comfort and full satisfaction from any which they had from him.   He would very often encourage us in confession with saying " My soul for yours," and that in such an expression as we might see it proceeded from a true and noble heart.'

Thomas Holland took his final vows at Ghent on May 26, 1634, and in the following year was sent into England, and worked there for more than eight years, mostly in London. Being obliged generally to keep within doors he lost almost all appetite for food and suffered much in health.   ' Sometimes for months together he was unable to venture out of his place of concealment, or to walk in a private garden, or to inhale the fresh air from an open window, for fear of being noticed by his neighbours.   Notwithstanding all these disadvantages, by a skilful division of the hours, he made this exercise of his patience agreeable to himself by a variety of prayers and occupations, and useful to the family in which he was residing by pious conversation.   His charity, moreover, urged him, in the dusk of evening or in the grey of the dawn, to go forth and console, instruct, and strengthen by

sacraments, such Catholics as did not venture or were unable
to keep priests in their houses ; and also to visit the sick.
He was very ingenious in disguising himself : he would
change his hair, his beard, and his clothes, so as to appear
sometimes as a merchant, at others as a servant, or even as
a man of the world. He could speak French, Flemish, or
Spanish, as occasion required, and thoroughly imitated a
foreign and imperfect pronunciation of his native English,
so that often, when assuming another character, even his
most intimate acquaintance did not recognise him before
he made himself known. By these artifices, rendered
necessary in those unhappy times, he was able to minister
much good to his neighbour, especially during the last two
years of his life among the destitute Catholics of London.'

The pursuivants were always on his track, for London—
especially under the Puritan rebels—was far more dangerous
than Lancashire ; and at last they arrested him in the street
on October 4, 1642, three weeks before the battle of Edge-
hill. He was in prison until his trial. There he lived ' with
such moderation in food, sleep, and all beside, and with such
singular innocence and gentleness of life, that he soon gained
the affection of all his fellow-prisoners, although many of them
were hostile to the faith. He very seldom used his bed for
taking his rest : sometimes he spent the night reclining in a
chair, sometimes in walking about his cell, praying or meditating on divine things, having taken off his shoes that he might
not disturb the repose of others. He used to take every
opportunity of collecting his thoughts ; and, betaking himself
to a cell, or to some unobserved corner of the prison yard,
would there recite his Office. The rest of the day he would
spend in profitable conversation. The Catholics affirmed
that nothing which he had said or done would not beseem
a holy man, and the Protestants were much grieved when
they heard that he was sentenced to death. Some of them

declared that they had never met with a more innocent man ; indeed, they said, if all Jesuits were like him, they did not understand how men could, with justice, revile them.'

On December 7, Father Holland was brought before the Court, indicted for the treasonable offence of being a priest in Roman Orders. Three of the witnesses against him were pursuivants, or, as we should say, detectives ; the fourth was an apostate priest, Thomas Gage, brother of the gallant and loyal Colonel Sir Henry Gage who was killed fighting for the King, near Abingdon, in January 1644, and of George Gage, a faithful Catholic priest. This miserable betrayer said that he had been with the accused at St. Omer's for five years, and gave other evidence. Holland admitted that he had been at the Colleges of St. Omer and Valladolid, but, without denying, said that it had not been proved against him that he was an ordained priest, or had celebrated Mass. The Judge said : ' Will you swear that you are not a priest now ? ' Holland replied : ' It is not the custom of the English law for the accused to clear himself by oath ; but either the crimes laid in the indictment must be clearly proved, or else the accused be acquitted and set at liberty.' He was a graceful speaker, and his defence was much applauded by those in Court.

On Saturday, December 10, Holland, at 8 A.M., was again placed at the bar, and asked what he had to say why sentence of death should not be passed. He repeated in a few words his defence that, according to the law of England, it ought to have been proved by witnesses that he was ordained a priest, or at least that he ' had exercised at some time sacerdotal functions by preaching, hearing confessions, or celebrating Mass. But my accusers have brought nothing of this sort against me, nor do I think they can do so now ; nor have they been able to mention the name of any one whom I have persuaded to change his religion, or whom I have in any way deceived.' 'I confess,' replied the Judge, 'that I find nothing in your life or morals to displease me. By the laws it is enacted that whosoever, being a subject of the King, takes Orders by authority of the Church of Rome, and returns into England, is guilty of high treason, and incurs the penalty of death. The jury have found you guilty upon this charge upon presumption, which at least is a legitimate and full proof, and nothing therefore remains for me, except, according to the form prescribed by law, to pass such sentence upon you as is appointed for priests and traitors. You will therefore return to the prison whence you came, and thence be drawn to the place of execution and there be hanged by the neck till you are half dead ; your bowels shall then be taken out and burnt before your face, your head cut off, and your body divided into four parts, to be exposed in the usual places in this city ; and so may the Lord have mercy on your soul.'

Father Holland, with grateful and humble joy, exclaimed 'Deo gratias,' and on his return to Newgate begged his Catholic fellow-prisoners to join with him in a Te Deum by way of thanksgiving.

This was on Saturday, and his execution was fixed for the following Monday, December 12, 1642. During these few hours 'many persons came to visit him of all nations, ages, sex, and condition—English, Spanish, French, Flemish —whom he received with religious modesty mingled with admirable cheerfulness and firmness. He addressed them in words full of piety, with a placid countenance, and the foreigners in their own language, aptly and skilfully, to the great admiration of all.' 'The prison,' says the narrator, 'assumed more the appearance of a fair than a gaol.' Some were brought there by curiosity, some by piety, some by grief, to bid farewell to so good a friend ; some to receive a last sacrament at his hands, since priests under sentence of death were allowed to say Mass openly in prison. Some

Catholics brought Protestant friends, hoping that they would be moved by the Father's discourse and example. To one such Protestant Father Holland said : ' You expect, I see, that I should say something to you. Now, should I tell you there is a plurality of Gods, you would justly deem me to be a lying man ; equally might you consider me a liar should I tell you that faith is not one. There is only one God, one faith, one religion, one Church, in which, and for which, I am about to die. Behold, therefore, how great an interest you have in following and embracing this one.' The Protestant was struck by these words, which, or the look of the martyr, led to his conversion to Catholicism. The Duke de Vendôme, of the French Royal House, who was in London, offered to intercede with the authorities, but Father Holland begged him not to take so much trouble for one so unworthy. A Portuguese nobleman, who said that he was descended from the Holland family—probably from the old Earls of Kent— sent a painter to take his likeness. This Father Holland at first declined, until the nobleman obtained an order from his religious Superior that he should comply.[1] At the end of this busy Saturday, which had begun with his sentence, the Father said to those present : ' Gentlemen and friends, allow me, I beg you, to collect my thoughts for a short time, and to pray to Almighty God for you and for myself. And you, again, who hear me, pray the same God to give you patience and perseverance at this time. Nor let the insolent and malicious pride of a few persons terrify you, who have it in their minds not only to take away the faithful servants of God, but even, if they could, to hurl God himself from his

---

[1] It is probably this portrait, or a replica of it, which the Teresian nuns at Lanherne in Cornwall still possess, though there is another and more singular story as to its origin. The nuns had the picture as long ago as 1645, when their house was at Antwerp The photograph in this chapter is from this miniature at Lanherne ; but as it is impossible to get a clear photograph from the old miniature it has gone through a clarifying process. In this is lost a very slight auburn beard which appears in the miniature, but which in an unclarified photograph comes out as a dark smudge

throne. Doubt not but that the blood of martyrs will appease their fury. Do you, in the meantime, remember me in your prayers, and I will not forget you.'

On the next morning—that of the Third Sunday in Advent—he heard several confessions, and, after celebrating Mass—(how moving these last celebrations must have been !) —he administered to many the Sacrament. During this day also he received many visitors. Among these was the Spanish Ambassador, to whom he promised that in gratitude for all the kindness shown by the Spanish Government to English Catholics, he would offer his last Mass for the King and Kingdom of Spain. He sat down to supper with his friends, but would take nothing but an egg and a little wine. This he said would give him a little more blood to shed for Christ. ' So, on Monday the 12th of December, Father Holland, having said Mass very early in the morning, before he had finished his thanksgiving, received the news that the hurdle was at the door ready to draw him to Tyburn. He descended with alacrity, giving his benedictions to the bystanders.' Neither of the Sheriffs of London and Middlesex were, as usual, present. It was believed that they considered it to be a judicial murder ; the Sheriff of London had applied to the Parliament Executive Committee for a respite, but had been refused. These gentlemen, who were themselves in active rebellion against their King, had usurped and abused his prerogative of mercy. A serjeant, who was officially walking beside the hurdle as two horses dragged it through the winter mud and over the stones, told people who asked about the prisoner that ' he was going to die contrary to law, right, and justice.'

At Tyburn was assembled a great crowd. The Spanish Ambassador was present, with his household. Another priest of the Society of Jesus, who had assisted Father Holland in prison, was there in disguise, and, taking his hand, said : ' Be of good cheer, and bear yourself bravely.' To whom he replied : ' By God's grace you have no cause to fear; my courage will not fail.'

When he was unbound from the hurdle he stood up and said to the people that he would speak to them, and say nothing offensive to any man. ' But what am I doing? I ought to begin with that sign by virtue whereof Christians may overcome their enemy.' Then fortifying himself with the sign of the Cross, he proceeded : ' No one can possibly be offended at this, being the sign of a Christian man.' Then he went on, ' in a firm yet sweet voice,' expressing his desire that God would pardon his enemies, but repeating his view that his condemnation had not been according to the English rules of the law-game. ' However,' he concluded, ' I confess before this assembly here present that I am a Catholic and a priest, and, by the infinite goodness of God, a religious of the Society of Jesus, and the first of that Order sentenced to death since the beginning of the present Parliament. For all which benefits conferred upon me, though undeserving of them, I give the greatest thanks to God immortal.'

He then began to explain to the people the true nature of the Roman and Catholic Church; but here he was interrupted by questions and statements made by the chaplain of Newgate, who was in official attendance. The chaplain then told him to speak no more to the people, but to say his prayers to himself, while he talked to the two robbers, who were also to be hung. ' Thus, whilst the minister was delivering a long address to the robbers, and praying extemporaneously and verbosely, singing also some psalms in English, Father Holland, turning another way, communed with God with a quiet and composed air. At length, when the minister had finished, he said : ' Mr. Minister, I have not interrupted you in your preaching and praying, and now in your turn let me pray to God with a loud voice that all may hear what I say.' The chaplain began to cavil, and say that it was unnecessary, because he had already prayed for him and the two others. 'But I will allow you,' he said, 'on one condition—that, whenever you fall into error, I may interrupt and correct you.' The Father accepted the condition, and, reverently kneeling down, signed himself with the sign of the Cross, using the Latin formula, and then began to pray in English, with a clear voice and earnest piety, first returning to God thanks for all His benefits from his birth, and especially for the greatest favour of dying for his religion and for the Catholic priesthood ; he then expressed the most lively sentiments of faith, hope, and charity, asking pardon for his sins, acknowledging that he was nothing of himself, and could do nothing without the help of God, offering to Him his memory, his understanding, and his will, and all his powers and faculties of soul and body, and lastly himself and his life as a sacrifice. 'Receive me,' he said, 'O Father of Mercies, as Thou seest me ; and receive these my unworthy sufferings which I most willingly offer to Thee in union with the most holy Passion of Thy only-begotten Son, to be, I hope, more acceptable by the virtue and in union of what my sweetest Redeemer Jesus suffered ; together with the merits of all who have been, or are, or shall be accepted by Thee.' Afterwards he said : 'I forgive my judge and his assessors who condemned me ; I forgive the jury who brought me in guilty on a capital charge ; I forgive my accusers and all others who in any way are the cause of my coming to a violent death.' He added prayers for the King, the Queen, their family and the Parliament and nation, for whose good, restoration to the faith, and eternal welfare, he said, 'if I had as many lives as there are hairs on my head, drops in the ocean, stars in the firmament, perfections in the Lord of Heaven, I would most willingly lay them all down for this purpose.' This the spectators applauded.

'Then, turning to the executioner, he said : 'Well,

Gregory, I also willingly pardon you for carrying out my sentence,' and he gave him all the money he had—two gold crowns. Then, reopening his eyes, which had been closed for a short time, he fixed them upon the priest of the Society of Jesus, his helper, who, on this signal, as had been previously agreed upon, gave him the last absolution, so that he heard the final words of the formula.'

The cart drove away from beneath him and he was left hanging. A Catholic bystander removed the cap which had been placed over his face, and revealed a countenance not at all distorted, but having an angelic expression. The Newgate chaplain, fearing the effect which might be produced on the people, called to the executioner to cut him down half dead, according to the sentence; but the more humane Gregory pretended to be busied with something until life was quite extinct, and the rest of the legally prescribed butchery could be effected upon a dead body.

The authorities had often been embarrassed by the undesired effect which these martyrdoms produced on the people. An official memorandum of 1586, endorsed 'The means to stay the declining in religion through the Seminaries offending in practice,' said, *inter alia*: 'The execution of them [the seminary priests], as experience hath showed, in respect of their constancy, or rather obstinacy, moveth many to confession, and draweth some to affect their religion, upon conceit that such an extraordinary contempt of death cannot but proceed from above, whereby many have fallen away. And therefore it is a thing meet to be considered if it were not convenient that some other remedy be put into execution.' It might be a memorandum by a puzzled Roman official with regard to early Christian victims of religious laws.

Thomas Holland suffered in the forty-second year of his age. 'In stature he was below the middle size; he had a handsome face, florid complexion, auburn beard, dark hair, large and prominent eyes—the expression of which was subdued by his sweet and pleasing manners.'

It was a proof of the respect felt for this martyr that no idle ballads, so usual on such occasions, were sung in the streets, nor were any insulting words uttered against him. A Catholic nobleman, in whose house Father Holland had lived, testified with tears that of all the priests he had known, he considered this Father most worthy of such a crown. A Protestant also was heard to say: ' When, in all our life, shall we see another—when shall we see anyone of our religion—die so nobly ? '

Father Corby concludes his account of Thomas Holland, in the ' Certamen Triplex,' by saying: ' His true character was that he had extraordinary talents for promoting the greater glory of God, and that he made extraordinary use of them. His knowledge in spirituals was such that he was termed the library of piety, *Bibliotheca pietatis*. And whenever he was in company, whatever the subject of the conversation happened to be, he would by a dexterous turn bring it to some moral or gospel instruction for the advantage of the company ; imitating the great St. Francis Xavier, of whom it used to be said that in his conversation with people of the world, ' he would go in at their door and come out at his own.'

Among the Stonyhurst MS there is a little volume, in handwriting, of an ascetical work by Father Thomas Cooke. Opposite the title-page this Father wrote a note that this book was entirely in the handwriting of Father Thomas Holland, Martyr, and that it was done while Father Holland was studying at Liège, where Father Cooke was at that time ' Confessor Domi.' He says : ' So far from my asking him to do it, or even thinking of such a thing, he, Father Holland, come to me and begged and intreated that, ill-suited—so his humility would have it—for theological studies, I would allow him to spend some of his time usefully in transcribing this book.' Two observations, it may be added, are made in the Annual Letter of the Rector of the College of Liège for the year 1642 : one, that the College gloried in the fact that Thomas Holland received Holy Orders in it ; the other, that he was the first of its *alumni* who had shed his blood for Christ, and that the news of his most holy death was received there with incredible joy.[1]

Another Lancashire gentleman, of the fine old Lancashire race of the Barlows, near neighbours of the Hollands of Clifton and Denton, who lived at Barlow Hall in Chorlton from the days of Edward I to the end almost of the eighteenth century, met the same fate as Thomas Holland, at nearly the same time. He was Edward Barlow, son of Sir Alexander Barlow, and was known in religion as ' Father Ambrose of the Order of ' Saint Benedict,' and in 1610 was at the English College of Valladolid. He was the truest possible saint, and his character is very beautifully described by Bishop Challoner in his ' Memoirs of Missionary Priests.' For twenty years he laboured in Lancashire, doing nothing but religious good to Catholics, and suffered martyrdom at Lancaster, to please or appease the then dominant faction, on September 10, 1641, at the age of fifty-five. He, too, was a martyr for the real and visible unity of the Catholic Church, which is, according to St. Augustine, the highest outward or sacramental form of Caritas.

The other Jesuit priests of the seventeenth century belonging to the Sutton family were Henry Holland, an uncle, and Alexander, a nephew, of the martyred Thomas.

Henry Holland was born in 1576. He went to the English College in Rome, where a note in the Rectorial Diary says that he was ' always modest, but too good friends with the disobedient.' He became a priest in 1603, went on the English mission in 1605, and entered the Jesuit Order in 1609. All his many years in England he was employed

---

[1] Foley's *Records*, vii. 188.

in his own county of Lancashire. There he made numerous converts, some of them persons of note. In a letter about his death, dated March 1656, the Rector of the College at Liège wrote : ' He alone among a great company of the gravest Fathers was selected to hear the first confession of that very celebrated man, justly ranked among the most learned men of his day—Mr. James Anderton of Lostock, the author of the very erudite work entitled " The Apology of Protestants." ' It was also said of him that ' by his candour of manner, innocence of life, and gentleness in dealing with his neighbour, he won the esteem of all and a high reputation for sanctity. So much so that the leading Catholics in all the places where he lived entrusted their concerns to him for his advice.'

The full and curious title of James Anderton's book is, ' The Protestants Apologie for the Roman Chvrch. Diuided into three seuerall Tractes.' The first edition was published in 1604, and led to some heavy, long-forgotten controversy. Rather more is known of another member of the same old Lancashire family, Lawrence Anderton, brother of Squire Christopher Anderton of Lostock. Five Andertons of the Lostock race fell later in the Civil War fighting for the King and the Conservative cause. They were connected by an earlier marriage with the Hollands of Denton. Lawrence Anderton was a scholar at Christ's College, Cambridge, where he took his degree in 1597, and so eloquent was he that he was called ' silver-mouthed Anderton.' Anthony à Wood says that he was disturbed by doubts as to the origin of the Reformation, and that ' his mind hanging upon the Roman Catholic religion he left that college, and, shipping himself beyond the seas, entered into Roman Catholic Orders, and became one of the learnedest among the papists.' He became a Jesuit in 1604, worked for forty years on the mission in Lancashire, wrote several books, and died in 1643 at the age of sixty-six. He must have been an intimate friend and colleague in that province of Father Henry Holland.

According to one account, Henry Holland was arrested in 1648, tried, and condemned to die, but had his sentence commuted to perpetual banishment. According to a more probable statement he was simply recalled by his superiors from England at that date because his age and growing deafness made him no longer suitable for active work in that dangerous period. He spent his remaining years in the College at Liège, and died there on February 29, 1656, at the age of eighty, having spent forty-seven years of his life in the Society. The Rector wrote of him after his death : ' Father Holland was a man of great innocence of life and extraordinary piety. He bore the affliction of his deafness with equanimity and cheerfulness, and endeared himself to all by his purity of life and sweetness of manners. His deafness prevented his enjoyment of conversation during the customary times of recreation, so that he spent nearly the whole of his time in prayer with God, his close union with Whom was frequently manifested by his raising his eyes and hands to heaven. He died rather from old age and decay of nature than from any real disease.'

Little is known of the third Jesuit priest of this family, Alexander Holland, nephew of the martyred Thomas. He was born in 1623, entered the Valladolid College in 1642—the year of his uncle's death—and obtained a university prize on the occasion of the funeral of Isabella, Queen of Spain. His name appears as one of the Jesuits of the College of St. Aloysius, in the Lancashire district of the English province, in the year 1655. He was then aged thirty-two, and had been for four years a priest of the Society of Jesus. He served in this mission until he died in Lancashire on May 29, 1677.

The Hollands of Sutton were, of course—as Catholics— engaged upon the Royalist side in the Civil War. At

the close of the war their estate was sequestered by
Parliament on account of the owner's—Richard Holland—
' recusancy and delinquency.' This was the second Richard,
nephew of the martyr, who, like his grandfather, had
married a lady named Anne. He died in 1649, and after
his death the ruined estate was seized for a time by
a creditor. His son and heir was Edward Holland, who
was twenty-four when he signed the pedigree for Dugdale's
Visitation of Lancashire in 1664. In 1679, when the popish
plot agitation was boiling, he was declared a recusant
together with Esther his wife, and in his old age—for he
was then seventy-six—he was on April 10, 1716, ' convicted
as a popish recusant,' at the Lancaster Quarter Sessions,
probably in connection with the recent Jacobite rising in
the north. When the Earl of Derwentwater, with his
Scots and Northumbrians, marched as far as Preston, he
was joined by many Lancashire Catholic gentlemen, though
the High Church Tories failed to consummate Jacobite
talk in action. Edward Holland died soon after, and, in
1717, Thomas Holland of Sutton his successor, registered
his estate as a ' Catholic non-juror.' He still possessed
Sutton Hall, but the Manor had been sold in 1700. Another
Jesuit ' of Lancashire,' Richard Holland, who was born in
1676, was professed in 1715 ; for many years in those milder
times lived at Wardour ; and was afterwards Rector of a
college, and died at Paris, July 1, 1740. He seems to have
been a younger brother of this last Thomas Holland. The
Hollands had been owners of land at Sutton for about four
hundred years. What became of them afterwards, or
whether they entirely died out, is not known. Baines, in his
' History of Lancashire', says that the Sutton Hall standing in
his time existed before the year 1567. It was in the Parish
of St. Helen, in the West Derby Hundred, in the plain
which is now no longer green and rural, but a dark industrial
region.

HOLLANDS OF DENTON AND HEATON

Thurstan de Holland, = Mary, d. of John Collyer.
eldest son of William de
Holland of Sharples (a
grandson of Sir Thurstan
Holland of Upholland)
and of Margaret de Shoresworth, heiress of Denton;
of full age 1316; still
living 1868.

Richard de Holland; = Aimeria, d. of Adam   William Holland = Marjory, d of Henry   Three other
b. about 1325, d 1402 | de Kenyon.   de Trafford   sons

Thurstan Holland, = Agnes, d. of ——   Hollands of Clifton, &c
b about 1360, d
1428

Thurstan Holland, = Margaret, d. of Sir Lawrence   Three other sons,
b. about 1390, d | Warren of Poynton. She d   Richard, Henry, and
before 1467. | before 1442 He also married   Thomas; all living in
                 | three other wives, s p   1430

Richard Holland; = Agnes, d. of ——
b 1432, d 1483 |

Richard Holland; = Isabella, d. of Sir William   Two other sons, Nicholas and Lawrence,
b. about 1450, d | Harrington of Hornby,   living 1510, and a d, Margaret, who m.
about 1501 | about 1466   Oliver Anderton.

Thurstan Holland, = Joan, d of John Arderne   Four other sons, William, Robert, Thomas,
b. about 1470, d. Oct. | She afterwards m Sir John   and Peter, and a d, Ellen, who m 1501 John
11, 1508. | Warren of Poynton.   Bradshaw.

Robert Holland, = Elizabeth, d of Sir   Sir Richard Holland, = (1) Anne, d of John = (2) Eleanor, d of Sir Ralp
b. about 1491, d s p | Richard Ashton.   b. about 1493, d. 1548 | Fitton of Gawsworth   bottle of Beamish, Durl
1513

(2) Cecily, d of = Edward Holland, = (1) Jane, d. of   Three sons, Richard,   Richard Holland,   Mary = Arthi
Edmund Trafford | b about 1520, d | John Carring-   Ralph, and Randle,   living 1548   Sir
and widow of Sir | Aug 22, 1570. | ton.   who all d s p, and a   Poole
Robert Langley of | d, Margaret
Agecroft in 1562

Richard Holland, = Margaret,   Edward Holland, = (1595), Anne, d of   John Holland,   Eight daugh
b. about 1516, d. | d. of Sir   b. about 1550, d | Edmund Gamull,   living 1571
March 2, 1619 with- | Robert   1631. | Alderman of
out male issue | Langley | Chester, and
                    | of Age- | widow of John
                    | croft. | Brock.

Edward Holland, = Anne   Thomas Holland   William Holland = Cecily, d. of   Two other sor
d s p   Rigby.   of Denton and   (Rev) of Denton | Alex Walt-   John and Heni
                          Heaton, d unm   and Heaton, b. | ham of   d. unm., and fi
                          May 22, 1661   1612, d 1682 | Wistaston,   daughters, Mai
                                                             | Cheshire   Elizabeth, Ani
                                                                                 Frances, ar
Edward Holland;   Richard, Frances, and   Jane, all marri
b. 1662, d. 1683   Jane, d children   Elizabeth = Sir John Egerton   into Cheshire ai
                                                        of Wrinehill,   Shropshi
                                                        Bart., Nov 27,   families
                                                        1684.

                                           Earls of Wilton,
Col Richard Holland = Katherine,   owners of Denton and Heaton.
of Denton and Heaton, | d. of Wm
M.P., &c.; b. 1596, d | Ramsden
1661. | of Lang-
                      | ley, Yorks

Edward Holland, = Anne, d of
d July 11, 1655, | Edward
before his father | Warren of
                  | Poynton.

CHAPTER XI

La vie champestre est la vraye vie d'un gentilhomme.
PIERRE MATTHIEU.

SIR THURSTAN DE HOLLAND (the second) born under
Edward I, and living far into the reign of Edward III,
founded the line of Hollands of Denton and their early
branch of Clifton. He was great-grandson to the first Sir
Thurstan de Holland, of Upholland. The eldest son of the
last-named Thurstan of Upholland was Sir Robert, ancestor
of the Earls of Kent and Huntingdon. One of the same
Thurstan's younger sons was Sir William de Holland, who
possessed the Manor of Sharples. This Sir William had a son
also named William, and also knighted. This second Sir
William was legally married to Joan de Pleasington, by
whom he had no children, but was less formally united to
an heiress of quality named Margaret de Shoresworth, and
by her became father to Thurstan Holland the second.

The informal nature of the union between Sir William
de Holland and Margaret de Shoresworth is shown by
various legal documents, from which it appears that
Thurstan was born when his mother, Margaret, was an
unmarried girl, a little before the year 1300. Margaret
was, after this, twice legally married: once to Henry de
Worsley, who died in 1304, and once to Robert de Radcliffe,
and had children by both. She died in 1363, when she must
have been about eighty, giving in that year to her son,
Thurstan de Holland, all her goods, movable and immovable.
In various documents and deeds Thurstan is referred to
sometimes as the ' son of Sir William de Holland,' sometimes
as ' the son of Margaret Shoresworth,' and sometimes as the
269

son of them both. In 1315. land in Pleasington was settled upon Sir William de Holland and Joan his wife, with remainder—in default of their issue—to Thurstan, son of William.[1] Thus Joan seems to have acquiesced. In 1316 Sir William de Holland, granted his inherited Manor of Sharples to ' Thurstan, son of Margaret de Shoresworth,' for life. A grant of land at Denton was made in 1325 to ' Thurstan, son of Margaret de Shoresworth,' and Sir William de Holland witnessed the deed. In 1330, by a deed dated at Denton on the Feast of St. Hilary, Alexander de Shoresworth, her uncle, granted to ' Margaret, daughter of Robert de Shoresworth,' all his messuages, lands, and tenements in the Hamlet of Denton, in tail. A few days later, Margaret de Shoresworth granted the same estates to Thurstan de Holland, her son, in tail, with remainder, in default of his issue, to William, son of Robert de Radcliffe and his heirs, and further remainders to other Radcliffes and Worsleys. Five years later, by another deed, Thurstan de Holland, calling himself ' son of William de Holland,' granted to ' Margaret, my mother,' a life interest in the Denton estate. In 1319, Sir Robert de Holland granted lands in Heaton to ' Thurstan de Holland, son of Margaret de Shoresworth.'

It has been suggested that Sir William de Holland had been married, without a dispensation, to Margaret, but that the marriage was within forbidden degrees, but there is no evidence of this. It is clear as day that Sir William, not having a son by his lawful wife, Joan de Pleasington, intended and took much trouble to found a family through Thurstan, his son by Margaret. For that purpose, he endowed him by grant with the Sharples estate, while Margaret's uncle, Alexander de Shoresworth, also not having heirs, endowed Thurstan with the Denton estate, a life interest for Margaret being subsequently arranged.

[1] There is a series of documents bearing on this subject in the appendices to Mr. Irvine's book, *The Hollands of Mobberley and Knutsford.*

Thus Thurstan de Holland was in a perfectly open way treated by every one as the son of Sir William, as in fact he was. If one studies chronicles and local histories, one sees that the position of 'natural' children was happier and better in medieval England than it is now, when such children usually suffer in darkness and loss of status for sins which are none of theirs. Medieval society was more sincere, and paid less devout homage to respectability, and such children—at any rate, if their mothers were ladies of some quality—were acknowledged and provided for, and if they belonged to good families they were openly and justly proud of the fact.

Since, however, Thurstan de Holland was not his father's legal heir-at-law, the entailed family land in the tenure of Sir William, passed at his death (about 1318) not to Thurstan, but to his uncle, Sir Robert de Holland, who apparently gave it, or some of it, back to Thurstan. The following table shows the derivation of Denton Manor.[1]

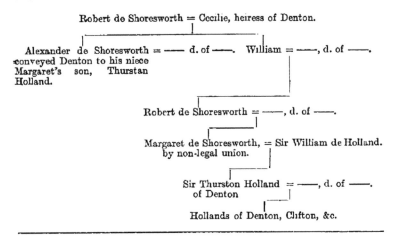

Robert de Shoresworth = Cecilie, heiress of Denton.

Alexander de Shoresworth = —— d. of ——. William = ——, d. of ——.
conveyed Denton to his niece
Margaret's son, Thurstan
Holland.

Robert de Shoresworth = ——, d. of ——.

Margaret de Shoresworth, = Sir William de Holland.
by non-legal union.

Sir Thurston Holland = ——, d. of ——.
of Denton

Hollands of Denton, Clifton, &c.

---

[1] See *Lancashire Inquisitions*, vol. i. p 150 ; *Chetham Society Papers*, vol. xcv. See also, *Vict. Co. History of Lanc.*, vol iv. pp. 312, 378, 395, and vol. v. p. 261. Also Irvine's *Hollands of Mobberley and Knutsford*. It is not quite clear whether Alexander was uncle or a great-uncle of Margaret

Denton Hall stood about five miles south-east of the old town of Manchester. The manor remained in the possession of Thurstan de Holland and his lineal male descendants from 1330 to 1686—about 350 years. Thurstan also acquired the Manor of Heaton, just north of Manchester, which at a much later date became chief residence of this family.

These Hollands of Denton always held the position of a county family on the higher level, and married into like families in Lancashire and Cheshire; but they played their part on the provincial and not on the national scene. No doubt they were sometimes in the Scottish wars, for it was the duty for the gentlemen in the nine northern counties to quell the Scots, while those of the south were engaged in the more pleasant and profitable trade of war in sunny France. Richard de Holland was, however, one of the Lancashire gentlemen summoned on March 28, 1373, to serve the Duke of Lancaster in an expedition to France.

Thurstan de Holland, son of William and Margaret, was in political trouble in the reign of Edward III, for, on June 12, 1346, that King issued letters patent to him from Windsor stating that, ' at the request of our cousin, Henry of Lancaster, Earl of Derby,' he pardons Thurstan de Holland for all felonies and transgressions committed against the King's peace prior to the 16th of June last passed.' History does not record what were these felonies and transgressions, but, ever since the affair of Boroughbridge, the Holland clan had no doubt been in disfavour with the potentate of the north—Henry of Lancaster. Probably Sir Thomas Holland, K.G., the near cousin of Thurstan and then in high favour at Windsor, negotiated this pardon. John Holland, youngest son of Thurstan, by the way, had been outlawed in 1338 for an assault, *vi et armis*, on William de Hulton, and all his cattle were confiscated.

Thurstan de Holland was of full age in 1316, and was still living in 1368; so that he attained to a considerable age. He was knighted before 1355. He married Mary, daughter of John Collyer, and was succeeded in the possession of Denton and Heaton, and other estates, by his eldest son, Richard, who was born about 1325, married Aimeria, daughter of Adam de Kenyon, and died in 1402. Sir Thurstan's second son, William de Holland, married Marjory, daughter and co-heiress of Henry de Trafford, and so acquired the manor of Clifton in Prestwich, and founded the line of Hollands who held it till the seventeenth century, and have left descendants to the present day.

The pedigree of the Hollands of Denton was very well kept, but their recorded history, like that of most county families, mainly consists of births, marriages, settlements, deaths, and transactions in land. They were squires of considerable standing, and married into neighbouring families of like degree. Sir Richard Holland of Denton, made a Knight by Henry VIII in 1544, died in 1548, leaving a large family of legitimate children by two wives, and also three illegitimate sons, whom, with the candour of that age, he commended by will—as they were then minors—to the care of his second wife. His eldest legal son, Edward, was born about 1520, and died in 1570. Edward's eldest son, Richard, was born about 1546. This Richard Holland of Denton was Sheriff of Lancashire in 1571, 1573, 1580, and 1595. He was 'much honoured by the Queen for his zeal against recusants,' and he took an active part against the Catholic gentry, then so numerous in Lancashire, among whom were some distant relatives of his own name, and in hunting down 'popish priests' and Jesuit missionaries. Edmund Campion, the brave and cultivated young Oxford Jesuit, who died at Tyburn in 1581, wrote in a letter from Lancashire, in 1580, that 'Holland of Denton is a rigid Puritan.'

Richard Holland died in 1619, leaving five daughters, but without male issue, and was succeeded in the possession of Denton and Heaton by his nephew, also named Richard, who was born about 1596. These Hollands attained at this period to their highest prosperity, and now began to live more spaciously at Heaton House than they had lived in their ancestral hall of Denton. The second Richard Holland, following the religious views of his uncle, took a leading part in the local civil war in Lancashire, on the side of Parliament. Most of the Lancashire gentlemen, headed by Lord Strange, who succeeded late in 1642 to the Earldom of Derby, were Royalists, and many of them, including the Hollands of Sutton and, probably, Clifton, were Catholics. But the small towns of south-east Lancashire—as Manchester, Wigan, Bolton, Warrington, already seats of young industries—were strongly Puritan, and so were some of the squires in that region, such as the Denton Hollands, the Rigbys, Bradshaws, Egertons.

At Manchester, in 1642, there was a small magazine of arms and munitions, which had probably been stored there— as that at Hull—with a view to the unsuccessful operations against the Scots. Lord Strange arrived from the royal headquarters at York on July 4, 1642, with a small armed force, and demanded the surrender of the magazine. The 'Committee of Manchester,' headed by Richard Holland, refused, and a skirmish took place. This was the opening bloodshed in the Civil War. One townsman was killed— Richard Perceval, a linen-webster (first, it is said, of all the thousands who died in this war)—and a few were wounded. On September 24, the Earl of Derby, as Lord Strange had now become on his father's death, returned to Manchester at the head of three or four thousand men and attacked the town unsuccessfully until December, when he retired.

Richard Holland was now at the head of the Manchester Defence Committee, and soon afterwards was appointed by Parliament to be Governor of Manchester. He had a special regiment of his own raising, and was known as Colonel Holland. Parliament appointed a Colonel for each hundred in Lancashire, and Richard Holland was Colonel for the Salford Hundred.

In October 1642, an attempt was made by certain Lancashire gentlemen—some on the King's side and some on that of the Parliament—to effect a *modus vivendi*, and to save, at any rate, local fighting and bloodshed between neighbours, relatives, and friends. Mr. Richard Shuttleworth of Gawthorpe—an ancestor of the present Lord Shuttleworth—and others, wrote to Richard Holland, and other Parliamentarians in the Salford Hundred, asking them to meet some Royalist gentlemen at Blackburn on Thursday, October 13. Holland and Peter Egerton replied that they could not go to Blackburn, but would meet the gentlemen at Bolton. Arrangements went so far that it was agreed that Richard Holland, Peter Egerton, John Bradshaw, Richard Shuttleworth, and two others, should meet an equal number of Royalists at Bolton on Tuesday, October 18, at 10 A.M. But in the interval, Holland received instructions from London, which prevented the holding of the conference. He wrote at Manchester on the 15th the following letter, preserved in the Gawthorpe Collection, with the seal of the Hollands attached to it. It is addressed to his 'much respected friends, Richard Shuttleworth and John Starkey, Esquires.'

'GENTLEMEN,—I have had a sight of a letter directed from Mr. Alex. Rigby, Mr. Ferington, and Mr. Fleetwood, touchynge a meetynge at Boulton uppon Tuesday next. 'Tis true Mr. Egerton and myselfe writt to you a letter to that purpose ; since when, wee have received commands both by letter and Declarations sett forth from Parliament, how much it is against their likynge to have any treatie, and have therefore declared their utter dislike of the accommodation in Yorkshire.

'I shall, therefore, not need to give you a reason why wee cannot well give a meetynge. As for the peace of this country, there is none, I dare answear, desires more the preservation thereof than wee hereabouts doc nor shall have a greater detestation of those that shall disturbe it. And thus leaving the premises to your consideration.

'I rest,

'Yo. very lovynge friend,

'RICHARD HOLLAND.'

Manchester, October 15, 1642.

In 1643 there was a good deal of fighting in Lancashire. A force under Major-General Sir John Seaton and Colonel Holland marched out of Manchester on February 10, joined other troops from Bolton and Blackburn, and stormed Preston after two hours' hard fighting, in which many men were slain. The Earl of Derby captured Lancaster in March. On April 1, the Manchester force, led by Colonel Holland, suddenly stormed the town of Wigan, which Lord Derby had left garrisoned under a Scot, named Major-General Blair. This was a great blow to the Lancashire Royalists. Wigan was near Lathom House, the glorious and ancient castle of the Stanleys, which Charlotte de la Tremouille, Countess of Derby was holding for her lord. On the day of Colonel Holland's capture of Wigan, the Countess wrote in her distress to Prince Rupert.

The letter is in French, and, turned into English, runs thus :—

' MONSEIGNEUR,—I have just this moment received the bad news of the loss of Wigan, six miles from this place ; it held out for but two hours, being terrified ; my husband was twelve miles off, and before he could make ready to succour it they surrendered. In the name of God, Monseigneur, take pity on us, and if you show yourself you will be able to reconquer it very easily and with great honour to Your Highness. I know not what I say ; but have pity on my husband, my children, and me. We are ruined for ever, unless God and Your Highness have pity on us.

'I am Monseigneur,
'Your very humble and obedient servant,
'C. DE LA TREMOUILLE.'

Lathom, April 1, 1643.

Warrington was next taken by the Manchester Puritan forces. The contemporary author of a 'Briefe Journall of the Siege against Lathom,' says :—

'Upon the surrender of Warrington, May 27, 1643, a summons came from Mr. Holland, Governor of Manchester, to the Lady Derby to subscribe to the propositions of Parliament or yield up Lathom House ; but her ladyship denied both : she would neither tamely give up her house nor purchase her peace with the loss of her honour.'

The Countess of Derby was born of one of the noblest houses of France, in a most energetic period of French history, and was a worthy compatriot and coeval of Anne de Bourbon, Duchesse de Longueville. Richard Holland was unfortunate in encountering such a heroine in Lancashire, for Romance was against him.

The rest of the war in Lancashire mainly turned on the attempts to reduce obstinate Lathom House. A force, commanded by Lord Byron, was defeated by Fairfax at Nantwich on January 25, 1644. Holland took part in this success, and his regiment was mentioned with honour by Fairfax in his dispatch. But Lathom House was still gallantly holding out in May 1644, and the arrival of Prince Rupert's army from the south was daily expected. On May 16, the Manchester Committee wrote to Lord Denbigh a pressing letter urging him to bring his force to assist or the siege might have to be broken up. Lathom was vigorously assailed at this time by a Parliamentary force under the command of Sir Thomas Fairfax himself, with Richard Holland serving under him. At the end of May, Prince Rupert relieved the place, and 1600 of the besiegers were killed and 700 taken prisoner. The Prince then stormed and sacked Puritan Bolton—' the Geneva of Lancashire,' as it was called—and passed away over the moors to his final defeat near York. Lathom House fell at last, but not till December 1645.

In the year 1643 an accusation was made against Colonel Holland's military conduct by one Rosworm. This kind of ' Dugald Dalgetty ' was of alien origin, and had served in the German wars, and understood how to make fortifications. Some citizens of Manchester—worthy drapers and others— were horribly afraid in the summer of 1642 that the town and their shops would be plundered by Lord Derby and his northern cavaliers, and entered into a solemn covenant with Rosworm that, if he secured them from this, they would pay him certain sums, which they collected by subscription. Rosworm, having this kind of independent municipal function, soon came into collision with Colonel Holland when the latter was appointed by Parliament to be Governor of Manchester. He accused him of wishing to surrender Manchester in 1642, and of weakness in the attack on War- rington, and generally of timidity and indecision, and because he refused to take good advice from a professional soldier. Holland had to go up to London in the summer or autumn of 1643 to appear before a Parliamentary Committee along with Rosworm and other witnesses. He was acquitted in consequence, says Rosworm, of the fact that ' his great friends prevailed for his escape ' in the House, but far more prob- ably because the allegations wholly broke down. In 1649

Rosworm printed a long, egoistic and rambling ' Historical Relation of Lieutenant Colonel Rosworm's Service and Rewards,' addressed to General Fairfax, John Bradshaw, President of the Council, and Lieutenant-General Oliver Cromwell, accusing Holland of all kinds of misconduct. In this Rosworm took to himself the whole credit of the capture of Wigan and said, with probable truth, ' Colonel Holland seemed troubled that I perished not in the action.' He said that Colonel Holland had afterwards deprived him, Rosworm, of part of his pay, ' upon the pretence that I had not taken the Covenant,' and he accused Holland of cowardice and vacillation on various occasions. ' Alas ! ' he wrote, ' Who can settle a trembling heart ? '

It seems to be true that at one time in 1642, Holland thought it would be necessary to evacuate Manchester for want of powder, and because the rustic soldiers in the town wished to get back to their villages, and because the enemy were growing in strength. But Colonel Holland's real offence seems to have been that he refused to be governed by Rosworm's opinions and prevented that mercenary engineer from getting all the pay that, in his own opinion, he deserved. Rosworm was the man with a professional grievance, who is always with us, too well known to every Governmental department. He and his grievance remain petrified for ever at full length in the Chetham Society volumes on the ' Civil War in Lancashire.'

Colonel Holland represented Lancashire in the House of Commons during those short Parliaments of 1654 and 1656 which Oliver Cromwell found so unsatisfactory. He was a moderate man of the Presbyterian party, opposed to the Independents. He was, probably, like all those moderate men, not exactly sorry to see the Restoration, although after that event the position of men like himself was unsatisfactory. As his friend, Henry Newcome, remarked, the moderate

Presbyterians were classed by the Royalists with the 'fana-tics' on the alleged ground of want of loyalty, and by the fanatics with the Royalists, on the ground of want of enthusiastic piety. This Henry Newcome was Presbyterian minister at Manchester, and was evicted after the Restoration. He was a weak man, tormented by innumerable petty religious scruples, which he recorded in a morbid diary, in which Colonel Holland figures from time to time. In 1659 Newcome was with Colonel Holland when one Nehemiah Poole was brought in and charged before the Colonel, as a magistrate, with the offence of being a Quaker. The Colonel ordered him to be sent to prison. Nehemiah had just arrived walking from Bristol to Manchester and was dripping wet, the water oozing above his shoes. He asked that he might first go home to his own house to change his clothes. 'The Colonel,' says Newcome, 'seemed to give no ear to him'; but at last, on Newcome's prayer 'condescended,' and Nehemiah did not on that occasion go to prison at all. With base ingratitude Nehemiah brought against Mr. Newcome a charge of persecution of the saints. Nehemiah was, however, soon afterwards sent to prison for three months for coming into the parish church during the sermon with nothing but a shirt on, and there lifting up his voice to testify.

On September 18, 1660, Mr. Newcome notes, after saying that he was clearly to be 'outed' from his living : 'Colonel Holland came and called on me, and sate with me an hour, and gave me his advice which I took very kindly of him.' On July 27, 1661, Colonel Holland lay dying at Heaton. The Lord Delamere took Newcome in his coach to see him, and on the way they discoursed much on the present state of affairs. Newcome, as they drove home again, 'had the hap to speak an improper word : it was this, that Mr. Angier [another divine] had great hopes of Colonel Holland because he had by many offices of love in times past, engaged the prayers of good people for him, and I had the hap to say that he was the *object* of many good prayers. I was sensible it was a wrong word, and it troubled me ill, and I thought it might make me ridiculous.' The point of this story is not very obvious, but it shows the esteem in which Richard Holland was held among his friends. Two days later, he died. Newcome notes in his diary on July 29 : ' Mr. Harrison and Mr. Angier called on me and told me they were present with Colonel Holland when he died, this day about three o'clock. A very prudent, able, Commonwealth man is now gone, and a true friend to good ministers.' He was sixty years old when he died.

Six years earlier, Colonel Holland had suffered a dreadful blow in the loss of his only son, Edward, who died July 8 1655, aged twenty-nine. Edward had married Anne, only daughter of Edward Warren of Poynton in Cheshire.[1] She was only sixteen when he died, and was left with one baby daughter, Frances Holland. Anne survived her husband for twenty-five years, and died on November 25, 1680. A tablet erected by Frances in the old Chapel Church of Denton, which long before had been built by the Hollands and their neighbours the Hydes, tells this mournful story of dying families and disappointed hopes. The touching inscription in elegant Latin testifies to the early genius of Edward Holland—his learning, his pleasing manners, distinguished probity, solid and unfeigned piety—and describes him as :—

' Familiæ suæ Decus et Ornamentum ;
Patriæ suæ Spes et Desiderium ;
Amicorum Delitiæ simul ac Solamen.'

---

[1] These Warrens of Poynton descended from an illegitimate son of the wicked Earl of Warenne in Surrey, whose second Countess was Isabel de Holland, sister of the first Earl of Kent. Thurstan Holland of Denton, in 1430, had also marrie Margaret, a girl of this Warren family.

His wife is described as 'Cara Deo, dilecta viro.' After erecting this monument the lonely Frances Holland vanishes into the night of oblivion.

The late Colonel Richard Holland had been the eldest son of a family of six brothers and five sisters. The sisters all married into good families of the squire kind in Cheshire and Shropshire. The second and third brothers, Edward and John, died, without children, before the Colonel. The fourth brother, Thomas, survived him for about three years, and became Squire of Denton and Heaton. The estate was then worth about £800 a year, which would mean a good deal more in our days. Thomas Holland was a bachelor about sixty years old, but, upon becoming Squire, resolved to marry. According to the diarist, Oliver Heywood, he 'found out a suitable gentlewoman—one Mrs. Britland—and their day of marriage was fixed. But before the day of marriage arrived, he fell sick and died, and the funeral happening on the same day that had been fixed for his marriage, the minister at the funeral preached from the same text that had been settled for the marriage, only substituting, 'There was a cry made,' for 'Behold the bridegroom cometh.'

Thomas Holland was buried in the Church of Nether Peover in Cheshire. There is a flagstone with the incription 'Here lyeth the body of Thomas Holland of Denton in the County of Lancashire, Esquire, who paid his latest debt to Nature, May 22, 1664. Here also lies the body of Frances, Lady Eyton, sister to the above-said Thomas Holland, who died June 23, 1691, aged 83.' In the next grave reposed another old sister, Jane Holland, who had married Thomas Cholmondeley of Cheshire. She died at seventy-eight, in 1696.

The houses and lands then passed to the third brother, the Rev. William Holland, Rector of Malpas in Cheshire,

who was aged fifty-two when he succeeded in 1664, and had not long been married. William had not at all sympathised with the Presbyterian views of his brother, Colonel Richard Holland. During the Cromwell Protectorate, he had preached a sermon on the death of a Cheshire cavalier gentleman ' not only replete with beautiful descriptions of the virtues and sufferings of the deceased, but reprobating with the most incautious zeal the heresies, schisms, and personated holiness of the ruling party.'

The Rev. William Holland, last of the Hollands of Denton and Heaton, died on April 29, 1682, at the age of seventy. By his will, he directed that his body should sleep with those ' of my fathers in the chapel of the Prestwich Church, which belongs to Heaton Hall and my family, and where so many of my ancestors have been buried.' He was succeeded in the estates by his son Edward, aged twenty, who survived him only a year. Then they passed to his daughter Elizabeth Holland, who, on September 27, 1684, married Sir John Egerton of Wrinehill in Northamptonshire, a maternal ancestor of the present Earls of Wilton. Thus, in the generation succeeding to that of Colonel Richard Holland and his five brothers, the estates were lost to the Hollands for want of male issue.

Heaton House continued to flourish, but what remained of Denton Hall sank at last, like so many old gentry houses, into the status of a farm. Only a fragment of it now remains, or lately remained. There is an elaborate description of it as it stood in 1856, with its carved coats of arms, old hall, and fine central fireplace, by Mr. Booker in ' Chetham Society Miscellanies,' vol. ii, p. 257. Mr. Henry Taylor, in his ' Old Halls in Lancashire and Cheshire,' wrote: ' Denton Hall was clearly at one time a fine quadrangular building, of which two sides now remain, the southerly or central portion containing the fine great hall and an eastern wing. Both portions have been much injured by the hand of man and by the ravages of time.' He thinks that the building was erected about the end of the fifteenth century, or perhaps earlier. ' We have here,' he says, ' in the great common hall, the complete arrangements for the lord and his retainers dining in common; but at the end of the sixteenth century' (to which another writer attributed it) ' a great hall like this, with a massive open timbered roof, and with a high table, canopy, and musicians' gallery, had gone out of fashion, and was very seldom built.' [1]

The Denton estate consisted of 549 acres, in the year 1810. In 1846 the Earl of Wilton's ' Denton Hall estate ' contained 603 acres. Heaton Hall was a residence of the Earls of Wilton, and in 1901 was sold to the Corporation of Manchester for £230,000, for dedication as a fine public park covering 693 acres. Elizabeth Holland had certainly brought to the Egertons and their successors a goodly heritage.[2] These Hollands would have become a very rich family if they had endured long enough and had held on as firmly as they always had done to those estates near Manchester, which had descended to them from Sir William de Holland and Margaret de Shoresworth.

[1] There is a very full description of Denton Hall in the *Victorian History of Lancashire*, vol. iv.

[2] The present Earls of Wilton are really a branch of the Grosvenors, one of whom married an Egerton heiress. They took the family name of Egerton in lieu of their own.

CHAPTER XII

Non mortui laudabunt te, Domine, neque omnes qui descendunt in infernum ;
Sed nos qui vivimus benedicimus Domino, ex hoc nunc et usque ad saeculum.
Ps. 113.

ANOTHER line of the Hollands, those of Clifton, branches
off from the earliest Hollands of Denton. Sir Thurstan
de Holland, son of Sir William de Holland by Margaret
de Shoresworth, the first owner of Denton Manor, who lived
in the reigns of Edward II and Edward III, had a younger
son named William. This William married Marjory, daughter
and co-heiress of Henry de Trafford, and through her
acquired the Manor of Clifton, a few miles north of old
Manchester. The Hollands, their descendants, possessed the
manor, hall, and land of Clifton from about the year 1350
till after the year 1670. This much is quite certain ; but
except for dim dealings with land, there is hardly any record
of what they did during these three centuries. It is clear
from documentary evidence that the second owner of the
manor was Otho, son of William de Holland and his wife,
Marjory de Trafford ; and that he was living in 1361. The
manor is shown by other documentary evidence to have been
held about the year 1440 by a second Otho Holland. There
must certainly have been at least one intervening owner, and
much more probably two, between these two Othos. Between
them, in all probability, came, for one, a certain Robert
de Holland, who by his violent actions plays a distinguished

285

HOLLANDS OF CLIFTON

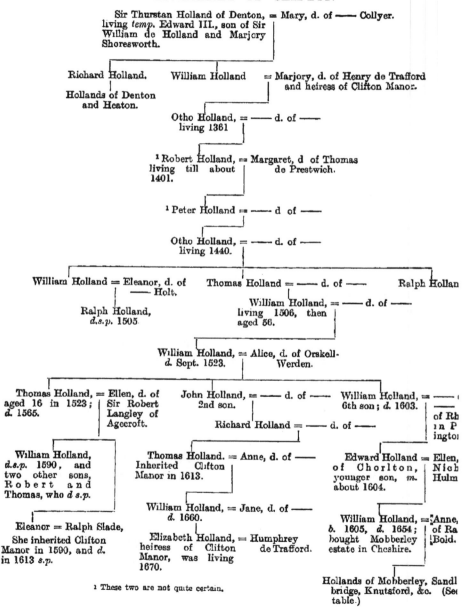

Sir Thurstan Holland of Denton, = Mary, d. of —— Collyer.
living *temp.* Edward III., son of Sir
William de Holland and Marjory
Shoresworth.

Richard Holland.

Hollands of Denton
and Heaton.

William Holland = Marjory, d. of Henry de Trafford
and heiress of Clifton Manor.

Otho Holland, = —— d. of ——
living 1361

[1] Robert Holland, = Margaret, d of Thomas
living till about de Prestwich.
1401.

[1] Peter Holland = —— d of ——

Otho Holland, = —— d. of ——
living 1440.

William Holland = Eleanor, d. of
—— Holt.

Ralph Holland,
d.s.p. 1505

Thomas Holland = —— d. of ——

William Holland, = —— d. of ——
living 1506, then
aged 56.

Ralph Hollan

William Holland, = Alice, d. of Orskell-
d. Sept. 1523. Werden.

Thomas Holland, = Ellen, d. of
aged 16 in 1523; Sir Robert
d. 1565. Langley of
Agecroft.

John Holland, = —— d. of ——
2nd son.

Richard Holland = —— d. of ——

William Holland, = ——
6th son; d. 1603.

——
of Rh
in P
ingto

William Holland,
d.s.p. 1590, and
two other sons,
Robert and
Thomas, who *d s.p.*

Thomas Holland. = Anne, d. of ——
Inherited Clifton
Manor in 1613.

Edward Holland = Ellen,
of Chorlton, Nich
younger son, *m.* Hulm
about 1604.

Eleanor = Ralph Slade,
She inherited Clifton
Manor in 1590, and *d.*
in 1613 *s.p.*

William Holland, = Jane, d. of ——
d. 1660.

Elizabeth Holland, = Humphrey
heiress of Clifton de Trafford.
Manor, was living
1670.

William Holland, =;Anne,
b. 1605, d. 1654; of Ra
bought Mobberley Bold.
estate in Cheshire.

Hollands of Mobberley, Sandl
bridge, Knutsford, &c. (Se
table.)

[1] These two are not quite certain.

part in the fourteenth century history of Prestwich. The seal
of William Holland of Clifton, attached to a deed of 1361, bore
the arms of the Hollands of Upholland, a ' lion rampant
gardant a field semé de fleurs de lys, over all a bend.' But
in 1533, as appears from the Herald's Visitation, the Hollands
of Clifton had carved on their house as arms, ' with a second
quarter sable, three maidens' heads couped two and one, with
the crest of a wolf passant,' no longer a lion rampant gardant.
There must have been some reason for this singular pheno-
menon, and it is said that the wolf crest and maidens' heads
belonged to a family called de Wolveley, who once owned the
manor of Prestwich next to that of Clifton.[1] Now, in the
year 1360, Margaret, daughter of Thomas de Prestwich, the
son of Alice de Wolveley (which Alice had been heiress of this
manor), took the veil at the age of fifteen in the convent of
Seaton in Cumberland. Margaret had no brother, and, but
for being a nun, would have been co-heiress with her sister
of Prestwich manor and two other manors. Her sister Agnes
died married, but without children, in 1362. Before this,
Margaret had eloped from the convent at the age of less
than seventeen, and had married Robert de Holland. Some
years later her father died, and on the ground that the escaped
Margaret was a professed nun, and so could not inherit, the
manors were transferred to her cousin, Roger de Langley,
then a minor, whose mother was a maternal granddaughter
of the original heiress, Alice de Wolveley.

Robert Holland by no means accepted the succession
of the boy, Roger de Langley. He seems at first to have
made some arrangement with Sir Thomas Molyneux, th
agent of the great over-lord, the Duke of Lancaster, for,

---

[1] The distinguished local historian, Mr. W. Langton, in the *Lancashire
Inquisitions* (vol. 99 of the Chetham Society Papers, p 135) discussed all this, and
is inclined to accept the conjecture. See also *Victorian History of Lancashire,*
v 77

by a letter from the Savoy Palace dated July 10, 1372, the Duke ordered Molyneux, notwithstanding any demise or lease of the manor of Prestwich made by him to Robert de Holland, to seize the manor and demise and let it to other persons than the said Robert and his wife. But in 1375 Robert de Holland assembled a troop of armed men and 'vi et armis contra pacem, etc.,' took possession of the manor. The Duke of Lancaster was fiscally interested because he was entitled to the profits of wardship during a minority, but apparently Holland kept possession for twenty years.

The case was at last tried before Mr. Justice Pynchbeck and his colleagues at the Lancaster Assizes in 1394. It was proved that Margaret, daughter of Thomas de Prestwich, son of Alice de Wolveley, was, before her marriage, 'a nun and professed in the House of the nuns of Seaton.' It was also proved that she had made her vows at the rational age of fifteen, 'on the morrow of St. Katherine the Virgin and Martyr, A.D. 1360, in the presence of Sir John Cragge, the Prior of the Abbey of Furness,' and several others named in the proceedings, and that 'the said Margaret on the said day confessed before the said persons that she was not coerced or compelled, but voluntarily entered the Order of St. Benedict in the said House.' On this point the case turned, for a nun, who of free will and at an age of dis‑cretion had taken vows, was disqualified for inheritance of land even if she came out of the convent and returned to lay life, unless she had a dispensation from Rome. Judgment was accordingly entered for the Duke of Lancaster in respect of the profits, but notwithstanding this decision, the Hollands asserted their claim some years longer. Very likely they obtained support from their southern cousins, the Earls of Kent and Huntingdon, then so powerful, and so closely allied with the Duke of Lancaster and King

Richard. In 1395 the feoffees of Robert de Holland and Margaret, his wife, made a deed of settlement dealing with Prestwich Manor as though it were indubitably family property. The trusts were to hold for Robert de Holland for life, and after his death for his son Peter and his issue, with remainders to the younger sons and daughters, Nicholas, John, Edmund, Marion, Catharine, and Alice.

At the end of 1401, the southern Hollands having tragically fallen, Robert de Holland reluctantly released to Robert de Langley (the son of the whilom minor Roger) all his claim upon Prestwich, and two other manors, and in 1416 his son Peter Holland agreed to give up his title deeds, and in 1418 released his claim ' to his manors ' to trustees for the Langleys. But peace was not re-established between Hollands and Langleys except after active war, for in May 1402 the King granted pardon to Robert de Langley, who was then twenty-four, for having captured and detained Robert de Holland. The latter had at various times invaded the Manor of Prestwich, and carried away some cattle and goods of Langley and his tenants into Cheshire,[1] not restoring them without payment. He had also come by night and carried some of Langley's cattle as far as Glossop (in Derbyshire), and being pursued, he entered the house of Master Wagstaffe, who must have been much annoyed, and defied Robert de Langley, wounding one of his servants with an arrow. The brother of the wounded man threw fire into the house, and Holland had to surrender, and was taken into Lancashire.[2] He had then already been outlawed for treason, probably in connection with the Holland movement of 1400.

The suggestion, to recapitulate, made by more than one student of local history, is that in order to assert the more

[1] Cheshire was a convenient place into which to drive cattle stolen in Lancashire, or vice versa, because the two counties were under entirely different jurisdictions, one reason why they were both lawless.

[2] *Victorian County History of Lancashire*, vol. v., quoting Agecroft documents.

ostentatiously his claim to the Wolveley inheritance during this conflict of thirty years, Robert de Holland, on the same principle as that on which the Kings of England assumed the French royal lilies, carved up the arms and crest of Wolveley, which the herald saw somewhere at Clifton in 1533. There was indeed no Otho among the children of Robert and Margaret, but the second Otho Holland, who owned Clifton about 1440, may have easily been their grandson, perhaps a son of the Peter named in the settlement of 1395. If this violent Robert de Holland were not the lord of Clifton, it does not appear who else he can have been, living at that time in the immediate vicinity of Prestwich. He may, on the whole, be fairly claimed, and not without pride, on account of his evidently strong and virile character, as a Holland of Clifton. There is certainly something in the style of these northern local proceedings, a Holland 'touch,' akin to the methods by which his cousin at two or three removes, John, Earl of Huntingdon, was in the same years endeavouring to promote the interests of the southern branch of the family.

After these troubles, the owners of Clifton, holding firmly to their manor and hall, proceeded obscurely on their way down history. Amid the darkness, the Lancashire Court records illuminate the fact that, one day in the year 1440, Ralph, son of Otho Holland of Clifton Hall, trespassed, with others, in the woods of Sir John Pilkington and took therefrom three hawks, valued at £20. Did Ralph redeem his woodland crime by fighting on the Lancastrian side at Towton Field in the Wars of the Roses, under the banner of his distant cousin, Henry Holland, Duke of Exeter? A novelist would be entitled to make him do so, but there is no record.

The pedigree of these Clifton Hollands can only, before the reign of Henry VIII, be defectively made out, and their marriages till then are mostly obscure, but early in the sixteenth century more light is thrown by two inquisitions *post mortem* : one made in 1506, which shows the descent for the two previous generations, and the second at the death, in 1523, of William Holland, then owner of Clifton. This William had married Alice Orskell Werden. The Werdens were a good old Lancashire family, some of whom, later, were Catholic Royalists in the Civil War. William Holland, in 1517, made a settlement in order to secure a dowry for his wife, and make provision for his younger sons and daughters. Richard Holland of Denton, and Nicholas Holland of Deane Hall, were two of the trustees of the settlement. William Holland died in 1523, and his eldest son, Thomas, then aged sixteen, succeeded to the Manor and Hall of Clifton. There were five younger sons and several daughters. The second son was named John and the sixth son William. The eldest son, Thomas Holland, married Ellen, daughter of Sir Robert Langley of Agecroft, a fine old hall which still exists near Manchester. This was the family with which Robert Holland waged so long a quarrel in the fourteenth century.

Thomas Holland died in 1565, leaving Ellen a widow with four children. His youngest and sixth brother, William Holland, who was born about 1517, was executor of his will, and was ancestor of the Hollands of Rhodes, Mobberley, Sandlebridge, and of the Viscounts Knutsford.

We might have possessed rather fuller details about this family had not Thomas Holland thoughtlessly been away when the Heralds called one day at Clifton in the Lancashire Visitation of 1533. .The Heralds, in consequence, made the barren note, ' Holland of Clifton was not at howme,' and merely recorded arms which no doubt they saw carved somewhere, and entered no pedigree.

The 'Lancaster Pleadings' (vol. xlix) contains a Bill addressed to Sir Ambrose Cave, as Chancellor of the Duchy of Lancaster, by Ellen Holland, widow of Thomas Holland, and William, Robert, and Thomas, and Ellmor Holland, children of the said Thomas *v.* William Langley, clerk, Parson of Prestwich. The complaint was that 'the said Thomas Holland, the father, left goods to the value of three hundred marks. The defendant was his trustee, being his wife's brother. He undertook to provide the said Thomas and his family with board and lodging during his own lifetime at the Parsonage of Prestwich; in consideration whereof, the defendant enjoyed all the goods of the said Thomas. Ever since Thomas' death, the defendant has refused these obligations. He has also driven out of the parsonage house his nephew and niece, Thomas and Ellinor, when they came to seek succour at the parsonage.'

This William Langley, Rector of Prestwich, was a queer and quarrelsome priest, always engaged in a number of lawsuits, about church property, with his neighbours. He was instituted in 1552, in the ultra-reforming reign of Edward VI, but conformed to the old religion during Mary's reign, and again to the new arrangements at the beginning of Elizabeth's. But presently he turned recusant, about the time he so maltreated the Holland children, and refused to attend his own parish church, and was finally deprived of the living in 1569. Prestwich was far too much of a Langley family living; it was held continuously by Langleys from 1417 to 1610.[1]

From this sad case of a cruel, though reverend, uncle, it seems that the Hollands of Clifton were in financial difficulties in the reign of Elizabeth, but they did not lose their social position as lords of a manor. The Derby household books record a visit to Lord Derby by 'Mr. Holland of

---

[1] One of his successors, as rector in the first half of the nineteenth century, was the Rev. John Booker, a most worthy antiquary, who wrote *Memorials of Prestwich Church*, &c., and contributed much to the *Chetham Society Papers.*

Clifton,' who came to stay at Lathom on February 10, 1588. The three sons of Thomas Holland died without surviving issue, and the manor then passed to their sister Eleanor, married to Ralph Slade. On her death without issue in 1618, the property reverted to a cousin, Thomas Holland, a grandson of John Holland, the second son of the William Holland who died in 1523. This Thomas Holland still owned the estate at the time of the Civil War. He was a Royalist; and the estates were sequestrated by Parliament for his own delinquencies, and more especially those of his son William, who had applied for a commission in the King's army, had fought as a defender of Wigan, when Colonel Richard Holland of Denton captured that town, and had also served in the garrison of Lathom House, and in other places.

The Hollands never recovered from this sequestration disaster, and had at last to sell their house, Clifton Hall, which in 1652 came into possession of the Gaskell family; but they retained for a brief space longer the manor and some land. William Holland, the last in the male descent, who died in 1660, had no son, but a daughter Elizabeth. Before 1671 she had married Humphrey Trafford, and thus the Manor of Clifton, which Marjory de Trafford had brought in Edward III's reign to the Hollands, was brought back over three hundred years later by Elizabeth Holland to the Traffords, now called again ' de Trafford.' These Traffords are one of the oldest Lancashire families that have a continuous recorded history. The grandfather of Humphrey Trafford was a strong Protestant and persecutor of recusants. His son, Humphrey's father, Sir Cecil Trafford, was reconciled to the Church of Rome in his youth about 1616, and ever after that the family adhered to that Church down to the present day. Sir Cecil died very old in 1673, and was succeeded in possession of the estates by Humphrey, who had married Elizabeth Holland. Elizabeth died, and Humphrey Trafford married again; his descendants spring from his second wife. Humphrey Trafford was in trouble in 1694, being implicated in a Lancashire Jacobite plot of that year, and he died at an advanced age in 1716. This marriage into a Catholic family makes it certain—unless (which is not very likely) Elizabeth was an individual convert—that the latest Hollands of Clifton were, like the Hollands of Sutton, not only Royalists but Catholics, though perhaps they may have thought it well, living as they did close to Protestant Manchester, to conceal the fact as much as possible.

It appears that the manor and lands of Clifton were mortgaged in 1685, and eventually were sold, so that their re-occupation by the Trafford family did not last long. Probably they were in financial difficulties at the time; but they would have done better to keep Clifton until the development of estates round Manchester in the nineteenth century.

While the elder line of the descendants from the William Holland of Clifton, who married Alice Werden and died in 1523, thus became extinct, a cadet branch continued to exist in a very modest but healthy and prolific way.

William Holland was sixth son of the William Holland owner of Clifton Manor, who died in 1523, and, since his eldest brother, Thomas, was born in 1507, and there were also sisters, he was probably himself not born earlier than 1517. He was in 1565 executor of the will of his eldest brother, Thomas, and he appears two years later in the pedigree given in Flower's Visitation.[1]   He married a Miss Parr who

---

[1] Mr. William F. Irvine, in his book called *The Family of Holland of Mobberley and Knutsford*, privately printed in 1902, denied the fact, previously accepted by all good authorities, that the William Holland who married Miss Parr of Rhodes was son of William Holland of Clifton, who married Miss Werden and died in 1523 I have given in an Appendix reasons showing that Mr. Irvine was in error on this point.

was co-heiress, together with a sister who had married John Foxe, of an ancient gentleman's estate called Rhodes, close to Clifton Hall. This William Holland's descendants in the elder line owned Rhodes till late in the seventeenth century.

HOLLANDS OF MOBBERLEY

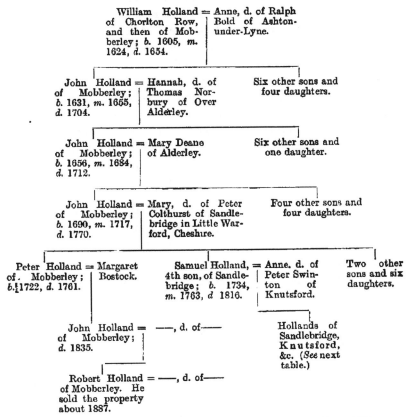

The Prestwich parish registers show that this William Holland died in 1603, at about the age of eighty-five, and that the second William Holland of Rhodes, his eldest

son, died in 1614, and was succeeded there by his son, John.
A younger son of the first-named William—namely, Edward
Holland—bought a house and land at Chorlton, close to
Manchester and five or six miles from Rhodes and Clifton,
and rather late in life married, about 1603 or 1604, Ellen
Hulme of Heyton. This Edward's only son, William Holland,
was born in 1605, and in 1624 married Anne, daughter of
Ralph Bold of Ashton-under-Lyne. About that time, his
father, Edward, died and William inherited the Chorlton
property. This he eventually sold, and bought, in 1650,
four years before his death, a property at Mobberley in
Cheshire, about fifteen miles from Manchester, near Knutsford. This was a small estate of 120 acres lying round a
house called Dam Head. Here his descendants in the
elder line lived on the land very quietly for a period of
237 years until the year 1887. The property was then sold
to Lord Egerton of Tatton, and is now a farm of the present
Lord.

The clash of arms has often been heard in the pages
of this book. It never disturbed the Hollands of Mobberley
save once, when, in 1745, the Highland Army passed within
five miles of them on the road from Manchester to Derby.
In a still extant diary of Mrs. John Holland, of that date,
are the following entries :

'Nov. 24, 1745. The week past has been attended
with a great deal of bad tideings from our armies, many
in great alarm and consternation.'

'November, ye last day. Every day brings fresh alarms,
our Rebel enemies drawing nearer and nearer ; six beside
our own family come for shelter.'

'December ye 8. Ye week past we had some intervall
from our fears. After many abuses in Maxfild [Maccles-
field] they went to Leek, pressed several to go with them,
from there to Ashburn, from there to Derby. A little number

behind meeting with ye King's forces, were frightened back to Ashburn, Leek, and poor Maxfild again. On Saturday night they begun to come in ; all the country alarmed again with great fear of them, one and twenty came this day by the Hall and Mill and made towards Altringham ; gave no disturbance to this neighbourhood.'

'April 26, 1746. We have joyful news from Scotland that the Rebels are defeated by the Duke on the 16th of this instant. We have had great outward rejoicings.'

John Holland, who died in 1770, husband of this lady, had a fourth son, named Samuel, who inherited from a maternal uncle a property of some three hundred acres, called Sandlebridge, about three miles from Knutsford. Samuel Holland married Anne, daughter of Peter Swinton of Knutsford. Their eldest son, Peter Holland, inherited Sandlebridge, and practised as a doctor at Knutsford. He died in 1855, and Sandlebridge passed to his eldest son, Sir Henry Holland.

The maternal grandmother of this Henry Holland was Catherine, a sister of Josiah Wedgwood, the famous potter of Etruria in Staffordshire ; so that he was, viâ the Wedgwoods, a second cousin of the great Charles Darwin, and related to all the amiable and lively Wedgwood clan. Henry Holland was born October 27, 1788. He went to London as a young physician, and there during his long professional career had a practice in the high social and political sphere, and was also a well-known man in society, a writer, and traveller. He was consulting physician to six prime ministers, including George Canning and Sir Robert Peel, and to Queen Victoria, and knew every one in the high political, professional, and literary world of his time. His name appears in many memoirs as a guest in the best society. He was President of the Royal Society, and of the College of Physicians. Probably none of his lineal ancestors had ever

HOLLANDS OF SANDLEBRIDGE AND KNUTSFORD, CHESHIRE

Samuel Holland = Anne, d. of Peter Swinton of Knutsford. of Sandlebridge, 4th son of John Holland of Mobberley (see last table); *b.* 1734, *m.* 1763, *d.* 1816.

Peter Holland = (1) Mary, d. of Rev. W. Willetts of Staffs of Sandlebridge and Knutsford; *b.* 1766, *d.* 1855

(2) Mary, d. of J. Whittaker of Manchester.

Samuel Holland = Katherine, *d.* of John Menzies of Liverpool. of Liverpool and Plas-yn-Penrhyn, Merioneth; *b.* 1768, *m.* 1796, *d.* 1851.

Swinton Holland = Anne, d. of Rev. W. Willetts of Staffs. of London; *b.* 1777, *d.* 1828.

Descendants (see Appendix I).

Four daughters.

Two sons and a daughter.

Descendants (see Appendix I).

eth, = William Stevenson.

eth, = Rev. W. Gaskell. *m* 865. Hist.

r daughters.

Sir Henry Holland,[1] Bt., M.D., = (1) Margaret Emma, d. of James Caldwell of Linley Wood, Staffs. of Sandlebridge; *b.* 1788, created Bart. 1853, *d* 1873.

(2) Saba, d. of Rev. Sydney Smith, Canon of St. Paul's.

Two daughters, Caroline and Gertrude, *d.* unmarried.

Emily, = Charles Buxton, M.P.

Sydney Charles, 1st Viscount Buxton, and other descendants.

Francis James Holland, = Mary Sibylla, d of Rev. Alfred Lyall of Harbledown, Kent. Canon of Canterbury; *b.* 1828, *d.* 1907.

Three living sons, Bernard, Francis, and Michael, and three grandsons, and one daughter, Agnes.

y Thurstan Holland = (1) Elizabeth, (2) Margaret, dlebridge; *b* 1825, *d.* d of Nathaniel d. of Sir G C.M.G. Created Baron Hibbert of Charles ord 1888 and Viscount Munden, Trevelyan, ord 1895. Herts. Bart.

Two living sons, Cecil and Lionel, and one daughter, Margaret.

Arthur Holland-Hibbert, = Ellen, d. of Sir Wilfred Lawson, *b.* 1855, of Munden, Herts. Bart. of Cumberland.

Edith = Charles Cropper of Westmorland

ey George Holland, = Mary d of 4th Earl 855, 2nd Viscount of Ashburnham. ford, of Kneesworth, lambridgeshire.

Two daughters, Lucy and

Thurstan Holland-Hibbert, = Viola, d. of T. Clutterbuck of *b.* 1888.

Wilfred Holland-Hibbert, *b.* 1893.

Elsie.

left England, unless some Holland of Clifton was in the Wars in France, and they had certainly rarely strayed from their flat green fields in Lancashire and Cheshire. Sir Henry Holland made up for this by travelling every year of his life, from the time he was twenty until he was eighty-five—in which year of his age he went first to Moscow and then to Rome, and died a week after his return to his London home in Brook Street on his eighty-sixth birthday, October 27, 1873. He was in the Spanish Peninsula in 1812, while Wellington was carrying on the War, and in North America for a month or two in 1863, in the Civil War, with a visit to General Grant's headquarters, having an insatiable curiosity about men and things. Perhaps it was the banked-up curiosity of his provincial ancestors! He left record of himself in a very cautiously composed 'Book of Recollections,' and there is also an account of him in the 'Dictionary of National Biography,' so that more need not be said here. He was made a baronet in 1853. He married, first, Emma, a fair and charming daughter of James Caldwell of Linley Wood in Staffordshire, and, secondly, Saba, daughter of the famous Canon, Sydney Smith.

Two uncles of Sir Henry Holland, sons of Samuel of Sandlebridge and younger brothers of Peter Holland, also attained distinction in their own lines.[1] One of them, the younger, Swinton Holland, became a partner in the great House of Baring. His eldest son, Edward Holland, at one time Liberal M.P. for East Worcestershire, owned the estate of Dumbleton in Gloucestershire. Among this Edward's sons were Frederick Holland, Vicar of Evesham, and Admiral Swinton Holland. Robert Martin-Holland, C.B., of Martin's Bank, Lombard Street, and Gloucestershire, is a grandson of Edward of Dumbleton, and son of Frederick of Evesham, and he has himself six sons. The sixth son of

[1] For their descendants see pedigrees in Appendix I.

Swinton Holland was George Holland, who married Dorothy, daughter of Lord Gifford, and became the father of Canon Henry Scott Holland, and of other children.

The other brother of Peter Holland, named Samuel, established a large financial and commercial business in connection with Liverpool and South America, and from him descends a numerous race settled in Lancashire, Wales, and the South. Sir Arthur Holland is one of them. He has five living sons.

A sister of Peter Holland, Elizabeth, married William Stevenson; and her daughter, also named Elizabeth, who married the Rev. William Gaskell, was the excellent authoress. Elizabeth Stevenson was born in 1810, and was mainly brought up at Knutsford, the model of the town in her novels, ' Cranford,' and ' Wives and Daughters,' and her uncle, Dr. Peter Holland, and his family can be recognised among the characters in her stories.[1] She married in 1832, and died in 1865.

Sir Henry Holland's success in London, and that in the commercial and financial world of his uncles Swinton and Samuel, placed this family upon a new, or restored, social basis. The Hollands never were so obscure, before or since, as in the eighteenth century. They had lived at Mobberley in a quiet way, much as substantial yeomen, farming their own land—their younger sons becoming nonconformist ministers, or provincial lawyers, or the like. They were, however, in virtue of their descent from a manorial family, described as ' gentlemen ' in legal documents, and they steadily used on their seals the old Upholland crest of the lion rampant grasping a fleur de lys, which was borne by Sir Robert de Holland, in 1307, on his banner at the Stepney tournament.

---

[1] The two Misses Browning in *Wives and Daughters* are the images of two old daughters of Peter Holland, who lived at Knutsford, and the two old sisters in *Cranford* have also a strong resemblance.

Like Colonel Richard Holland of Denton, but unlike the Hollands of Sutton and the main line of Clifton, the Hollands who settled at Mobberley were Presbyterians during the Commonwealth and after the Restoration. But Presbyterianism never flourished in England as it did in Scotland. Eventually, like most English Presbyterians, they became Unitarians, and so continued until the nineteenth century, when most of their descendants gradually reverted to the Church of England. One or two of them even became distinguished members of the Anglican clergy —such as the late Canon Francis Holland of Canterbury and Canon Henry Scott Holland, formerly of St. Paul's and now of Christ Church, Oxford, and Regius Professor of Divinity.

While they lived in Lancashire and Cheshire these Hollands married into families of the same kind of middle-class social standing and religion, never going for wives beyond the borders of those counties, until Peter Holland went as far as Staffordshire for that purpose. They led unemotional and unadventurous, virtuous and temperate lives, which both earlier and later Hollands would have thought intolerably dull, and they almost invariably in consequence had large families and attained to advanced ages. The late Lord Knutsford, who died at eighty-eight, in 1914, was the fifth in lineal succession of men who passed the eightieth year, such was the stored-up and yet un-expended vitality of the race.

On Sir Henry Holland's death in 1873, the estate of Sandlebridge, which he had doubled in extent by purchasing adjoining land, descended, together with the baronetcy, to his eldest son, Henry Thurstan Holland.[1] This son was born in 1825, and educated at Harrow and Trinity College,

---

[1] The house and land at Sandlebridge were a few years ago sold to the City of Manchester for the purpose of some melancholy Institution.

Cambridge. He was first at the Bar, and then held a high post in the Colonial Office. He married, first, Elizabeth, daughter of Nathaniel Hibbert of Munden House in Hertfordshire, and, by her mother, a granddaughter of the above-mentioned Sydney Smith, by whom he had three children ; and, secondly, Margaret, daughter of Sir Charles Trevelyan, Baronet, and niece of Lord Macaulay, by whom he had four children. After his father's death, he left the Colonial Office and entered the House of Commons as a supporter of Lord Beaconsfield's administration. He became Financial Secretary to the Treasury in Lord Salisbury's short government in 1885 and, in the latter part of 1886, in his next administration, was Vice-President of the Council for Education. In the ministerial changes at the beginning of 1887, caused by the revolt of Lord Randolph Churchill against Lord Salisbury, Sir Henry Thurstan Holland became Secretary of State for the Colonies, and held that great office until the Unionist Government went out of power in 1892. He had the honour of presiding over the first Colonial Conference, held in 1887 in connection with Queen Victoria's Jubilee. He was raised to the House of Lords as Baron Knutsford in 1888, and advanced to be Viscount in 1895. Lord Knutsford owed his success to restless industry combined with charm of manner and goodness of heart. He died in 1914, and his eldest son, Sydney George Holland, who married Lady Mary Ashburnham, daughter of the fourth Earl of Ashburnham, succeeded to the peerage, which he now holds with distinction.

The younger son of Sir Henry Holland was Francis James Holland. He was at Eton and Trinity College, Cambridge, and then took Orders. He first held the living of St. Dunstan's, Canterbury ; was then for twenty years incumbent of Quebec Chapel in London, and for the last twenty-five years of his life was a Canon of Canterbury Cathedral. He also was chaplain to Queen Victoria and to King Edward VII. He was certainly one of the best of all his race. Like his father he was a great traveller, and died at Sorrento in Italy, when he was just seventy-nine, on his way back from a journey in North Africa, in the year 1907. After a solemn service in Canterbury Cathedral he was buried at Godmersham in Kent. His wife was Mary Sibylla, daughter of Alfred Lyall, rector of Harbledown in Kent, and sister of the distinguished Anglo-Indians, Sir Alfred and Sir James Lyall. He left sons and grandsons now living.

One of the sisters of the first Viscount Knutsford and Francis Holland was Emily, renowned for her beauty and intelligence in early Victorian days, and she was living till the year 1908. She married Charles Buxton, M.P., of Fox Warren in Surrey, and one of her sons is Sydney Charles, from 1905 to 1914 a member of the Liberal Cabinet, and now first Viscount Buxton, and Governor-General of South Africa.

One of Sir Henry Holland's daughters by his second marriage was Caroline, who inherited much of the cheerful and indomitable vigour of her maternal grandfather, Sydney Smith, and was well known in London for her social and philanthropic energies, until her death in 1909.

PEDIGREE OF THE HOLLANDS OF CONWAY[1] (*abbreviated*).

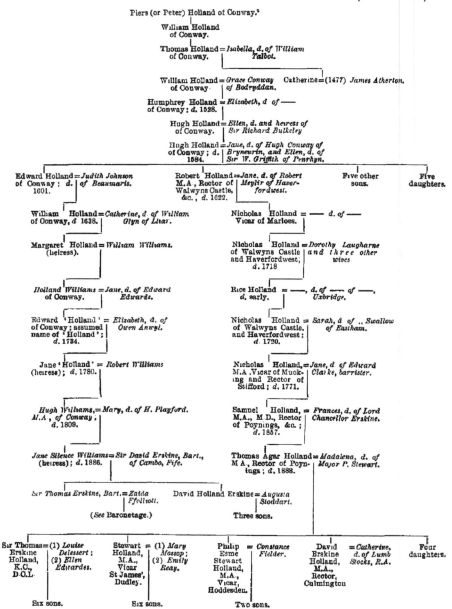

Piers (or Peter) Holland of Conway.[2]

William Holland of Conway.

Thomas Holland = *Isabella, d. of William Talbot.* of Conway.

William Holland = *Grace Conway* of Conway of Bodryddan.   Catherine = (1477) *James Atherton.*

Humphrey Holland = *Elizabeth, d of ——* of Conway: d. 1528.

Hugh Holland = *Ellen, d. and heiress of* of Conway.   *Sir Richard Bulkeley*

Hugh Holland = *Jane, d. of Hugh Conway of* of Conway; d.   *Bryneurin, and Ellen, d. of* 1584.   *Sir W. Griffith of Penrhyn.*

Edward Holland = *Judith Johnson* of Conway; d.   *of Beaumaris.* 1601.

Robert Holland = *Jane. d. of Robert* M.A., Rector of   *Meylir of Haver-* Walwyns Castle,   *fordwest.* &c.; d. 1622.

Five other sons.

Five daughters.

William Holland = *Catherine, d. of William* of Conway, d 1638.   *Glyn of Lliar.*

Nicholas Holland = *—— d. of ——* Vicar of Marloes.

Margaret Holland = *William Williams.* (heiress).

Nicholas Holland = *Dorothy Laugharne* of Walwyns Castle   *and three other* and Haverfordwest;   *wives* d. 1718

Holland Williams = *Jane, d. of Edward* of Conway.   *Edwards.*

Rice Holland = *——, d. of —— of ——,* d. early.   *Uxbridge.*

Edward 'Holland' = *Elizabeth, d. of* of Conway; assumed   *Owen Anwyl.* name of 'Holland'; d. 1734.

Nicholas Holland = *Sarah, d of .. Swallow* of Walwyns Castle,   *of Eastham.* and Haverfordwest; d. 1720.

Jane 'Holland' = *Robert Williams* (heiress); d. 1780.

Nicholas Holland = *Jane, d of Edward* M.A .Vicar of Muck-   *Clarke, barrister.* ing and Rector of Stifford; d. 1771.

Hugh Williams, = *Mary, d. of H. Playford.* M.A., of Conway; d. 1809.

Samuel Holland, = *Frances, d. of Lord* M.A., M.D., Rector   *Chancellor Erskine.* of Poynings, &c.; d. 1857.

Jane Silence Williams = *Sir David Erskine, Bart.,* (heiress); d. 1886.   *of Cambo, Fife.*

Thomas Agar Holland = *Madalena, d. of* M.A., Rector of Poyn-   *Major P. Stewart.* ings; d. 1888.

Sir Thomas Erskine, Bart. = *Zaida Ffolliott.*

(*See* Baronetage.)

David Holland Erskine = *Augusta Stoddart.*

Three sons.

Sir Thomas Erskine Holland, K.C., D.O.L.

= (1) *Louise Delessert;* (2) *Ellen Edwardes.*

Stewart Holland, M.A., Vicar St James', Dudley.

= (1) *Mary Mossop;* (2) *Emily Reay.*

Philip Esme Stewart Holland, M.A., Vicar, Hoddesden.

= *Constance Fielder.*

David Erskine Holland, M.A., Rector, Culmington

= *Catherine, d. of Lumb Stocks, R.A.*

Four daughters.

Six sons.

Six sons.

Two sons.

CHAPTER XIII

HOLLANDS OF WALES

I.—THE CONWAY FAMILY

'The highest tides have their falls and ebbs, and, after great tempests and darkest days, the sun shineth.'—REV. ROBERT HOLLAND, Dedication to the 'Holie Historie.'

A BRANCH of the Hollands, long settled at Conway in Wales, and still continued, in the male line, in England, is said by some good authorities to descend from Alan Holland, a son of Robert Holland of Upholland and a brother of Robert, the first Lord Holland, who was beheaded at Henley, in 1328. This Alan is stated to have had a son named John, who was the great-grandfather of Peter, or Piers, Holland of Conway. From this Peter the descent of the family to the present day, shown in the pedigree herewith, is clear and certain. Peter himself served in the household of King Henry IV.

The ancestor of these Hollands came, it appears, to Conway, to which English colonists had been brought, in the first instance, by Edward I, after his conquest of the wild Celtic country. These settlers were described in Latin as 'Advenae.' R. Williams, in his 'History of Conway' (1835, p. 43), says : 'The town had obtained the great privileges mentioned above from Edward I. In order that he might have a body of Englishmen, besides the garrisons of his castles, to maintain his power in Wales, all that held office in his towns of Aberconway, Caernarvon, and Beaumaris were exclusively English.' And further on, he says : ' The exclusive advantages enjoyed by Englishmen, from the time of the first Edward for several centuries, brought here a great number of adventurers, and the names of almost all the inhabitants were extraneous : such were the Hookes, Stodarts, Actons, . . . Hollands, &c. The last who bore any of these names was Owen Holland of Plas-isav, Esq., who died in 1795 . . . and even within the last two centuries Sir John Wynne of Gwydir mentions that they were called " the lawyers of Carnarvon, the merchands of Beaumaris, and the gentlemen of Conway." '

Besides their town house, called Plas-isav, these Hollands owned most of Conway and much property in the neighbourhood, in particular Bodlondeb and Marle, holding also the Castle, by tenure of a dish of fish to Lord Hertford when he passed through. The ferry belonged to them, and they are said to have received a large sum in compensation when Conway Bridge was built.

The arms of this family are ' *azure* seme de fleurs de lys, a lion ramp. gard, *arg.*' Crest: ' out of a flame *ppr.* an arm issuant habited in a close sleeve *sa* the fist *ppr.* holding a lion's gamb. barwise erased *or* the talons to the sinister side.' [1] Their motto, at least as early as the reign of Elizabeth, was *Fiat Pax, Floreat Justitia*, and is so still.

An interesting deed exists, dated 17 Edward IV (1477), whereby ' Thomas de Holond ' settled his property at Conway on his son William and his daughter Catherine, wife of James Atherton, successively in tail, with ultimate remainder to the burgesses of the town ' for the maintenance of a fit and proper priest to say masses in Conway Church for the salvation of the soul of the said Thomas de Holond and of

---

[1] This crest is said by some to have been borne by the Hollands before the family was ennobled. (Harl. MS. 2076, f. 26.)

Isabella, his beloved wife, and of his ancestors, relatives, and heirs, as the burgesses shall answer for it before the most high Judge in the Day of Judgement.'

In the church at Conway there are a great many monuments of the family. The inscription on one of these runs as follows : ' Edward Holland, Armiger, posuit hoc memoriale Hollandorum ad requisitionem Hugonis Holland, Arm., patris sui, paulo ante obitum, qui obiit 13 die Maii, A° D'ni, 1584.' The Edward who thus commemorated his father was himself commemorated, on his death in 1601, in another Latin inscription in the same church, by his own son, William.

This son, William Holland, of Conway, married Catherine, daughter of William Glynn, of Lliar, and with him ended the male succession of this elder line. He had, however, a daughter and heiress, Margaret, who married William Williams. Their son was christened Holland, and his children assumed the surname of ' Holland,' but the male descent of this family again came to an end in the following generation, on the death of Owen Holland, of Plas-isav, Conway, in 1795. He died without issue, and the property passed eventually to the younger son of his sister Jane, who had also married a Williams, Robert Williams, owner of the charming estate of Pwllycrochon. This son, the Rev. Hugh Williams, of Conway and Pwllycrochon, left a daughter and heiress, Jane Silence Williams, who, in 1819, married Sir David Erskine, of Cambo, Fife, the great-grandfather of the present baronet of that name. The Welsh property passed by this marriage to the Cambo family, and was sold by them in 1865 for about £212,000. The Conway family has, however, been continued in the male descent, to the present time.

Edward Holland, of Conway, who erected the monument in the reign of Elizabeth, had a younger brother, Robert, who married Joan, daughter of Robert Meylir and of Catherine, heiress of Howell ap Rees Vawr, of Haverfordwest, in the County of Pembroke. Robert Holland was a very strongly Protestant clergyman, M.A., of Jesus College, Cambridge, and Rector of Prendergast, holding afterwards two other Crown livings in Pembrokeshire. Some account of him, as also of his brother Henry, M.A., ultimately Vicar of St. Bride's, Fleet Street, is given in the 'Dictionary of National Biography.' Robert published in 1594 a little book entitled ' The Holie Historie of our Lord and Saviour Jesus Christ's Nativitie, etc., gathered into English Meeter, and published to withdraw vaine wits from all unsauerie and wicked rimes and fables, to some love and liking of spirituall songs and holy Scriptures.' He remarks in the same preface that the ' Booke of God delivereth the receiver from the poisoned cup of that great. Circe, the Bishop of Rome, which hath infected so many thousand, and turned them into swine '; but, none the less, he says, in those days many bestowed ' months and years ' on reading romances, ' but scarce bestow one minute on the Bible, albeit the booke of God.' The Dedication and Address to the Reader are followed by twenty-eight lines of commendatory verses by H. Smartus, Oxoniensis, ending :

> ' Ergo manent Hollande tibi coelestia serta
>   Carpere, namque Theon nullus obesse queat.'

Two other poets, John Canon and John Pine, contribute laudatory verses in English.

Robert wrote also three books in Welsh, one of them designed to discourage recourse to so-called witches. His ' Epistle Dedicatory ' to King James I, prefixed to a genealogy of that monarch, ' gathered by George Owen Harry, Parson of Whitchurch, at the request of Mr. Robert Holland,' printed in 1604, is so apposite to family history of the present kind that it must be quoted here, especially since it lacks neither style nor dignity.

' It is the desire of immortality in every man's brest, which inforceth all men by all meanes to propagate their names to posterity, so as it may never die (if it were possible). Hence it is that some erect magnificent monuments for their Tombs . . . that other some desire to leave an heire of their name, whom they endow with great livelihood, in whose descent they think still to live. Hence is it that other derive the memorie of their names backward from antiquitie as far as they can : who, as they wish they might draw their first stemm from all beginnings, so do they desire to propagate their memorie without ende.

' Thus the restless soul, knowing her own worth and Immortality, seekes these by-pathes to finde out her own Pedigree, which though it errs in the object, by not aspiring to heaven, whence she had her first origin, yet is this desire being naturall no way discommendable, for that it shews the generosity of the minde.'

One of Robert Holland's sons, Nicholas, also took Holy Orders, and in 1618 was presented by the Crown to the Vicarage of Marloes in Pembrokeshire. His descendants, from father to son, for more than a century practised law at Haverfordwest, holding estates at Walwyns Castle, Walton West, and other places in that county. It will be seen, from the pedigree annexed, that the family has never ceased to be carried on in the male line, though it is no longer represented in Wales, having for nearly two hundred years been settled in England, where they have evinced a marked predilection for Oxford and for taking Holy Orders, first in the person of the Rev. Nicholas Holland, M.A., born in 1713, Vicar of Mucking and Rector of Stifford, in Essex. He married Jane Clarke of the Ikenham family. His elder sons, Thomas, a Colonel in the Indian Army, and William, an

Indian merchant, left no male issue. Not so his third son, Dr. Samuel Holland, a distinguished divine, who, besides holding two or three other livings, was Rector of Poynings in Sussex, and after 1817 Precentor and Prebendary of Chichester Cathedral. His grandson, Sir Thomas Erskine Holland, says of him : ' Landscape gardening was indeed a favourite amusement with him, and he was a considerable botanist. He kept up his classics, and was a man of wide general reading. He was, after the fashion of those days, thoroughly religious, always taking a selection of devotional works in the old-fashioned chariot in which his frequent journeys were made between Poynings and Chichester. He firmly believed in the advantages of the system which accumulated preferment upon the superior clergy, and was strongly opposed to Methodism, maintaining these views in sermons which attracted a good deal of attention. He was a Rural Dean, and zealous in the discharge of the duties of the office.'

Dr. Holland married Frances, daughter of Lord Chancellor Erskine, and had two sons, who both became clergymen, and four daughters. In 1846 he resigned the living of Poynings, in which he was succeeded by his eldest son, Thomas Agar Holland, M.A., previously Rector of Greatham, Hants, who held it till his death in 1888. A short account of him is given in the ' Dictionary of National Biography.' He wrote much verse throughout his life, and one of his earlier poems, ' Dryburgh Abbey,' was warmly praised by Sir Walter Scott. He also published prose writings. He married Madalena, daughter of Major Philip Stewart, and had five sons, three of whom became clergymen, as have also two of his grandsons. His eldest son, the distinguished international jurist, Sir Thomas Erskine Holland, K.C., D.C.L., F.B.A., Fellow of All Souls College, sometime Chichele Professor of International Law at Oxford, has several sons, one of them holding a high position in the Indian Civil Service.

Sir Thomas Erskine Holland is intimately acquainted with the history of his family. As long ago as 1866 he contributed an article, with pedigree, on the 'Hollands of Conway,' to the 'Archaeologia Cambrensis,' series 3, vol. xii, and has subsequently printed for 'private circulation only' a full history of their fortunes during five hundred years.

The present writer is indebted and grateful to him for information on the subject contained in the preceding pages.

II.—The Hollands of Denbighshire and Anglesey

In addition to the Hollands of Conway there was in Wales a group of families of the same name, bearing the same arms with a different crest, but of more doubtful descent. Its various branches were established at Pennant, Kinmel, Teyrdan, Hendrefawr, Denbigh, and Berw.

In the reign of King Charles I, the right of Sir Thomas Holland of Berw to his arms was actively challenged. The result was a special heraldic inquiry, resulting in the following ' Confirmation ' :

' To all and singulare to whom these presents shall come, John Borough Knight Garter Principall King of Armes sendeth greeting : Upon complaint made unto me that Sir Thomas Holland of Berrow in the county of Anglesey, Kt. did unduley beare for his armes azure a lyon rampant gardant between five flowers de lice argent, w^h armes (as was conceived) properlie belonged to the family of Holland some time Duke of Exeter, the said Sir Thomas Holland having notice given him of ye said complaynt repayred unto me, and produced divers and sundry auncient evidences, pedigrees, bookes of armes, letters patents and other authentique testimonies of credible persons : whereby it manifestly appeared that the said Sir Thomas Holland is lineally descended from Hoshkin alias Roger Holland, who by computation of time lived in or neer the raigne of Edward the third. He the said Sir Thomas being the sonne of Owen, sonne of Edward, sonne of Owen, sonne of John, sonne of Howell, sonne of the above named Hoshkin Holland, and that John Holland, sonne of Howell Holland aforesaid was household servant to King Henry the sixt, and Owen Holland great-grandfather to the said Sir Thomas was sheriffe of the county of Anglesey for tearme of his life as by letters patents under the seales of King Henry the seventh and King Henry

the eighth and certain deeds of Charles Brandon, Duke of
Suffolke, and other muniments, appeareth. And further
that by sundry matches and marriages the said Sir Thomas
is allied to many families of undoubted gentry in and near
the said county, who acknowledge the said Sir Thomas for
their allie and kinsman : beside ye testimony of divers
gentlemen of the name of Holland issued from the aforesaid
Hoshkin alias Roger their common ancestor : and as touching
the arms above mentioned, it is manifest by sundry pedigrees
and bookes of armes remayning in the custody of George
Owen, Esquire, Yorke Herauld, that the ancestors of the
said Sir Thomas did beare the same as they doe above emblazoned. In consideration of which premises and for that
the said Sir Thomas Holland is not only dignified with
knighthood, but likewise a justice of the peace and one of
the deputie lieutenants in the county where he liveth : I have
thought fit at his request to signifie and declare by these
presentes that the said Sir Thomas Holland and his heires of
that family resp'ly may use and bear the foresaid armes each
with his proper difference according to the law and usage of
armes. In witness whereof I have hereunto affixed the seals
of mine office and subscribed my name. Dated the five and
twentieth day of November in the eleventh year of the reign
of our Sovereign Lord Charles by the grace of God King of
Great Brittaine, France, and Ireland, Defender of the Faith,
etc., and in the yeare of Our Lord God, 1635.'

The argument of the Herald appears to rest upon the
social position of Sir Thomas, and no attempt is made to
trace the pedigree above Hoshkin or Roger Holland. It is,
however, alleged by reputable authorities that this Roger
was the great-grandson of a Sir Thomas Holland who married
Joyce daughter of Sir Jasper Croft, and lived in the reign
of Edward I. This Sir Thomas was alleged to be a son of
the first Sir Thurstan Holland of Upholland, and therefore

brother of Sir Robert Holland, father of Robert, first Lord Holland. The name of such a Thomas does not occur in the Lancashire records, but this is perhaps not enough to prove his non-existence. Thurstan had, however, a son named Roger, but nothing is known of him, or any descendants of his. Roger may possibly have gone to Wales.

Other origins have been attributed to these Hollands, but no doubt are mythical. Pennant, in his ' Tour of Wales,' 1784, says (vol. ii, p. 354) : ' The pedigrees derive them from a Sir Thomas Holland, who, tradition says, came, with another brother, into Wales in troublesome times. I have reason to suppose them to have been William and Thomas, the two younger sons of John Holland, Duke of Exeter, who died in 1446, and left to each of them an annuity of £40. They were of a most unpopular family, therefore probably retired to shun the miseries they might experience in that age of civil discord.' William and Thomas were, in fact, illegitimate sons, and were so described in the Duke's will ; but nothing in the least authentic is known as to their lives. John Williams, in his ' Denbigh,' says that ' the Hollands of these parts have a family tradition that they are descended from a Lord Holland who, having committed high treason, fled to Wales, and, when in exile, living in the Snowdonian Wilds, married a Welsh peasant, the daughter of a pedlar.' These wild legends are by no means chronologically compatible with the Herald's Report which traces the origin to Roger or Hoshkin Holland, who lived in the reign of Edward III, and no credit whatever is to be attached to them.

A full pedigree accompanies the article, contributed in 1867 by Sir Thomas Erskine Holland to the ' Archaeologia Cambrensis ' (series 3, vol. xiii.), upon this widespreading family of Hollands of Denbighshire and Anglesey. It is to this article that the present writer is indebted for the above account of them, but it did not seem necessary to reproduce here the copious pedigree of these probably extinct folk of dubious origin. They seem all to have died out in the male line, in the course of the eighteenth and nineteenth centuries. They were an extremely provincial race, and, almost without exception, married into Welsh Celtic families.

Only one of their offspring is distinguished enough to appear in the 'Dictionary of National Biography.' This is Hugh Holland,[1] who was born at Denbigh, educated at Westminster School, a Scholar in 1589, and afterwards a Fellow, of Trinity College, Cambridge. He travelled to Rome, Jerusalem, and Constantinople, and on his return studied in the Oxford libraries. He died in 1633, at the age of seventy, and was buried, without any monument, near the door of St. Benet's Chapel in Westminster Abbey. He wrote: (1) The not very brilliant sonnet prefixed in 1629 to the first folio of Shakespeare, and therefore the best known of his compositions; (2) Verses prefixed to a musical work entitled 'Parthenia,' 1611; (3) Verses prefixed to the 'Roxana of Alabaster'; (4) 'On the Death of Prince Henry'; (5) 'On Matthew, Bishop of Durham'; (6) 'Verses Descriptive of the Cities of Europe'; (7) 'Life of Camden'; (8) 'A Cypress Garland for the Sacred Forehead of our late Sovereign, King James.' He dedicated the 'Cypress Garland' to George Villiers, Duke of Buckingham, who, he says in the magniloquent and obsequious style of the age 'led me by the hand, not once, nor twice, to kiss that awful hand [of James I] to which I durst not else have aspired. With what sweetness and bravery the Great Majesty of Britain embraced then his meanest vassel our young Sovereign, then Prince of my country [Wales] Your Grace, and the honourable lords then present, perhaps remember; sure I am I can never forget, and, if I do, let my right hand forget her cunning' etc.

[1] His descent is quite clear. See *Arch. Camb.* mentioned above.

This is pretty strong, and so it is when Holland in the poem calls James ' a mortal God.' It must have made Buckingham smile. Hugh Holland is also guilty in this poem of this account of the ravages recently made by death in the ranks of the English nobility.

> How many great ones here not meanly graced
> In thirteen months the dance of Death have traced !
> Three Earls, two Dukes, a Marquis, and a Baron,
> Who then may 'scape thy boat, uncourteous Caron ?

The same 'Cypress Garland' contains a sad little fragment of autobiography :

> Cursed be the day that I was born, and cursed
> The nights that have so long my sorrows nursed,
> Yet grief is by the surer side my brother
> The child of Pain, and Payne was eke my mother,[1]
> Who children had, the Ark had men as many,
> Of which, except myself, now breathes not any,
> Nor Ursula, my dear, nor Phil, my daughter,
> Amongst us Death hath made so dire a slaughter ;
> Them, and my Martin, have I, wretch, survived. . . .

Fuller, in his ' English Worthies,' expresses the opinion that Hugh Holland was ' no bad English, but a most excellent Latin poet.' He also says that he was ' addicted to the new-old religion,' and when in Italy ' let fly freely against the credit of Queen Elizabeth,' for which *scandalum Reginæ*, when he arrived at Constantinople, on his way back from Palestine, Sir Thomas Glover, ambassador there for King James I, had him put into prison for a while. He was disappointed, says Fuller, on his return to England, at not getting an official post, expecting to be made Clerk of the Council at least, and ' grumbled out the rest of his life in visible discontentment.' The poet certainly ought not to have expected any official promotion after letting fly so

---

[1] Hugh Holland's mother was a Miss Payne by birth

freely at Queen Elizabeth. Fuller, however, had a prejudice against Hugh Holland, on the ground that the poet was more or less a Catholic, and his remarks may therefore lack verity. Anthony à Wood, who was no Puritan, says ('Ath. Oxon.,' vol. ii, p. 560) that Hugh Holland 'died within the City of Westminster (having always been *ex animo Catholicus*), in 1633, whereupon his body was buried in the Abbey Church of St. Peter there, near to the door entering into the monuments, on the three and twentieth day of July in the same year. I have seen (Wood adds) a copy of his epitaph made by himself, wherein he is styled, "Miserrimus peccator, musarum et amicitiarum cultor sanctissimus." ' Rather a touching self-inscription.

Hugh Holland had an interesting, if not very fortunate, life, and he evidently belonged to the best literary society of the time—that which included Ben Jonson and Shakespeare. He could tell them tales of Wales, Cambridge, Rome, Jerusalem, and Constantinople.

HOLLANDS OF NORFOLK

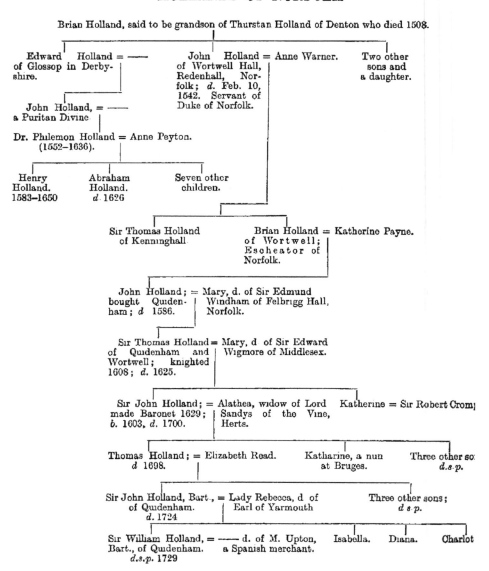

Brian Holland, said to be grandson of Thurstan Holland of Denton who died 1508.

Edward Holland = ——
of Glossop in Derby-
shire.

John Holland, = ——
a Puritan Divine

Dr. Philemon Holland = Anne Peyton.
(1552–1636).

Henry
Holland.
1583–1650

Abraham
Holland.
d. 1626

Seven other
children.

John Holland = Anne Warner.
of Wortwell Hall,
Redenhall, Nor-
folk; d. Feb. 10,
1542. Servant of
Duke of Norfolk.

Two other
sons and
a daughter.

Sir Thomas Holland
of Kenninghall

Brian Holland = Katherine Payne.
of Wortwell;
Escheator of
Norfolk.

John Holland; = Mary, d. of Sir Edmund
bought Quiden- | Windham of Felbrigg Hall,
ham; d 1586. | Norfolk.

Sir Thomas Holland = Mary, d of Sir Edward
of Quidenham and | Wigmore of Middlesex.
Wortwell; knighted
1608; d. 1625.

Sir John Holland; = Alathea, widow of Lord
made Baronet 1629; | Sandys of the Vine,
b. 1603, d. 1700. | Herts.

Katherine = Sir Robert Crom|

Thomas Holland; = Elizabeth Read.
d 1698.

Katharine, a nun
at Bruges.

Three other so:
d.s.p.

Sir John Holland, Bart., = Lady Rebecca, d of
of Quidenham. | Earl of Yarmouth
d. 1724.

Three other sons;
d s.p.

Sir William Holland, = —— d. of M. Upton,
Bart., of Quidenham. a Spanish merchant.
d.s.p. 1729

Isabella.

Diana.

Charlot

CHAPTER XIV

I.—HOLLANDS OF NORFOLK

Homo, vanitati similis factus est, dies eius sicut umbra prætereunt.

Ps. 143

A FAMILY of Hollands, settled in Norfolk, claimed descent from the Lancashire Hollands of Denton, and bore as arms the lion and lilies, with the motto *Secreta mea mihi*. Their claim was vouched for and pedigree given in the sixteenth-century ' Visitations of Norfolk ' (Harleian Society, vol. xxxii, p. 158). Here they are made to descend from Brian Holland of Denton, who, in Blomefield's ' History of Norfolk ' (1739, vol. i, p. 231), is said to have been a grandson of Thurstan Holland of Denton, who died in 1508, by his third son, John. No such son John is, however, mentioned in the Denton pedigree. The son of Brian, named John Holland, owned Wortwell House in Redenhall, Norfolk. He was a ' trustee and servant of the Duke of Norfolk.' He died February 10, 1542.[1] His son, Brian Holland, was Escheator of Norfolk—

---

[1] Another Holland, George, was secretary to the same Duke, when he was arrested for treason in 1547, and the officials found in the house Elizabeth Holland, a mistress of the Duke. But George Holland was certainly one of the Hollands of Estovening, Lincolnshire, and so, probably, was Miss Elizabeth, descendants from Sir Thomas Holland, who mostly lived in the Holy Land, and his wife, Elizabeth, the "devilish dame." In the seventeenth century the Hollands of Quidenham were for two generations trustees of the Howard estates in Norfolk.

the local official who looked after the financial interests of the Crown in each county. This respectable Escheator can hardly be the Brian Holland of Norfolk, who in 1572 received a pardon from Queen Elizabeth for treasonable action committed in 1569 when he and others assembled in arms at Cringleford ? Their motives, if mistaken, were truly patriotic, for they gave out their intention in these words : ' We will procure the Commons to rise and exprese the strangers out of the Cyty of Norwich and other places in England, and when we have levied a Powre, we will loke about us, and so many as will not take our partes, we will hange them up.'

The son of Brian Holland the Escheator was named John, and acquired Quidenham, in Norfolk, and married Mary, daughter of Sir Edmund Windham of Felbrig, near Cromer. His son Thomas was knighted by King James I, at Greenwich, on May 24, 1608, together with two other Norfolk gentlemen—Sir Rotherem Willoughby and Sir Anthony Pell. He died in 1625. John Holland, of Quidenham, the son of this Sir Thomas, was born in 1603, and on June 15, 1629, was created a baronet by King Charles I.[1] Afterwards, he sat in the House of Commons as a member for Norfolk, and ungratefully joined the Opposition. He became a Presbyterian during the Civil War, and served as a Colonel in the Parliament's Army, and on many committees. He was once sent by the Parliament as a Commissioner to treat with King Charles I, and from February to May 1660, he was a member of the new Council of State, which arranged the Restoration.[2] He married Alathea, widow of Lord Sandys of

---

[1] Sir John Holland had a sister Katharine, called on her monument at Quidenham ' Filia pulcherrima Thomae Holland.' She married Sir Robert Crompton, and died in 1653, aged 34.

[2] *Complete Baronetage*, by G. E C., 1902, vol. ii, p. 74.

the Vine, and lived till January 19, 1700, when he died at the age of ninety-seven.

His wife, Alathea, had died in 1679. Her monument in Quidenham Church says that she had by Sir John Holland six sons and five daughters, and with him 'lived happily 50 years within three months and then, the 69th year of her age, upon the 22nd day of May, 1679, she cheerfully rendered up her pious soul to God that gave it.' Sir John, according to the inscription upon a monument which he erected for himself, seventeen years before his death, was a 'benefactor to his family,' and ' eminent for his particular abilities and integrity.'

Sir John Holland and his wife Alathea had a daughter named Catharine, who was born in 1635. Sir John was a strong Protestant, and severe in temper. His wife was a zealous Catholic, and good and amiable. Her husband had married her, after the death in 1629 of her first husband, Lord Sandys of the Vine, for worldly and interested motives, but was sensible of her worth, and used to call her 'the mirror of wives.' He would often say to his daughter, 'Imitate your mother in all but her religion.' Sir John removed his children from their mother's tuition, and looked after their education himself. He taught Catharine to read and write, and made her when she heard a sermon write it down afterwards, as nearly as possible word for word, and punished her severely if she made mistakes. Catharine Holland spent her time with girls of her own quality who were absorbed in pleasures, but she would often say to herself, ' The religion I follow seems to be but an empty shadow ; there must be one true and only faith ; where can I find it ? ' Sir John, after the execution of the King and the seizure of power by the advanced Republicans, quarrelled with his party, and in 1651 removed his family abroad, living first at Bruges. Here Catharine for the first time saw Catholic worship, and said to herself, ' Here is God truly served,' and prayed that He would enlighten her mind. She was now sixteen years old. Sir John then removed his children into Protestant Holland, leaving his wife in Brabant. After two years, however, he allowed Catharine to return there to see her mother. Within two years from then she had resolved to become a Catholic, and wrote so to her father, who was now back in England. He was very angry, and did his best to prevent it. After the Restoration he brought his family back to England, where he made Catharine talk to the Bishop of Winchester, whom, in her own opinion, she completely defeated in argument. Sir John lived in Holborn, and a door opened from his garden into Fetter Lane. Here, as Catharine discovered, lodged two Catholic priests belonging to a religious Order. She consulted them, and they advised her to follow her conscience, but would do no more, because their superiors thought that if they received her into the Church, the whole Catholic body would suffer, as Sir John Holland was a man of much influence. Catharine, therefore, fled from her father's house and got to Bruges, where she made her profession as an Augustinian Nun on September 7, 1664, at the age of twenty-nine. Sir John at last relented, upon the intercession of Henry, Duke of Norfolk, and even gave £400 to his daughter, as a religious dowry. The Duke himself led Catharine to the Altar.

Catharine Holland wrote three books: (1) Spiritual dramas, and fugitive pieces of poetry; (2) Translations from French and Dutch books of piety; (3) Reasons why she became a Catholic, from which the facts of her life are derived.

She died at Bruges in the year 1720, at the age of eighty-five, having been a Nun for fifty-six years, in that somnolent city of the plain. They must have passed even more like a dream than the years of most lives.

The first Sir John Holland of Quidenham was succeeded in the estates and baronetcy by his grandson, also named John, having outlived his son, Colonel Thomas Holland. This second Sir John married the Lady Rebecca Paston, daughter of the second Earl of Yarmouth, by his wife Charlotte Boyle, or Fitzroy, an illegitimate daughter of King Charles II. This Sir John died a young man in 1724. His son, Sir William, succeeded, and then the baronetcy became extinct for lack of male issue.

John Holland, of Wortwell, the ' servant of the Duke of Norfolk,' had a brother named Edward, who lived at Glossop in Derbyshire. A son of this Edward was John Holland, a Puritan divine, who, on account of his religion, had to fly to the Continent in the reign of Queen Mary, but returning home, under Elizabeth, became Rector of Dunmow Magna, in Essex, and died there in 1578. His son was Dr. Philemon Holland, a mighty scholar and indefatigable translator. Of him, that insatiable devourer of books, the poet Robert Southey, wrote that ' Philemon, for the service which he rendered to his contemporaries and his countrymen, deserves to be called the best of the Hollands.'

Doctor Philemon may not have been this, but he really was a great man in his own line. He was born at Chelmsford in Essex, in 1552, and educated at Trinity College, Cambridge. In 1595 he settled at Coventry, and lived there for forty years. At first he practised medicine, without much success, and, next, in 1608, became an usher in the Coventry Free School, and in 1627 he rose to the position of head master. The great day of his life was in 1617, when King James I visited Coventry, and Philemon, as the best Latinist in the place, was selected to address the learned monarch in a Latin oration. The municipal annals of Coventry record that the King was met outside the Bishop's gate by the mayor and aldermen in scarlet gowns, and that ' Dr. Philemon Holland, drest in a suit of black satin, made an oration, for which he had much praise.' Dr. Holland's shirt cost the town £1 3s. 1d., and the suit of black satin, with trimmings, cost £14 7s.[1]

Philemon Holland, it is recorded, suffered from poverty, but ' always kept good hospitality. *Sic tota Coventria testis.*' He was evidently a fine old fellow. Although he lived till he was eighty-five, and read and wrote incessantly, he never used spectacles in his life. He turned from Latin into English, Pliny, Plutarch's 'Morals,' Suetonius, Livy, Camden's 'Britannia,' and other books. The appearance of Suetonius produced this epigram :

> ' Philemon with translations does so fill us
> He will not let Suetonius be Tranquillus.'

He translated all ' the Romane Historie ' of Livy, and some shorter works, with a single quill pen : ' a monumental pen,' says Fuller, ' which he solemnly kept.' A lady, who was his friend, had it set in silver for him. Philemon composed about it the following poem :

> ' With one sole pen I wrote this book,
> Made of a grey goose quill,
> A Pen it was when I it took,
> A Pen I leave it still.'

Until his last illness, he was ' indefatigable in study.' Fuller says of him : ' He was the translator-general in his age, so that the books alone of his turning into English are sufficient to make a country gentleman a competent library.'

Philemon appears in Pope's picture of a heavy and solemn library in the 'Dunciad' :

---

[1] J Nichols, *Progresses of King James*, vol. iii, p 423

'But, high above, more solid learning shone,
The Classics of an Age that heard of none.
There Caxton slept with Wynkin at his side,
One clasped in wood, the other in strong cow-hide.
There, saved by spice like mummies many a year,
Dry bodies of divinity appear ;
De Lyra there a dreadful front extends,
And here the groaning shelves Philemon bends.'

Philemon Holland died February 9, 1636, aged eighty-five. He composed for himself a long Latin verse epitaph, inscribed over his tomb in Coventry Church. The first four lines contain a very bad pun upon his family name :

'Philemon
Holland hic recubat rite repostus humo.
Si quaeras ratio quaenam sit nominis, haec est,
Totus terra fui, terraque totus ero.'

That is, 'I have been *whole land*,' &c. This seems to show that Holland was still then pronounced as if spelt Holand. Philemon married Anne, daughter of William Peyton of Perry Hall, Staffordshire, and she died in 1627, at the age of seventy-two, after forty-eight years of marriage. Three daughters and seven sons had she given to Philemon. She also had a Latin inscription in Coventry Church, composed by her son Henry, the London bookseller and antiquary. Here are some lines of it. The first is mellifluous :

'Hic recubat dilecta Philemonis uxor Holandi,
Anna pudicitiæ non ulli laude secunda,
Quadraginta octoque annos quæ nupta marito,
Septem illi pueros enixa est, tresque puellas,
Lactavitque omnes, genetrix eadem est pia nutrix
Septuaginta duos vitæ numerararat annos
          .   .   .   .   .   .
Quodque unum potui, supremi pignus amoris,
Filius hoc dedit Henricus ad carmina marmor.'

Henry Holland alone of Philemon's seven sons survived his octogenarian father. He was a man of some mark also. He wrote books of an antiquarian-historical-genealogical kind, and was a publisher and bookseller in London.[1] One of his books was a treatise on Holland pedigrees, published in 1615. A more pretentious work of his was called ' Hero-logia Anglica,' published in 1620. It is a set of short accounts written in inflated Latin of some English worthies, and unworthies, beginning with King Henry VIII down to his own time. It contains much coarse and virulent abuse of the See of Rome and of the old religion of England. He says that he has travelled in several papist countries, and found absolutely no good in any. He says that the ' Babylonica Circe converted Sir Thomas More into a pig,' and so forth. He described himself as a ' zealous hater and abhorrer of all superstition and popery, and prelaticall innovations in Church government, ' and was imprisoned by order both of the High Commission Court and Star Chamber, in Laud's time. Afterwards, however, he declared himself adverse ' to all late sprung up sectaries,' only approving of the earlier kinds. In 1643 he served in the Midlands in the life-guards of the Earl of Denbigh, the General of the Parliament then commanding in those parts, and was ' eldest man of the troop, being sixty years old'—well over military age. Subsequently he was ruined by lawsuits and seems to have become a wreck, mentally and bodily. In one writing of his he says that he is now aged sixty-two. He claims descent from the Hollands of Upholland in order to show his affinity to the extinct ducal branch. He is proud of being acknowledged cousin by Sir John Holland, Baronet, of Quidenham, from whom he gives a letter addressed to him at ' the Falcon ' in Cheapside. He calls God to witness that he is descended from Brian Holland and is cousin of Sir John, but, he says, he

---

[1] See account of his works in *Dictionary of National Biography*.

does not know from whom Brian descended, 'so careless
have the heralds been of late,' though he has gone over
300 years, and searched not a few books. After these
mundane vanities he becomes pious and talks of his ' heavenly
heritage,' and seems altogether sadly doting, although he
had been an industrious man in his time.

Another son of Philemon, who died before him, named
Abraham Holland, wrote pompous poems : a list of which
is given under his name in the ' Dictionary of National
Biography.'

II.—HOLLANDS OF DEVONSHIRE

The pedigree of this family, for nine generations down to
1576, is fully set out in the ' Visitations of County Devon,'
printed in the Harleian Society publications, vol. vi, p. 345.
The information was given to the Heralds by Joseph Holland,
who was the representative of this family at that time. He
is described by John Prince, in his ' Worthies of Devon,'
published in 1697, as ' a gentleman, sometime of the Inner
Temple, a laborious antiquary, and excellently skilled in
armory,' especially in the arms of Devonshire families. The
arms of these Hollands were the ' *azure semée of fleurs de lys,
a lion rampant of same.*' They are stated to have descended
from John, a fourth son of Sir Robert de Holland, of Upholland, first Lord Holland. This John does not appear in
the Lancashire histories or elsewhere, but may have lived
none the less—possibly an illegitimate son of the illustrious
Robert. He married a South Devon heiress. John Prince
says that Margaret, the daughter of Augustine, son and
heir of Sir Walter de Bath, brought Bath House at Weare,
near Topsham, and other estates in South Devon, to her
husband, Sir Andrew Metstead, whose daughter and heiress,
Eleanor, brought them ' to her husband, John Holland, of

the same noble family with the Duke of Exeter,' and that their ' posterity is yet (1695) in being in this county, though much shorn of the splendour of their ancestors.'

Sir Walter de Bath was High Sheriff of Devon in 1238, and lived till at least 1252. So that his granddaughter, in point of time, may well have married a man who was son of Robert, Lord Holland, and younger brother of the first Earl of Kent. Except for Joseph, the Elizabethan antiquary, this family produced no one of the slightest distinction, and it gradually declined in social standing, and seems to be now extinct in the male line.

III.—HOLLANDS OF SUSSEX

This branch is stated in the ' Visitations of Sussex ' (Harleian Society publications, vol. liii, p. 17) to descend from Sir Richard Holland, owner of Denton in the reign of Henry VIII, through Richard Holland, one of his sons by his marriage with Anne Fitton. According to the Denton pedigree, this son Richard died without issue, but, if this be correct, the Sussex Hollands may, perhaps, have descended from another son of Sir Richard, by another marriage, also called Richard (see pedigree). These Hollands had an estate at Westburton in Sussex. This is their descent given in the ' Visitations of Sussex ' :

Sir Richard Holland of Denton, = *Anne Fitton.*
  temp. Hen. VIII.
Richard Holland, 3rd son . = ——
Thomas Holland, 2nd son . = ——
John Holland .   .   . . = *Elizabeth Parsons.*
William Holland   .   . . = *Frances, dau. of*
                                Henry Shelley of
                                Wormingrove.
Frances, dau. and sole heiress = *John Ashburnham.*

This John Ashburnham (1603–1671), of Ashburnham near Battle, was a Sussex Squire of ancient lineage, and was the faithful and intimate servant of King Charles I during the last sad years of his life. He was with him in his flight from Hampton Court, and it was through his error of judgment that the King was recaptured. From him and his wife, Frances Holland, descend the Earls of Ashburnham.

Henry Shelley, above mentioned, is ancestor of all the Sussex Shelleys of Michelgrove, Field Place, &c. —a very antique Sussex family. These Hollands did not bear for their crest the Holland lion, but an ash-tree rising out of a ducal coronet, and their arms were *gules, a fesse* between six *mullets argent*. These were also the arms and crest of the Ashburnhams. The reason for this does not appear.

There was in Sussex another family of Holland living at Angmering, whose pedigree for five generations, in the sixteenth and seventeenth centuries, is given by Berry. This family had the same crest and arms as the Hollands of Conway; but Berry, in his ' Sussex Genealogies,' does not say that they were derived from these, or from the Hollands of Upholland. The first of them mentioned is a William Holland of Calais.

IV.—HOLLANDS OF SHROPSHIRE

There was also a Shropshire family of Hollands, of Burwarton and other estates in that county. They used the lion and lilies in their arms; but their descent from the Lancashire Hollands cannot be ascertained. They were still extant at the Shropshire Visitation of 1623, and are there traced upwards through six generations living in the same district.

Dr. Thomas Holland, one of Fuller's ' Worthies,' was probably of this family, since he was born at Ludlow

in Shropshire. He died in 1611. He was Fellow of
Balliol, Professor of Divinity, and for twenty years
Rector of Exeter College, Oxford. He was a heavily erudite
divine. Anthony à Wood says of him (in ' Ath. Oxon.') :
' This learned Doctor Holland did not, as some, only
sip of learning, or, at the best, drink thereof, but was
mersus in libris, so that the scholar in him drowned
almost any other relations. He was esteemed by the
precise men of his time as another Apostle, so familiar with
the Fathers, as if he himself had been a Father ; with the
Schoolmen, as if he had himself been another Seraphical
Doctor.'

The originator of the terms in the last sentence was
Henry Holland in his ' Hero-logia Anglica.' He vaguely
claims relationship to Dr. Thomas Holland.

Such was the learned doctor's reputation among the
Puritan party. He was very Protestant. Anthony à
Wood says that when going on any long journey he used
to take this solemn valediction of the Fellows of the
College : ' I commend you to the love of God, and to the
hatred of Popery and Superstition '—*Commendo vos dilec-
tioni Dei et odio papatus et superstitionis.* Amiable sentiment ! In 1592 Queen Elizabeth visited Oxford in state,
and as part of the programme of entertainments, Dr.
Holland, at 9 A.M. on Monday, September 25, read
a divinity lecture ' at which were present '—this is not
surprising—' *but a few of the nobility,* and many scholars.'
On September 27, he argued before Her Majesty on
the question : ' An licet in Christianâ republicâ dis-
simulare in causa veritatis.' He preached at St. Paul's
Cathedral, on November 17, 1599, a panegyric on the
Virgin Queen, which was printed in 1610 together with
a later discourse on the same topic delivered at Oxford.
In the latter he says of the late Queen : ' By whose honorable

stipend I have been relieved these many years in this famous University, and by whose magnificence, when I served the Church of God in the Netherlands, being chaplain to the Earl of Leicester, his Honour, I was graciously rewarded.' [1]

On August 28, 1605, King James I was at Oxford, and, to amuse him, various doctors held a debating tournament in Latin, the learned monarch attentively listening and frequently intervening. One of the questions was this : ' Whether, if the plague should increase, the pastors of churches are bound to visit the sick ? ' Dr. Holland maintained the negative, discharging two syllogisms, which was nothing to another disputant, much praised by the King, who had a battery of twenty.[2] On another day Dr. Holland, before the King, went through the ritual of some degree-creation so tediously that His Majesty was bored and the proctor had to cut the Doctor short half-way.

Dr. Holland was no doubt a famous scholar, and Wood mentions two or three foreigners who came over to study at Oxford attracted by the repute of Holland and Prideaux. But he must have been one of the men whose power of writing is killed by too much reading and accumulation of detail, for he left no great work behind him to load with dull weight the book-shelves of posterity. There is such a thing as being too learned to write.

Except for this Dr. Holland, if, as probable, he belonged to them, the Shropshire Hollands produced no man of fame. One may say of an obscure and vanished family of this kind

---

[1] Of this Earl of Leicester, the betrayer of Amy Robsart, a Protestant historian, Dr. Heylin, said that ' he was a man so unappeasable in his malice, and insatiable in his lusts ; so sacrilegious in his rapines, so false in his promises, and treacherous in point of trust ; and, finally, so destructive of the rights and properties of particular persons, that his little finger lay far heavier on the subjects than the loins of all the favourites of the last two kings ' (viz. James I and Charles I). Dr. Holland must have neglected his opportunities as chaplain, in a spiritual sense.

[2] Nichols, *Progresses of King James*, vol. i, p. 548.

that which Fuller, in his ' Profane State,' says of the average squire :

' Within two generations his name is quite forgotten that ever any such was in the place, except some Herald in his Visitation pass by, and chance to spell his broken arms in a Church window. And then how weak a thing is gentry than which, if it wants virtue, brittle glass is the more lasting monument !'

Some such reflections must occur to anyone who peruses county histories, or investigates the history of modest families; yet there is something tranquillising in observing the uneventful flow of rural life, and soothing in comparing things transitory with things eternal. It seems to me that, wherever it is possible, the histories of families should be written, so that descendants at least may have some dim idea of those who bore the name before them, and who now have fallen into almost complete oblivion. That is why I have erected this ' *Memoriale Hollandorum*.'

APPENDIX I (A).

HOLLANDS OF LISCARD VALE, ETC.

Samuel Holland = Anne, d. of Peter Swinton
of Sandlebridge, | of Knutsford; b. 1740,
Cheshire, 1754– | d. 1814.
1816. See Table, |
p. 208 ante. |

[2] Samuel Holland = Katherine, d. of
of Liverpool and | John Menzies
Plas-yn-Penrhyn, | of Liverpool.
Merioneth, second |
son; b. 1768, d. |
1851. |

Charles Holland = Elizabeth, d. of William
of Liscard Vale, | Gaskell of Warrington
Cheshire; b. 1799, |
d. 1870. |

Menzies Holland;
b. 1802, d.s.p. 1817.

Samuel Holland, M.P.;
b. 1803, d.s.p. 1892.

Three
daughters.

Menzies = Harriet Neill,
of Den- | d. of John
b; b. 1839, | Neill of Bel-
| fast.

sons and four daughters.

[1] Sir Arthur = Barbara, d. of
Holland of | F. Schwann
Wimbledon; | of London.
b. 1842. |

Five sons and one daughter.

[1] Walter = Alice, d. of
Holland of | Lieut.-Col.
Carnatic | Wray.
Hall, near |
Liverpool; |
b. 1842, d. |
1915. |

Four sons and
three daughters.

William = Mary, d. of
Gaskell | T. Rees,
Holland | of Smyrna.
of Denbigh- |
shire; b. |
1843, d. 1910. |

One son and
four daughters.

Edgar
Swinton
Holland;
b. 1847,
d. 1896.

Four
daughte

[1] Arthur and Walter were twins

HOLLANDS OF DUMBLETON, ETC.

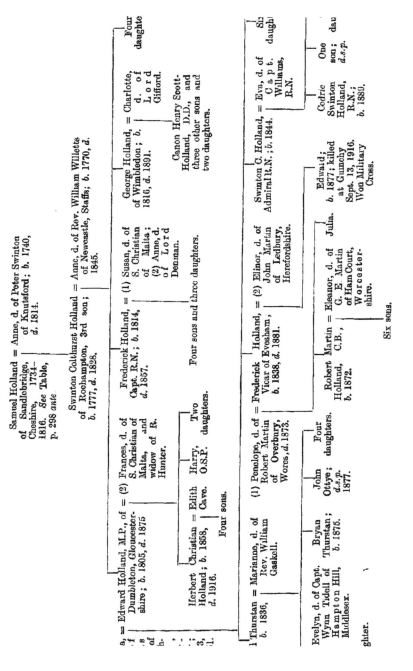

Samuel Holland = Anne, d. of Peter Swinton of Sandlebridge, Cheshire, 1734–1816. *See* Table, p. 298 *ante*. | of Knutsford; *b.* 1740, *d.* 1814.

Swinton Colthurst Holland = Anne, d. of Rev. William Willetts of Rochampton, 3rd son; *b.* 1777, *d.* 1828. | of Newcastle, Staffs; *b.* 1770, *d.* 1845.

a, = Edward Holland, M.P., of Dumbleton, Gloucestershire; *b.* 1805, *d.* 1875 = (2) Frances, d. of S. Christian of Malta, and widow of R. Hunter.

George Holland, of Wimbledon; *b.* 1816, *d.* 1891. = Charlotte, d. of Lord Gifford.

Canon Henry Scott-Holland, D.D., and three other sons and two daughters.

Four daughte

Frederick Holland, Capt. R.N.; *b.* 1814, *d.* 1857. = (1) Susan, d. of S. Christian of Malta; (2) Anne, d. of Lord Denman.

Four sons and three daughters.

Herbert Christian = Edith Holland; *b.* 1858, Cave. *d.* 1916.

Harry, O.S.P.

Two daughters.

Four sons.

1 Thurstan = Marianne, d. of *b.* 1836, Rev. William Gaskell.

(1) Penelope, d. of = Frederick Holland, = (2) Elinor, d. of Robert Martin Vicar of Evesham, John Martin of Overbury, *b.* 1838, *d.* 1881. of Ledbury, Worcs. *d.* 1873. Herefordshire.

Swinton C. Holland, = Eva, d. of Admiral R.N.; *b.* 1844. Capt. Willeams, R.N.

Si daught

Robert Martin = Eleanor, d. of Julia. Holland, C.B., G. E. Martin *b.* 1872. of Ham Court, Worcestershire.

Edward; *b.* 1877; killed at Gunnehy Sept. 13, 1916. Won Military Cross.

Cedric Swinton Holland, R.N.; *b.* 1889.

One son; *d.s.p.*

dau

Evelyn, d. of Capt. Wynn Tidell of Hampton Hill, Middlesex.

John Ottye; *d.s.p.* 1877.

Four daughters.

Bryan Thurstan; *b.* 1875.

Six sons.

ghter.

APPENDIX II

I

THIS note is intended for members of the Clifton-Rhodes-Mobberley-Knutsford line, and will not be of interest to others.

The Rev. John Booker, Vicar of Prestwich, a learned Lancashire antiquary who specialised on the Manchester district, and wrote about 1850, says, in his 'Memorials of Prestwich,' p. 214, as to the estate called 'Rhodes,' or sometimes 'The Rodes': 'From the old local family it passed in marriage with an heiress into the family of Parr, from whom it was conveyed by two sisters and co-heiresses—one portion to William, son of William Holland of Clifton, in right of his wife, Jane Parr, and the remainder to Foxe of Lathom, who had espoused the other sister.'

It appears, however, from later information, that Jane Parr married John Foxe, and that it was the other sister (name lost) who married this William Holland. John Foxe was in occupation of Rhodes in 1541, so that he must have married Jane Parr before then. His widow, Jane, died in 1580. Her will is abstracted in the Chetham Society Papers, new series 1, p. 210, 'Lancashire and Cheshire Wills.' It is a will of 'Jane Foxe, widow of John Foxe of The Rhodes in Pilkington.' She left to 'Henry, my son, a ring. Item to Hollande,' &c. 'My son William and his son John to be my executors.' Unluckily the Christian name of the 'Hollande,' is not decipherable in the MSS.

The Rhodes estate must have been divided, and there may have been two houses, for both Hollands and Foxes of Rhodes occur in the parochial register in the seventeenth century.

Now Mr. W. F. Irvine in his otherwise excellent book, called 'The Family of Hollands of Mobberley and Knutsford'—which was printed for private circulation in 1902, but is now to some extent in the book market—says, on p. 30, that the William Holland who married Miss Parr of Rhodes could not have been, as Mr. Booker and others have said, son of the William Holland of Clifton, who married Alice Werden, and died in 1523. This statement, he says, is 'demonstrably false.' Why ? Because, he says, ' the William Holland, son of William Holland of Clifton and Alice Werden, went into Shropshire and there founded a family, as will be seen by reference to the ' Visitation of Shropshire, 1623,' and so obviously cannot have also settled at Rhodes and died there in 1603.

Mr. Irvine's memory unluckily played him false on this occasion. A reference to the ' Visitation of Shropshire, 1623,' published in the Harleian Society Papers, will show that there was in Shropshire at that time only one Holland family—that of Burwarton—and that they had been settled there for generations : before either the William Holland of Clifton, who died in 1523, or his sixth son, William, were born.

Their then living representative, who signed the pedigree in 1623, was indeed named William, but had obviously nothing to do with the Hollands of Clifton, and could not possibly have been the son of the William Holland of Clifton who died in 1523. He would, for one thing, in that case, have been over one hundred years old. Mr. Irvine has entirely admitted this mistake to me in a letter.

Again, Mr. Irvine had not, unfortunately, before him, when he composed his book, an old vellum pedigree which was made about 1652 for the William Holland who bought Mobberley, and is now in my possession. It is good evidence, at any rate, of what he and others then believed to be the fact. This pedigree states that William Holland of Mobberley was the son of Edward Holland of Chorlton, who was the son of William Holland of Rhodes, who was the sixth son of William Holland of Clifton who married Alice Werden. This represents the belief of William Holland of Mobberley, in 1652, and the information which he could then obtain. The Prestwich parish register shows that Hollands of Heaton, Clifton, and Rhodes were baptised, married, and buried at that church in the seventeenth century, and so must have known each other extremely well. Clifton and Rhodes lie close together, not half a mile apart, on either side of the river Irwell. Chorlton, where William Holland lived until he bought Mobberley, is only about five or six miles distant from Rhodes and Clifton. The elder line of Hollands of Clifton were living at Clifton Hall until about 1650, and held land there still

z

longer. If William Holland of Mobberley was right in the view expressed in his pedigree in 1652, he was a second cousin of Thomas Holland—his living contemporary, the Squire of Clifton. But if, as on Mr. Irvine's theory, he was entirely mistaken, then the only blood connection between them would have been through (as their common ancestor) Thurstan Holland of Denton, who lived three hundred years earlier.

Now a man like William Holland of Mobberley, a conscientious Puritan, but sufficiently interested in family history as to have an expensively illuminated pedigree made out, and living most of his life at Chorlton within an hour's ride of Clifton Hall, which, again, was within a rifle-shot of Rhodes where first his uncle and then his first cousin resided, could not possibly have made such an error as to mistake and solemnly enter in a pedigree as his near cousins the family at Clifton, if their connection with him, on Mr. Irvine's theory, was so remote. It is, to say the least, highly probable that William Holland, in 1652, knew better who were his own second cousins, in his immediate neighbourhood, than did a gentleman writing about the year 1901. There is no reason at all to suppose that Edward Holland of Chorlton erred in supposing William Holland of Clifton to be his grandfather, and he must have handed-down this fact to his son, William of Mobberley.

The descent, then, was certainly as follows :

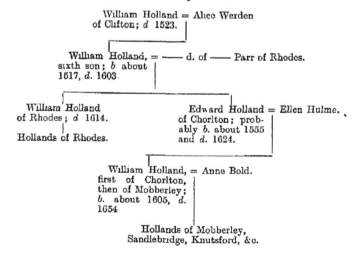

```
        William Holland = Alice Werden
        of Clifton; d 1523.  |
              ┌───────────────┘
    William Holland, = —— d. of —— Parr of Rhodes.
    sixth son; b about  |
    1617, d. 1603.       |
      ┌──────────────────┴────────────────────────┐
 William Holland                        Edward Holland = Ellen Hulme.
 of Rhodes; d 1614.                      of Chorlton; prob-
    |                                    ably b. about 1555
 Hollands of Rhodes.                     and d. 1624.
                              ┌──────────────────┘
                        William Holland, = Anne Bold.
                        first of Chorlton,  |
                        then of Mobberley;  |
                        b. about 1605, d.   |
                        1654                 |
                              Hollands of Mobberley,
                              Sandlebridge, Knutsford, &c.
```

The vellum pedigree of 1652, when it gets behind William Holland of Clifton, certainly falls into error, which our present information makes obvious. It states that this William was the son of a Laurence Holland, who again was a younger son of Thurstan Holland of Denton, who lived in the reign of Edward IV, and married Miss Joan Arderne (see the Denton pedigree).

But we now know that the Manor of Clifton, held by William Holland at his death in 1523, descended to him; not from such late Hollands of Denton, but from a Holland—a younger son of the first Thurstan Holland of Denton—who lived a century earlier, in the reign of Edward III. The root of this tiresome mistake is no doubt in Flower's 'Visitation of Lancashire, in 1567,' a public record which evidently misled the expert who drew up the pedigree for William Holland of Mobberley in 1652. Flower says that William Holland of Clifton (died 1523) was 'the second sonne of Holland of Denton.'

It is pretty clear what happened. The Hollands of Clifton were sadly careless as to matters of pedigree—not even taking the trouble to be at home when the Herald called on his Visitation—but they held firmly the tradition that they were descended from Thurstan Holland of Denton. This was true, because they did in fact descend from the Sir Thurstan Holland of Denton (son of Sir William de Holland and Margaret Shoresworth), who lived in the reigns of Edward II and Edward III, whose younger son William acquired Clifton by marrying Marjory de Trafford. Flower, the Heraldic Visitor, on the second Visitation in 1567, hearing of this tradition and not knowing exact facts, ascribed their descent to 'the second son of Holland of Denton,' cautiously not saying which Holland. The expert (probably Randle Holmes) who drew up the vellum pedigree of 1652, knowing his Flower and also hearing of the Thurstan tradition, imputed the descent to the nearest Thurstan Holland of Denton, who by his date would do for the grandfather of William Holland of Clifton, who died in 1523. He found this in the Thurstan Holland of Denton, who lived about 1470–1508, and married Joan Arderne. From this Thurstan, accordingly, he started his pedigree, evidently impossibly, since the Manor of Clifton could not have come from him.

The Rev. Joseph Hunter of the mid-nineteenth century, in his book called ' Familiæ Minorum Gentium,' also gives this erroneous derivation; but he states that he got the information from the family, and does not vouch for it. He evidently regarded it with suspicion.

On the whole matter, then, it is quite clear that—

1. William Holland, sixth son of William Holland lord of the Manor of Clifton, was born about 1517.

2 He married one of the neighbouring Parr co-heiresses of Rhodes—probably before 1545, since the other was married to John Foxe before 1541.

3. He was the executor of the will of his eldest brother, Thomas Holland of Clifton, in 1565, and died at age of about eighty-five years in 1603, leaving an elder son William, who inherited Rhodes, and died in 1614.

4. One of his younger sons was Edward Holland of Chorlton, the father of the William Holland who bought Mobberley in 1650.

I have been forced to make this tedious disquisition on these very uninteresting Hollands by the error made and printed by Mr. Irvine, and still more by the fact that his statement was accepted on this point without further investigation by the editors of the admirable 'Victorian County History of Lancashire.' Mr. Irvine, after erroneously rejecting the descent of the Hollands of Mobberley and Knutsford from those of Clifton —a descent which had been fully accepted by such considerable previous authorities as the Rev. John Booker, Mr. James Croston, (in his ' History of Samlesbury Hall '), and Mr. Holland Watson— then proceeds to suggest a different line of descent from Sir Richard Holland of Denton, *temp* Henry VIII, which rests on no evidence whatever, and is, as he himself admits, pure conjecture.

II

The following Inquisition made after the death, in 1523, of William Holland of Clifton (of whom William Holland of Rhodes was sixth son) is not, as is the Clifton Inquisition of 1506, printed in the collection of Lancashire Inquisitions, but I have had it copied from the original parchment in the Public Records Office. I print it here at some length, though with considerable abbreviations, as it is a good example of how a squire in the reign of Henry VIII made provision for a widow and a large family of boys and girls, and it illustrates also the ideas of spelling entertained in Lancashire at that time. The Report of the Jurors is in Latin, but the will of William Holland, annexed to it, is in English.

DUCHY OF LANCASTER INQUISTIONS. POST MORTEM.
VOL. V. No. 49

The document recites that the Inquisition was taken at Chorley in the County of Lancashire, on the Saturday after Easter, in the fourteenth year of the reign of King Henry VIII, before James Borseley, the King's 'Escaetor' for Lancashire, and that the Jurors were Lever de (?), Charles Somner of Leyland, John Bardesworth, Philip Strange, Hugo (?), Richard Edmondson, (?) Eccleston, Robert Aghton, John Werden, Richard Charnock, Richard Croston, Charles Farrington, and William Allenson.

They say on oath that William Holland, of Clyfton, did not die seised of any lands or tenements held from the King, or from the Duchy of Lancaster, but that he was seised of the Manor of Clyfton, with some other property mentioned. They then state that by an indenture, dated April 17, in the eighth year of King Henry VIII, the said William Holland had conveyed the Manor of Clyfton, while he was so seised of it, and the other houses and lands at Manchester, Swynton, Leyland, and Farryngton, to certain trustees—namely, to Richard Holland of Denton, gentleman, Thomas Longley, Charles Whitill, Edward Sudhill of Walton-in-le-Dale, Clerks, Nicholas Holland of Deane Hall, and Robert Parr of Worseley to hold for the purpose of performing the will of the said William Holland declared and contained in a schedule thereto annexed. The Jurors state that this will was in the following words :

' Whereas I William Holland of Clyfton in Salfordshire in the Countie of Lancaster, Gentleman, of grete confidence and speciall truste that I have in Richard Holland of Denton Esquire, Thomas Longley, Charles Whitill, Edmund Sudhill of Walton in le Dale, Clerks, Nicholas Holland of the Deane Hall, and Robert Parr of Worseley, Gentlemen, have given, graunted, and confermed by this my present dede indented. Whereunto this present cedule indented is annexed the aforesaid persones their heirs and assignes for ever. All my manor and lordship of Clyfton aforesaid and all and every my messuages,' &c. &c., ' in Clyfton aforesaid,

Manchester, Swynton, Leyland and Faryngton in the County of Lancaster or ellswher, within the said Countie to the entent that they should execute the Will of me the said William Holland to them in that behalfe specified published and declared as by the said Dede indented more playnely it doth appere. Be it knowen to all Cristen people this present writting indented of a Will declared . . . in manner and forme insuying; Fyrst I will and declare that the aforenamed persones and their heirs shall stand and be feoffees peasabully seised of and in all and any of the premises to the use and behofe of me the said William Holland for terme of my life, and shall suffer me or my attorneys peasabully to perceyve take and have yerly All and every the issues, rents,' &c., &c., ' there of to mine owne use during all the terme of my life without eny interruption,' &c., &c. 'Allso I will that my said feoffees shall make by their dede indented at my request a sure and laful estate and feofment of parcells of the premises in Clyfton, Leyland and Faryngton aforesaid to the yerly value of fyve pounds xvi^s. iii^d to Alice nowe my wif or to feoffees for her use for terme of her lif in the name of hir joynture and dower, the remeynder thereof after hir decess to me the said William Holland duryng all the terme of my lif. Allso I will that my said feoffees within xx days after my decess shall make a sufficient graunte by their writting indented to the said Alice or to feoffees,' etc. ' of a parcell of my demeyne of Clyfton aforsaid such as I shall name and appoint to byld an house and a barne upon with the best of foure kyen both somer and wynter, within my said demeyne if she kepe hir sole and unmarried after my decesse toward the norrishing fyndyng and exibition of all my children mulier [i.e. girls] except myn heir. And if the said Alice after my decesse [here follow provisions for making void this gift if the said Alice should sue for anything more in a court of law, and then comes a gift of certain titles at Clifton to Alice for life while unmarried] to the use and behofe of hir and my yonge children mulier.' If Alice married again she was to lose all benefits, which would then go to ' only my yonge children mulier begottyn.' The document then declares that ' my said feoffees shall make at my request by dede indented such convenient estate and feoftment of parcell of the premises at myn appoynting . . . as it shall happyn me to graunte hereafter to be made by indenture at the mariage of my said son and heir. And if it happen me to decesse afor my said son and heir shall be committed by me to be maried in my lif then I

will that my said feoffees with the consent and advyse of the aforsaid Alice my wyf if she kepe her unmaried shall marie my said son
and heir in convenient place and to such a gentlewoman as they
shall best think by their discretion.' And they were to make such
grants from the estate on such an occasion as they thought advis-
able. The feoffees were also directed within twenty days after
William Holland's decease to convey certain specified houses in
Clifton, Manchester, and Swinton 'to my yonge sons of my body
by the aforsaid Alice my wyf nowe begottyn or to be gottyn evenly
and equally to be departed and divided among them for the terme
of their liffes all. Provided that if it happyn any of my said yonge
sons to dye or to be promoted by benefice, prebend, chauntry or
mariage to the yerly value of 17 marks over all charges and reprises
for the terme of life.' [In that case the life-gift of the share in house-
rents is to become ' extinct and of none effect '] ' And if the said
Alice kepe hir sole and unmaried after my decesse then I will that
she shall have the custodie, rule, governance and possession, if it
shall please hir, of all my said yonge sons and any of them and their
said anunytes with all their goods so long as thei or any of them will
be so contented and pleased to be and abide with hir. And if it
happyn me the said William to dye afor my said son and heir shall be
of the age of xviii yers completed.' [The feoffees are then to allot the
executors of his last will to raise 40 marks and use them in accord-
ance with instructions to be given by his last will and subject to the
dower and annuities to younger sons, the feoffees should then hold the
residue of the estate to the use of his son and heir. His wife Alice,
if she keeps unmarried, is to have the custody, rule, and governance
of the son and heir until he is twenty-one. William Holland then
reserves to himself the right of altering the provisions of this his
present will at any time thereafter]

The Jurors at the Inquisition, after stating the above will,
and describing the various properties with their existing annual
value, repeat that the said William Holland died on the Wednesday
before the Feast of St. Michael the Archangel last, that Thomas
Holland is his son and heir, and that at the date of the Inquisition he
was sixteen years old and over.

The minuteness of the portions given to the younger sons is
worth noting. They only get very small rents for life, and even
these are to cease if they get slender ecclesiastical preferments or
marry a girl with a little money. No wonder that so many younger

sons of squires could not marry, or disappeared into utter obscurity. There was then no army or navy, or home or Indian civil service, or colonies, to give them a career. Such would have been the fate of my ancestor William Holland, sixth son of Squire William Holland of Clifton, had he not chanced, in middle life, to pick up a small co-heiress, the daughter of Parr of Rhodes.

APPENDIX III

I

CHRONICLES.

Walsingham.	Grafton.
Higden.	Froissart.
Malverne.	Jean de Wavrin.
Hardynge.	Enguerrand de Monstrelet.
Hall.	Jean le Fère.
Holinshed.	Philippe de Commines.
Fabian.	Chronique de Normandie.

II

GENERAL HISTORIES

BARNES, JOSHUA : History of Edward III and the Black Prince. (Cambridge : 1688.)

BAKER's Chronicle. (London : 1660.)

CARTE's General History of England. (1747.)

KENNET : Complete History of England. (London : 1706.)

GUTHRIE : History of England. (London : 1747.)

SANDFORD : Genealogical History of the Kings of England. (London : 1707.)

TURNOR : History of England during the Middle Ages. (1830.)

LINGARD : History of England. (1849.)

STUBBS, BISHOP : Constitutional History of England. (1880.)

WYLIE, J. H. : History of England under Henry IV. (1896.)

    „   „   „   „   „   Henry V. (1911.)

RAMSAY, SIR J. H. : Lancaster and York. (1892.)
„ „ Genesis of Lancaster. (1913.)
OMAN, C. : Political History of England from 1377 to 1485.
MOWETT, R. B. : The Wars of the Roses. (1914.)
STEVENSON : Wars of the English in France.
BARANTE : Histoire des Ducs de Bourgogne. (1825.)
QUICHERAT : Rodrigue. (1879.)

III

COUNTY AND LOCAL HISTORIES

BAINES : History of Lancashire. (1836.)
Victorian County History of Lancashire.
Chetham Society Publications.
Surtees Society Publications.
Camden Society Publications.
Harleian Society Publications. Visitations, &c.
STOW'S London. (1707.)
CROSTON : History of Samlesbury Hall. (1871.)
HUNTER : History of South Yorkshire.
„ Familiæ Minorum Gentium (Harleian Society, 1894–6).
BOOKER, REV. J. : Memorials of Prestwich, and other works.
ORMEROD : History of Cheshire.
HASTED : History of Kent.
BLOMEFIELD : History of Norfolk.
DALLAWAY AND CARTWRIGHT : History of Western Sussex.
BRAY : History of Surrey.
POLWHELE : Devonshire. (1793.)
JONES : History of Denbighshire.
WILLIAMS : History of Conway.
Archæologia Cambrensis.
Archæologia Cantiana.
PENNANT : Tour in Wales. (1778.)
PRINCE, JOHN : Worthies of Devon. (1698.)
FULLER : English Worthies. (Ed. 1811.)
„ Warwickshire.
WM. F. IRVINE : The Family of Hollands of Mobberley and Knutsford. (1902.)

IV

OTHER WORKS

BURKE : Peerage.
    „   Extinct Peerages. (1883.)
    „   Vicissitudes of Families. (1869.)
    „   Rise of Great Families. (1873.)
    „   Royal Families of England, &c. (1848.)
DOYLE : Baronage of England. (1886.)
METCALFE'S Book of Knights. (1885.)
DUGDALE, SIR WILLIAM : Baronage.
    „   „   Monasticon.
    „   „   Warwickshire.
RYMER : Fœdera.
WEEVER, JOHN : Funeral Monuments. (London : 1631.)
BELTZ : Memorials of the Most Noble Order of the Garter, 1821.
FENN : Paston Letters.
Calendar of Inquisitions *post mortem.*
Register of Papal Letters : Cal. State Papers.
BERRY : Genealogies.
ROWLAND, DAVID : Family of Nevill. (1830.)
G. E. C. : Complete Peerage. (London : 1887–1898.)
    „   Complete Baronetage. (Exeter : 1900–1904.)
NICHOLS : Progresses of Queen Elizabeth and of King James I. (Ed. 1828.)
FOXE : Acts and Monuments. (Book of Martyrs.)
CHALLONER, BISHOP : Memoirs of Missionary Priests. (1742.)
FOLEY : Records of the English Province of the Society of Jesus.
GILLOW : Biographical Dictionary of English Catholics.
The Dictionary of National Biography.
Dictionnaire de Biographie Universelle.
ANTHONY À WOOD : Athen. Oxon. (1692.)

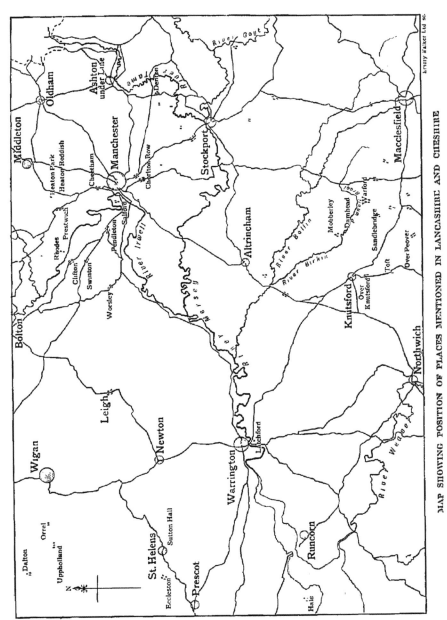

MAP SHOWING POSITION OF PLACES MENTIONED IN LANCASHIRE AND CHESHIRE

Emery Walker Ltd sc.

INDEX OF PERSONS

(The Names which are only given in Pedigree tables and are not also mentioned in the text, are not included in the Index)

Milton Keynes UK
Ingram Content Group UK Ltd.
UKHW020624071223
433866UK00005B/100